A magical story anthology from nine northern romance authors

Mary Jayne Baker • Sophie Claire • Jacqui Cooper
Helena Fairfax • Kate Field • Melinda Hammond
Marie Laval • Helen Pollard • Angela Wren

Published by OPS Publishing

ISBN 978-0-9930356-3-0

Cover design and typesetting by Fully Booked Design
(cover illustrations © DepositPhotos)
Edited by Helena Fairfax

A CIP record for this book is available from the British Library.

CONTENTS

MAP OF HAVEN BRIDGE 5

A Glitch in Time
By Jacqui Cooper 7

Caught Red-Handed
By Sophie Claire 43

Three Butterflies
By Marie Laval 76

GU 1909
By Angela Wren 110

The Secret of Greymoor Hall
By Kate Field 135

The Treasure Seekers
By Mary Jayne Baker 166

Ginny's Ghost
By Helen Pollard 204

I Shall Wear Purple
By Melinda Hammond 239

Music, Love and Other Languages
By Helena Fairfax 273

Artwork by Livi Gosling (livigosling.co.uk)

A Glitch in Time

By Jacqui Cooper

Nicola

'I'm looking for a dress, Miss Moonshine. Something special, though I don't really know why I'm bothering,' said Nicola. She and Mark were barely speaking at the moment, so dinner with his family tonight was going to be interesting.

Miss Moonshine looked as if she was considering which of those two statements to respond to first. 'I have some lovely dresses on the rail at the back.'

'Vintage?'

'Age is just a number, dear. So why are you bothering but not bothering?'

'It's Mark,' sighed Nicola.

'What awful thing has he done now? Bought you chocolates when you were dieting? Wine when you'd vowed off?'

Nicola forced a smile. 'Put like that, he is awful, isn't he?' She reached the rail and began to sift through the dresses. 'Actually, he painted the kitchen while I was away on a training course.'

'How dare he?' Miss Moonshine made it a question.

Nicola spotted a dress, plucked it out, studied it and rejected it. 'You should see the colour he chose,' she said, still annoyed. And maybe just a little bit guilty, too, at the way she'd reacted to his 'surprise'. But what had he expected? Seriously, what had possessed him to turn her cosy kitchen into a dark and gloomy cave? Even now she could feel her indignation stir.

'I mean who paints a room without checking colour charts and the feng shui and – oooh, I like this one!' Forgetting about the kitchen, she drew a pale pink dress with grey polka dots from the rail. It was sleeveless with a nipped-in waist and full skirt and felt like silk. Very 1950s.

'Someone who wanted it to be a surprise?' suggested Miss Moonshine. The phone on the counter, an old Bakelite model with a rotary dial, began to ring. 'Excuse me,' she said.

Nicola held the dress against her. It really did look perfect. Miss Moonshine was deep in conversation, so she signalled to ask if she could use the changing room and got the go-ahead.

She knew no one would understand about the painting incident, but the truth was it had really got to her. For her, the conversation about tarting up the house to put it on the market had just been idle chat, something they would do 'one day'. So to come home a few days later to find Mark already pushing ahead had been a real shock.

Her reaction hadn't gone down well. And of course she knew the colour – vile though it was – wasn't the real issue.

She had to wiggle into the dress but once on it fitted like a glove. Mark's parents would wonder why she was wearing an old dress, and his sister would come right out and ask. But the material was so sumptuous and the colour flattered her fair colouring.

She was stepping out of the changing room for a second opinion when the overhead lights began to flicker. For a second the air around her seemed to crackle and she rubbed at the goosebumps prickling her arms.

That was when she noticed that the dress looked different. Instead of being pink with grey spots, it now appeared red with black spots, which of course was impossible. It had to be a trick of the light. Surely she couldn't have got something like that so wrong? She was holding the skirt out in front of her, studying the material, as she stepped into the main shop.

'Miss M, what kind of material is this? I mean I love the

colour, but it's like one of those internet illusions. You know, is the dress blue or gold? Or in this case, red or pink? Miss M?'

Miss Moonshine was still on the phone, though she appeared to be on hold. She glanced over at Nicola – and promptly dropped the handset with a clatter that drew a growl from her little chihuahua, Napoleon.

A bus trundling past the shop caught Nicola's eye and she walked over to the window for a better look. 'I haven't seen a double-decker bus in Haven Bridge for years,' she said. 'Vintage, too. Look! There's a conductress at the back. Do you think it's for a wedding? I hear that's becoming fashionable… oh! There are loads of old cars on the road too. Maybe it's a rally.'

Nicola's two older brothers had been obsessed with vintage cars and steam trains when they were little. For years, as the youngest, she'd been dragged around transport museums until she was old enough to put her foot down. But some of the information must have stuck, because she recognised various models of car: Austin, Hillman and Morris, to name but a few.

And then she noticed something else; all the people in the street were in costume. 'Miss M, have you seen this?' she said excitedly. 'Is it a film company, do you think? I wish I'd known. The am-dram society usually tells us when something like this is going on. I might have got a job as an extra.'

Miss Moonshine didn't reply and when Nicola turned the old woman was staring at her with a very odd expression.

'Miss M? Are you OK?'

'Oh dear,' said Miss Moonshine weakly. 'Oh dear, oh dear. What date is it?'

'Date?' Nicola had gone back to watching the scene unfolding outside. 'Why? Did you get a flyer? Can I see? Does it say who's in it?'

'What date is it?' repeated Miss Moonshine in a small voice.

'The sixth, I think.'

'No. What year?'

Now Nicola was beginning to worry. Miss Moonshine was old, but she was as sharp as a tack. She abandoned her post by the door. '2021. Look, do you want to sit down?' She glanced around for a chair but instead caught sight of a display of hats she hadn't noticed before. And those handbags too. Where had they come from? Surely they hadn't been there before? They were going to need some serious inspection–

'2021? Oh dear, oh dear,' said Miss Moonshine again. 'I am so sorry. I should have been paying more attention.'

'To what?'

'To you. To the dress. Oh, this is such a mess.'

'What's a mess?' asked Nicola, bewildered.

Miss Moonshine shook her head. 'This won't do. It won't do at all.'

'Look, can I get you a cuppa, Miss M?'

Instead of answering Miss Moonshine crossed to the door, locked it and turned the sign to 'Closed'. Nicola's jaw dropped.

'Make the tea, dear, by all means, but I rather fear we may need something stronger.'

Concerned, Nicola hurried into the back shop and looked around for supplies. There was no electric kettle, only a blackened kettle sitting on a gas ring. When she tried and failed to light it, Miss Moonshine came in to assist.

'What do you think they're filming?' asked Nicola again.

'Whatever it is, it will be in black-and-white,' muttered Miss Moonshine.

'What?'

'Sit.' Miss Moonshine handed her a cup of tea. A proper cup and saucer and not a mug. How posh was that? 'Now you need to listen to me, Nicola. Listen and not interrupt.'

Nicola nodded and smoothed her dress. Which reminded her. 'Didn't this look pink–?'

'Shhh. The dress is red because it's new.'

'Oh? Does that mean it's more expensive?' Or was vintage dearer? Nicola had no idea. 'How much is it?'

'One pound ten-and-six,' said Miss Moonshine.

Nicola worked out the old money. 'I don't get it.'

'No. I can see why you might not. Let me put it this way.' Miss Moonshine appeared to gather her thoughts. 'Sometimes in this shop, time gets a little bit… well… confused, shall we say. It doesn't happen often and normally I have it marked on my calendar but today… well, today no one reminded me.' She looked pointedly at Napoleon.

Time wasn't the only thing that was confused. Nicola was really worried about the shopkeeper now. 'Miss M, maybe you should take the afternoon off.'

'Nicola, there is no filming in Haven Bridge today. I'm sorry to be so blunt, but you've travelled back in time. It's1951 and we have a very big problem.'

Nicola said nothing, because she had no idea what to say. Had Miss M been at the sherry? Come to think of it, what age was Miss Moonshine? She cleared her throat and chose her words carefully. 'My mum told me my gran used to get what she called senior moments. Maybe –'

'I knew your grandmother very well,' said Miss Moonshine sharply. 'Lily Boddington. She wore that very dress in 1951 the day your grandfather proposed.'

This was just weird now. 'Miss Moonshine, is there someone I could call?' Even as she asked, she realised she'd been coming to Miss Moonshine's shop since forever and had no idea if the old woman had any family.

'Listen to me, Nicola,' said Miss Moonshine impatiently. 'This is important. Sometimes, as I say, this shop… well, it slips in time a little bit. And that, I'm very much afraid, is what has happened today.'

Nicola sat back. Should she phone Mark? He was a vet rather than a doctor, but maybe he'd be able to advise.

Her thoughts were interrupted by someone knocking on the door of the shop.

Miss Moonshine looked over and groaned. 'The butcher's boy. I'd better answer. He's very persistent.'

'Hi, missus. Why's the door locked? Brought you some sausages and a nice bit of liver. Be glad when this rationing's over, eh? Who's that you got with you?'

Miss Moonshine had been trying unsuccessfully to block his view of the shop's interior, but she lacked the height to be very effective. He stood on tiptoe, straining his neck, spotted Nicola and uttered an appreciative wolf whistle. 'Well *hello*, doll.'

Nicola blinked. Doll? Had a skinny fifteen-year-old just called her *doll?* She opened her mouth to deliver a lecture, but Miss Moonshine was already pushing him out of the door. When he was gone she locked it firmly again and turned back to Nicola.

'I really don't have time to explain this. Perhaps this will help.' She selected a mother-of-pearl-backed hand mirror from a dressing-table set and handed it to Nicola. 'Take a look.'

Nicola did. Instead of her short, neat, blonde pixie cut, her hair was black. And there was a lot of it. Much more than there should be. Confused, she reached up and touched it to find it back-combed to within an inch of its life and rigid with hairspray.

She turned the mirror over. And back again. The hair was still there, and now she also noticed something else.

'That not my face,' she said weakly.

'No,' agreed Miss Moonshine. 'It's Lily Boddington's.'

Nicola was still staring at the mirror. Her reflection showed lips painted a bright scarlet and lashes so thick with mascara it looked like she'd stuck two caterpillars to her eyelids. 'W – what's going on? I think I need to sit down.'

'You are sitting down. I've just explained it to you,' said Miss Moonshine, not unkindly. 'You've gone back in time. Oh, and of course there's the tiny matter of a body swap too. Don't worry. It's not permanent. As I remember, it ends at midnight.'

'Body swap? Wait… Y – you remember? This has happened before?'

Miss Moonshine dropped her gaze, looking somewhat sheepish. 'In 1951. Poor Lily went into the changing room and came out wearing a faded pink dress. She was most distraught, though I thought it looked rather good on her. As did your haircut. She, however, was terrified that she'd gone bald. The crying was quite intense for a time. She kept saying she looked like a man. Do you remember, Napoleon?'

If the little dog did remember, he gave no sign.

Nicola would have liked to tell her she was talking crazy. But crazy was looking back at her with a stranger's face from a mother-of-pearl-backed mirror.

'I don't believe a word of this,' she said slowly. 'But if I did, I only have to last till midnight?'

'You have to last till midnight and not change anything,' clarified Miss Moonshine. 'There are laws that govern time, of course, and it would not be good to break them. Not good at all.'

'So I'll just stay here with you then.' There were loads of interesting things in the shop to keep her occupied. 'If I hide one of those bags can I pick it up in about seventy years or so –'

'Didn't you hear me?' said Miss Moonshine. 'Your grandfather proposes tonight.'

'To me?' Nicola screwed her face up. 'That's just wrong on so many levels.'

'Not to you. To Lily Boddington.'

'Lily Boddington was my grandmother's name.'

Miss Moonshine rubbed between her eyes. 'I do not

understand why these temporal glitches take so long to sink in. Always it's the same.'

'Well, maybe because you've just told me I've gone back in time and warned me not to do anything to change the future,' said Nicola defensively. 'It's not exactly a normal Saturday afternoon, is it? And what do you mean I can't change anything? What will happen?'

'What will happen? You have to ask? Haven't you seen *Back to the Future*? I strongly encourage you to avoid changing the timeline at all costs. Countless Dr Whos have explained this to your whole generation,' she continued, sounding increasingly exasperated.

'Sorry,' mumbled Nicola. 'It's a bit much to take in.'

Miss Moonshine appeared to concede that. 'It is. But sadly you get used to it. Right. If I am correct, William Travers will be here to pick you up at seven. You go to see a film at the Picture House. You have a choice of Gene Kelly or Humphrey Bogart, I think. You will watch the film, young William will propose and you will accept. Then you will come back here and everything will be sorted out at midnight. That is the only possible outcome. For all of us.'

'But –'

Miss Moonshine held up her hand. 'No more questions. In fact it's probably best if you keep all talking to a minimum.'

'Yeah, the thing is, I'm not very good at that.'

'Try, dear. Try very hard. DO NOT CHANGE A THING. Thankfully it's 1951 and no one really wants to know what you think. Now, how do you fancy some sausages? I seem to remember the butcher now is particularly good…'

At 7.30 they heard a tap on the door. A young man stood there, fresh-faced, hair combed and Brylcreemed in place. He was wearing what Nicola assumed was his Sunday best suit, along with a neatly pressed white shirt and tie and an eager smile.

'That's William,' said Miss Moonshine. 'Except you call him Will. A nice boy. Very bright. He's wasted at the mill in my opinion. Now remember, say very little. Be demure.'

'Demure?'

'It means –'

'I know what it means. I just don't know if I can do it.'

'You wanted a part as an extra,' said Miss Moonshine, as she threw open the door. 'Consider this an audition.'

'Evening, Miss Moonshine,' said Will. 'Lily's dad said she was here…'

'She's been helping me,' said Miss Moonshine, inviting him in. 'To, er… take stock.'

Will grinned. 'That could take a while in this shop.'

'You have no idea,' said Miss Moonshine grimly.

But Will had spotted Nicola and his eyes lit up. No, his whole face. 'Lily. You look smashing.'

Smashing? He was so genuine, Nicola felt herself blush for the first time in years. She glanced at Miss Moonshine in rising panic. 'Er, thank you.'

'Off you two go, then,' said Miss Moonshine. 'Just remember what I told you, Nicola.' She closed the door.

'What did she tell you?' asked Will.

'Umm. Behave?'

Will laughed. 'They all say that. Not that we have to pay any attention.' He gave her a cheeky grin then planted a quick kiss on her cheek. 'I meant what I said, you know. You look lovely.'

Nicola's boyfriend Mark was good with compliments, but no one had ever looked at her the way Will Travers was looking at her now. The man was completely smitten.

'Come on,' he said, grabbing her hand. 'We don't want to be late.'

The streets of Haven Bridge were surprisingly busy for a Saturday evening – much more so than in her day, when people didn't go out till later. Nicola would have loved to linger and look at the clothes and the shops. Shops that were now charity shops looked thriving and bustling. She spotted a bakery she remembered from her childhood. And a hosiery shop! Imagine a shop that just sold tights. No – she peered in the window. Stockings. Eww.

Will turned into a street and she came to a halt. The shops may have changed but not the cinema. 'I thought we were going to the Picture House?'

'That's what you told your dad. Have you forgotten that we're meeting Eddie and Molly and going dancing?'

Dancing? Her first thought was: Ha! Miss M didn't know everything! Her second was: No, stick to the plan. Her third was: Wow, Grandma, you minx!

The sound of a car horn drew their attention. 'Will, Lily. Over here!'

On the other side of the street was a sleek black car, all chrome and gleaming paintwork. It was in a completely different class from the Morris Minors and Austins on the road. The driver's window was down and he beckoned them over with a lazy wave. He was a different class too. Instead of a tie he wore a silk cravat tucked into the collar of his shirt. His hair was slicked back like Will's and his pencil moustache was so fine, it could have been drawn on. He looked like a film star.

Nicola heard Will mutter something under his breath, but he guided her across the road.

'Hello, Jack,' he said, without enthusiasm. 'Can't stop, I'm afraid. We're meeting some people.'

Jack leaned back to show them his passenger, who gave a rather sheepish wave.

'Eddie?'

'Hello, Will. Lily. Guess what? Jack saw us at the bus stop and offered us a lift. He's coming dancing with us.'

'Just like me to save the day, eh?' drawled Jack. 'Hop in, both of you. Lily, why don't you sit up front with me? There's more room for those delectably long legs of yours.'

Nicola glanced at Will, uncertain as to what was going on and looking for a cue, but he was stony-faced.

'Hey,' said Eddie. 'Steady on, old man. I'm in the front.'

'But I know you won't mind shifting, Eddie. Can't you see Lily's admiring my bodywork?' said Jack. 'Impressive, eh, Lil? And the view from up front is always best.'

His gaze lingered a fraction too long on her cleavage. Eww.

Will still hadn't said a word, so Nicola did. She eyed the car critically. 'Lanchester Ten standard, isn't it? Personally I'd have chosen the fixed-head coupé. Or the sports saloon with the new electric windows.' She had no idea what she was saying. They were just words she'd heard her brothers utter. But she had the satisfaction of seeing Jack's jaw drop. Will and Eddie's too, for that matter.

She hadn't noticed the woman in the back seat until she scooted over and threw the door open. 'Don't be such a tease, Jack. Come and sit with me, Lily.'

Lily did, and Will squeezed in beside her.

'Hello, Molly,' muttered Will.

Molly greeted Will then grabbed Lily's arm and squealed. 'You bought the dress! It's gorgeous! The red really suits you. Miss Moonshine never disappoints, does she?'

Molly was wearing a black taffeta skirt and tight fitting broderie anglaise blouse. Bras were rather pointy in the fifties, Nicola concluded. The natural look was a long way off.

By keeping quiet and listening closely to the conversation, Lily managed to work out the relationship between the four people. Eddie and Molly were a couple. Everyone worked at a mill, but Jack seemed to have a position of authority over the others, no matter how much he laughed or cracked jokes. It was not a very comfortable journey.

Jack pulled up right outside a large concrete building that had been derelict for as long as Nicola could remember. Now, though, it was painted baby pink and had a huge illuminated sign saying *Lux.* They joined the crowd flocking up the steps. It seemed dancing on a Saturday night was a popular pastime.

While the men queued for the cloakroom and tickets, Molly dragged Nicola off to the powder room. It actually *was* a powder room. The air was thick with the stuff, and it set Nicola off coughing, waving a hand in front of her face.

'Do you need a cigarette?' offered someone.

'No. No, thank you,' she gasped.

'So,' demanded Molly. 'What are you going to do about Jack?'

'Er…'

'Did you tell Will? No, of course you didn't. He'd punch him right in the nose, wouldn't he, and then there'd be trouble and no mistake. Oh, dear. He can't keep his eyes off you, can he?'

'Who?' said Nicola, struggling to keep up. 'Will?'

'Jack!' said Molly impatiently. 'What a nerve, him turning up like this. Poor Eddie tried to say we'd rather take the bus, but you know no one dares say no to Jack Laithwaite.'

Laithwaite? Wasn't that the name of the old mill in Haven Bridge? Nicola was sure she remembered seeing it on the side of the tall chimney.

'Lily!' said Molly.

'Sorry. What?'

'Are you listening? I asked if you want to borrow my lipstick. You need some colour.'

The men were waiting in the foyer when they got back.

Jack gave a mocking bow. 'May I have the pleasure of the first dance?' he asked Lily. 'Will doesn't mind, do you, old chap? He's going to hog you for the rest of the night, whereas this might be my only chance before the floozies swarm all over me.'

'Don't flatter yourself,' said Nicola's mouth before she could stop it.

'Come on, Lil,' he coaxed, unfazed.

'Actually, I've promised this dance to Will,' she said sweetly. 'Maybe later, Jack.' Or more like never.

She could see Jack didn't like it. 'Well, all right then. But I'm sure you won't grudge me this!'

And he grabbed her and kissed her right on the mouth.

Mark

Mark watched Miss Moonshine, unsure what to do. The old woman looked perfectly normal. Her pupils were fine. She clearly thought she was making sense, but she so wasn't. Truth was, he was worried about her. She'd been talking complete and utter nonsense since he'd arrived an hour ago, after her phone call telling him that Nicola needed to cancel their plans for tonight and that she would see him in the morning. No further explanation had been forthcoming, so of course he'd rushed straight round. Miss Moonshine had tried to keep him out, but there'd been no chance of that. Not until he'd seen Nic and knew she was OK.

She was not OK. His gaze returned to her as she wandered round the shop, cuddling Miss Moonshine's little dog, picking things up, putting them down again, all the while with a slightly vacant expression on her face.

'Have you two done anything unusual?' he asked Miss Moonshine. 'Eaten something? Smoked something?'

Miss Moonshine arched an eyebrow. 'No, we have not. I've told you what happened. I've told you three times, to be exact.'

And Mark did not want to hear *that* outlandish story a fourth time. 'Drunk anything?' he asked.

'Of course not,' said Miss Moonshine. 'Well, perhaps some herbal tea.'

'What kind of herbs?' He spied the teapot, picked it up, took the lid off and sniffed. Chamomile. But then he noticed the bottle of gin it had been hiding.

Miss Moonshine followed his gaze. 'OK, the tea may have been fortified,' she admitted. 'But Lily was rather hysterical. She didn't take it as well as Nicola did. I think she's still in denial about her hair.'

Lily. She'd been calling Nicola Lily since he'd arrived. 'You're really serious about this, aren't you?' said Mark. 'You really believe this nonsense.'

'Look at her,' said Miss Moonshine. He did. Nicola was pulling tissues out of a box. Every time she took one, another popped up, and she gave a little shriek. 'Does that look like your Nicola to you?'

The face, the hair and the body were Nicola's. But… 'There's something wrong with her,' admitted Mark. 'I should take her to a doctor. I should take you both –'

'I do not understand why this is so difficult to grasp,' sighed Miss Moonshine. 'You've been brought up on stories about time travel. I mean, how many times did you see *The Terminator* as a child?'

'That was science fiction.'

'Was it?'

They'd been going round in circles like this for half an hour.

Nicola came to a halt in front of a shelf of toys. She reached out tentatively and touched a plastic dinosaur. It emitted a loud roar, its eyes flashing red, its tail lashing, and she screamed, and Napoleon started barking, and Miss Moonshine picked up the gin and drank it straight from the bottle.

When it had finally all calmed down again, Mark looked at Miss Moonshine. 'OK. Let's pretend you're right. So if she's not Nicola, who is she again?'

'Lily Boddington. A sweet young girl who is completely lost in this time. That's why I phoned to cancel your date. How do you think it would go, meeting your parents?'

He and Nic were barely speaking after that debacle with the painting. He'd already been worrying about that, never mind this. 'I've called them and rearranged.'

'Probably for the best. Look, this is all going to work out fine. Nicola will be back by midnight. I'm sure of it.'

Mark hoped he'd imagined that tiny hesitation. 'This isn't a joke? Or a prank?'

'Have you ever known me to play a prank, young man? Or be anything other than truthful?'

That stopped him. He'd known Miss Moonshine all his life. His mum had brought him into the shop when he was a baby. He'd spent his pocket money here. He'd delivered her newspapers when he was twelve.

Now he remembered the many tales of odd doings in Haven Bridge which all seemed to have Miss Moonshine and her shop at the centre. Feeling the colour drain from his face, he swore softly.

'Language!' Miss Moonshine scolded and Nicola/Lily looked equally disapproving.

'So what should I do?' he asked.

'I'd much prefer you to go home and do nothing, but I can see that's not going to happen. So why don't you take Lily out for a walk? Along the canal, maybe. That won't have changed much. It might reassure her that she hasn't been stolen away by fairies.'

'Fairies?'

'It was her second theory.'

'What was the first?'

'Spacemen.'

'It's OK to take her out?' asked Mark. 'I thought you were

all about disruption to the space-time continuum, glitch in the matrix stuff.'

'As long as you don't let her see the winning lottery numbers or suggest she invest in bitcoin it should be fine. Look at her, poor girl; she's barely taking things in. I'm more worried about Nicola changing things. She is rather outspoken and 1951 probably won't sit too well with her.'

Mark had to agree.

He went over to Nicola – or should he say Lily? Because although she looked identical to his Nic, deep down he knew she wasn't. Deep down he knew that, crazy insane though it was, Miss Moonshine was telling the truth.

He whirled in panic. 'What if Nic doesn't come back? What if she gets stuck?'

'She won't.'

'Are you sure?'

'It's never happened before.'

'This has happened before?'

'My lips are sealed.'

He turned back. 'Lily?'

'Yes?'

'How do you feel?'

'As if I'm in a Hollywood film. In fact, that's what I'm telling myself. Miss Moonshine says it will be fine and she's usually right, isn't she?'

'She is. She says it's OK if we go for a walk.'

Her eyes clouded. 'I have a young man. Will. He'll be wondering where I am.'

Mark glanced back at Miss Moonshine. 'I think you're right. I think we should trust Miss Moonshine.'

'Then I'd like to go for a walk. Thank you.'

So they went out. It was early evening in Haven Bridge and the shops were closing up. Lily stopped dead to stare at a single-decker bus, the on-screen display flashing through all the stops. 'I thought there would be flying cars by now,' she said, and he laughed, until he realised she wasn't joking.

A short walk took them to the canal. They stopped on the bridge to look at the view.

'Is it very different?' asked Mark, curious.

'The clothes certainly are.' It was summer. With all the shorts and bare midriffs on show, Mark could believe that. 'And the hair,' she said, stroking her own short locks and wincing. 'But the ducks are the same. And the boats, of course.' Suddenly she smiled. 'And that bench over there is the same. It's where Will and I sit. It's our special place.'

While they were talking, a canal boat passed below them with a black-and-white collie on deck. Bonnie the dog was one of Mark's patients, and the boatman, Seth, waved when he saw them.

'A friend of yours?' asked Lily.

'Kind of.' Mark led her down to the towpath, taking the opposite direction to the one in which the canal boat was going. Seth was pretty chatty. He'd have stopped to talk and Lily – well, Lily would be hard to explain.

Or maybe not. Mark half-remembered some implausible tale about how Seth had met his wife Laura, a local artist. The story had involved Miss Moonshine's shop, so maybe not that far-fetched.

Lily suddenly stopped. 'That's the same.' She pointed to a tall chimney rising into the blue sky. The name Laithwaite could still be made out faintly on the side. 'Although the air is so much cleaner than I've ever known it.'

'The mill is a warehouse now,' Mark said, sure he wasn't giving too much away. Still, probably best not to tell her that most of the mills were gone, converted to other purposes. Here in Haven Bridge, they were filled with artists.

'So what would you be doing tonight if this hadn't happened?' he asked her.

'On a date with Will,' she said promptly. 'We go dancing every week with some friends.' She giggled. 'Father would have a fit if he knew. He thinks we're at the pictures. Do you think that's very naughty of us?'

'He doesn't approve of dancing?'

'He's the doctor, so his family have to be above reproach. The dance halls are full of factory and mill workers. Salt of the earth, of course, but Mother thinks they can be a bit… common.'

'But… I thought you worked at the mill?' he said, trying to remember what he knew of Nic's family.

'In the office. My choice was nurse or secretary, but it seemed silly training for years to be a nurse and then giving it all up to get married and have babies. The secretarial course was much shorter.'

'Nowadays women can do both,' said Mark. 'Marry, have a family and still have a career. They can have it all.'

Lily laughed. 'That sounds like very hard work, assuming there are still only twenty-four hours in the day.'

Mark had no answer to that. 'What about Will? What does he do?'

'He's a baler at the mill. Father wouldn't normally approve of us walking out, but he's known Will since he was a baby. He doesn't mind me spending time with him.'

There was something in her voice that suggested her father wasn't as happy with the arrangement as she was making out. 'Are you and Will serious?'

She hesitated. 'Yes.'

Mark felt panic start to rise. Weren't Lily and Will supposed to get married? What if they didn't? What would happen to Nic? Would she just disappear off the face of the earth because she'd never been born? 'You don't sound too sure,' he said, pleased his voice was so steady.

'Mother would rather I married someone else.'

No, no, no. 'Who?'

'Jack Laithwaite.'

His gaze went to the chimney. 'The mill owner?'

'His son. Jack's very handsome, but he's a beast.'

This was said with real feeling. 'He's not nice to work for?'

'He's not nice to work *with*. He thinks he's God's gift, that women are just there for his entertainment.'

'Ah,' said Mark uncomfortably. 'Like that, is it? Have you told anyone?'

'Who?' she snapped, then immediately looked contrite. 'Sorry. Actually I told my father. He suggested I wear less make-up to work and a thicker cardigan.'

'Oh. Right. What about Will? Have you told him?'

'No!' Then more calmly, 'No. It's difficult. He and Jack were friends as boys and used to play together. Things are different now.'

'Because Jack is the boss?'

She nodded. 'What would the other… What would Nicola do?'

He couldn't help smiling. 'She'd not put up with anything like that,' he said with certainty. 'Boss or no boss. But then she has the law on her side. Sexual harassment is illegal now in any way, shape or form.'

Lily raised an eyebrow. 'No pinching bottoms? Sometimes I can be black and blue after a day at work.'

'No unwanted touching at all. Even wolf-whistling can cost you your job.'

Lily absorbed that. 'Women in the future know nothing about hair or make-up and they must work extraordinarily long days, but I suppose it isn't all bad.'

Mark laughed. 'Look, do you fancy a drink?'

'In a public house?'

'We could sit in the beer garden.'

'Is that like a ladies' lounge?'

'It's for families. People take their kids.'

'Children in a public house?' She was scandalised but stoic. 'If you think it's suitable, then of course.'

He smiled.

'Did I say something wrong?'

'No, of course not. I was just trying to picture Nic saying something like that.'

'Doesn't she let you choose how you spend your time together?'

He had to think about that too. 'I don't know if *let* is the word.' Come to think of it, he didn't think *choose* was the right word either. Nic was such a ditherer, unable to make up her mind about what to watch on TV or what to have for tea, never mind where to go on a night out. Left to her, they'd never go anywhere.

They went to The Packhorse and found a table in the sunshine.

'What will you have?'

'Would you be shocked if I had a gin and tonic?' Lily asked shyly.

'After the day you've had, I'd be shocked if you didn't.'

He was back a few minutes later with their drinks.

'So what do you and Nicola do on a Saturday night?' she asked him.

'Not dancing. Sometimes we meet friends for a meal. There's the cinema, of course, or a show. But usually it's just Netflix. We stay in and watch television,' he translated.

'With your parents?'

Did she sound a bit sorry for him? 'We have our own house.'

'I don't understand.'

'Nic and I share a house. Up there.' He nodded to the hill behind the town.

'Just the two of you? And your parents don't mind?'

'Actually, we never asked them.'

'But you and Nicola aren't married?'

'Not yet.'

'But you're not at the moment,' she pressed. 'Why would you marry her if you can… if she'll let you…' Her cheeks flamed and she lowered her voice. '*You know*, any time you want?'

The thought of Nic agreeing to 'you know' on demand had him laughing so hard he choked on his pint.

Lily finished her drink, crunching noisily on the ice. 'That was lovely. May I please have another?'

Mark had the impression she wasn't much of a drinker and he remembered the 'herbal tea' at Miss Moonshine's. 'Are you sure that's a good idea? Maybe you should have a soft drink this time. Lemonade?'

'Of course,' said Lily quickly. 'Whatever you think is best.'

A couple of women were passing and one shot Mark a dark look. Lily was sitting, eyes downcast, looking at her hands, the picture of feminine compliance. 'Perhaps just one more, then,' he said uncomfortably.

When he came back a man in a biker jacket and boots was sitting at the table chatting to Lily and they were both smoking.

Nicola

She was too stunned to react to the kiss. Presumably so was Will. In fact, everyone was staring.

Jack laughed it off. 'Consider it payment for the ride here.'

'Are you going to kiss Eddie and Will too?' Nicola demanded, only just resisting the urge to wipe her mouth with the back of her hand.

Jack sauntered of. 'I'll hold you to that dance.'

'Sheesh.' Nicola rolled her eyes. 'What an ego.' Will was glaring at her. 'What?'

'Why do you lead him on like that?' he demanded.

'Why do I…? Wait? What?' Eddie and Molly melted away. 'He kissed *me,*' said Nicola, outraged.

'You didn't exactly fight him off!'

'Well, you didn't exactly speak up either!' She couldn't believe she'd just said that. Since when did she need a man to fight her battles?

Will held his glare a moment longer, then visibly sagged. 'I know. I'm sorry. I shouldn't let him get to me. Not tonight.'

Not tonight? What was so special about tonight? And then she remembered. Will was going to propose.

Which might explain why he was so uptight, but it didn't give him the right to blame her for Jack's behaviour.

She, too, pulled herself together. This wasn't her life to mess with.

When Will asked her if she wanted to dance, she agreed. Taking her hand, he forged a path onto the packed dance floor. He was a good dancer. Far better than Nicola.

'Just let me lead,' said Will, exasperated as they stumbled yet again.

She didn't know how to let him lead. It didn't feel natural, like being pushed around.

'What's wrong?' he asked.

'You have to ask?'

There was a moment's silence. 'I know. I'm sorry. Jack shouldn't have done what he did and I shouldn't have said what I said. But well. A man has limits, Lily. That's all I'm saying.'

'What's that supposed to mean?'

His face was flushed and she realised he was actually deeply upset. 'I've heard the talk,' he muttered. 'Everyone has.'

'About…?'

'You and Jack in the office together with the door closed.'

'Oh. That.' Heavens. What was Lily up to, if anything? Nicola's mind raced as she tried to dredge up everything she knew about her grandmother. Lily had gone to secretarial college, hadn't she, before getting a job in the office at the local mill?

'You know how noisy the looms are,' she said, remembering a school trip to the industrial museum. 'It's impossible to hear myself think when they're running.'

'I know,' said Will. 'But I just wish you'd be more careful. Jack's not the same lad we used to play with when we were kids. When we did our National Service he earned himself a bit of a reputation for being a ladies' man.'

'I suspect that was only in his head,' said Nicola.

'What?'

'Nothing.'

'He was always bragging about his conquests,' said Will. 'I don't want your name… I mean I couldn't bear if people were thinking…' His face flushed in distress.

He was so upset. And so sweet. Suddenly Nicola could see what Lily saw in him. He was worth ten Jack Laithwaites.

'Do you trust me, Will?' she asked.

'Of course,' he said, with no hesitation.

'I swear there is nothing between me and Jack,' she said, crossing her fingers.

Will looked relieved. 'I know that. I do. I'm just jealous that he sees so much of you at work. And I'm sorry you have to put up with him.'

'I can handle myself,' she said confidently.

'Don't underestimate him,' Will warned. 'He's far too used to getting his own way. He's got all that money. His looks. That car.' He frowned. 'Actually, since when do you know so much about cars?' He stared at her, his frown deepening. 'In fact, are you all right, Lil? There's something different about you tonight…'

Quickly she pressed a finger to his lips. 'Let's stop talking about Jack. He shouldn't be allowed to spoil our evening.' There was a proposal on the cards, after all.

Once Nicola gave herself over to the dancing and relaxed, she really enjoyed herself. Women in the fifties might have odd ideas about hair, but they knew how to have a good time and they'd never need a gym! She liked the way the dress swished deliciously around her legs while she danced, too. It was weird that she and her grandmother had the same taste.

Eventually an interval was called.

'Phew,' said Will. 'I'm ready for a break. I'll get the drinks. What do you fancy? Grapefruit or shandy?'

A beer would go down a treat right now and she was disappointed it didn't seem to be on the cards. 'Shandy.'

Will joined a growing queue at the bar while Nicola headed to the powder room in search of Molly. Before she could reach it, though, Jack Laithwaite stepped in front of her, blocking her way.

He flashed her a grin. 'Come outside with me,' he urged. 'Just for ten minutes.'

His stance and proximity were designed to intimidate, but there were plenty of people around, so Nicola wasn't worried. 'No thanks.' She made to go round him.

Jack stepped too, still in her way, and lit a cigarette.

'Those things will kill you,' said Nicola.

'Very funny. Come on. Come outside. Just for a bit. Pretty please. See? Jack Laithwaite doesn't often beg. That's what your teasing reduces me to.'

Her teasing? That was his interpretation of *no*? 'Get out of my way, Jack.'

'Look, you're annoyed. I get it. Perhaps I was a bit fresh. But that's just because you drive me wild. What do you say?' he wheedled.

'Will –'

'Will knows how this works. And so do you. Or at least you should.' His voice had an edge of impatience now, as if it was beginning to dawn on him that things might not actually go his way.

'Do I? Perhaps you should spell it out to me.'

'It goes along the lines of, you scratch my back, I won't sack your boyfriend.'

This was unbelievable. Jack leaned in and she just knew he was going to kiss her again. All Miss Moonshine's words flew out the window as instinct took over. Jack was coming in for a smacker. He was off balance. Nicola used his own momentum against him and instead of pushing him away, pulled him closer. She had one second to see the triumph in his eyes before she caught his wrist and spun him round. A second later he had his face pressed up against the wall, and his arm twisted up his back.

It was all too easy, but then Jack Laithwaite wasn't to know she was a police officer.

'No means no,' she said in his ear.

'Why you –' Jack tried to wrench free and she tightened her grip.

It was only then she realised the error of her move. Usually the next step was to bring out her handcuffs, but of course she didn't have any. Without backup he was going to turn on her the moment she released him.

'Lily?'

She turned her head to see Will standing there, taking in the scene, his face white with shock.

With her attention diverted Jack easily shook himself free.

'Why you little –' He took a menacing step towards Lily, but Will immediately shouldered between them.

'Back off,' he snarled.

It took Jack a moment to regain control. He looked at Will, at Lily, and their growing audience. Then he brushed down his jacket and straightened his cuffs. 'Or what, Travers? Are you going to take a swing at me? What do you think my father will have to say about that?'

'What do you think the back-shift at t'mill on Monday will have to say about you being bested by a girl?'

That was met by silence. Then Jack pulled out another cigarette. 'You can make your own way home,' he said and strolled off.

Will watched him go, fists clenched. Nicola put a hand on his arm and could feel the tension coursing through him. 'Let him go,' she said quietly. 'He's not worth it.'

With an effort, Will pulled himself together. 'Are you all right?' he asked anxiously.

'Yes.'

There was a very odd look in his eyes. 'For heaven's sake, Lily. Where did you learn to do that?'

Oh, dear. Nicola thought on her feet, dredging up even more family history. 'Er, you know my sister was a nurse in France?'

'Deborah, yes?'

'Well, she had to deal with more than a few too many drunken soldiers who didn't always respect boundaries. She taught me a few moves.'

'Well, thank goodness for Debs. Look, what do you say we split? I need to get out of here. I'll find Eddie and Molly and tell them they're on the bus.'

'OK.'

Ten minutes later they were out in the cool evening air. Will immediately removed his jacket and draped it over her shoulders. It was such a natural gesture for him, she accepted it without a word. But she couldn't help remembering when she and Mark first started going out and he'd offered the same thing. She squirmed a bit, remembering how she'd laughed and he'd never offered again.

'Do you want to go for a drink?' Will asked.

Boy, did she need one. 'Yes, please!'

Unfortunately he led her to a café round the corner. His idea of a drink wasn't the same as hers.

Nicola recognised the place. Her mum used to bring her to town shopping when the shops in Haven Bridge couldn't supply what she needed, and they'd stop here for lunch. Then, as a teenager, she'd come with her friends on a Saturday afternoon, making a milky coffee last for hours. She'd seen the café go through many transformations, from wood to Formica and back to wood again. But never had she encountered this thick carpet or someone playing a piano.

'I'm sorry for causing all that bother,' she said after they were seated, hoping it was the sort of thing Lily would say.

'You did nowt wrong,' said Will grimly.

'Will you have much trouble on Monday?'

'I might,' he admitted. 'But Old Man Laithwaite's pretty straight up. And he's bailed Jack out of enough bother to have any illusions about him, so who knows?'

Nicola couldn't think what to say. Had she ruined everything? She had a vague feeling that jobs were easy to come by in the fifties, but what if they weren't? Would Will still ask her to marry him if he was worried he couldn't support her?

'The thing is,' said Will. 'I was thinking of leaving anyway.'

'Leaving Haven Bridge?' No! Her gran had always lived here. Miss Moonshine was going to have a fit!

'Leaving the mill,' Will clarified. 'We both know the best I can hope for there is overlooker when I'm about forty.'

'What will you do?'

His sudden smile lit up the room. 'You remember I wasn't keen on going into the RAF for my National Service? But the truth is, I really enjoyed it, especially the training they gave us in electronics.'

He paused for her response and all she could do was nod.

'I know it's a completely new field, but I haven't been able to get it out of my head since.' His enthusiasm was growing. 'I've been speaking to Miss Moonshine and she –'

'Miss Moonshine?' said Nicola sharply.

Will looked sheepish. 'I was buying a gift for Ma and we got talking. Miss Moonshine thinks there's a big future in electronics. That it's a much better gamble than the mills.'

Oh she did, did she? Don't change anything, be damned! Nicola was going to have a serious word with the old shopkeeper when she got back.

'Actually, she's been helping me apply for technical college,' said Will. 'I'm sorry I didn't say something sooner, but I thought it best to wait and see if anything came of it. But now this has happened, I reckon you need to know. If I go to college it would mean me leaving the mill in any case and getting a job working nights while I studied. And it'd also mean I couldn't afford to marry you for a while.'

'Marry?'

His face turned puce. 'Oh. Aye. Didn't I mention that?'

'No, you did not.'

'Well, of course I'd be doing it for you. For us. But we couldn't get married until I could support you, obviously. Oh, I've made an awful mess of this.'

Actually, he hadn't. Nicola had never had a marriage proposal before but she suspected this was actually a very good one.

He reached into his pocket and offered her a small package, one of those little jewellery boxes Miss Moonshine used in her shop. Not a ring box, though.

She took it. Opened it. Inside was a delicate gold chain with a tiny wishbone pendant. Her breath caught. She'd been given this pendant, or one identical, at her christening. From her grandmother.

'Oh, Will, it's beautiful.'

'It's not a ring,' he said, still blushing furiously. 'I can't ask you to wear my ring when we can't wed for a while yet. But I wondered… I thought if we made each other a promise…'

'Yes,' she said. 'I'd like that.' And because it was only fair to Lily, Nicola added, 'But you have to propose again when the time is right. On one knee, mind.'

He grinned. 'You're the best girl a man could ever have, Lily. I love you so much.'

They caught the last bus back to Haven Bridge, sitting on uncomfortable wooden seats. Resting her head on his shoulder, Nicola thought about everything that had happened. Will had made all these plans and apparently not said a word about them to Lily. She thought about Mark and the row they'd had over the kitchen. She hadn't been annoyed about the colour. She'd been annoyed because he'd taken that first step towards selling the house, moving somewhere bigger, starting a family…

She gulped. She loved Mark, but the speed with which he had moved had frightened her. She wasn't ready for that kind of commitment, but instead of explaining, she'd picked a fight. Lily and Will had some talking to do. But then so did she and Mark.

'Can you get away tomorrow afternoon?' she asked Will. 'Then you can tell me all this again. It's too much for me to take in right now.'

He kissed the top of her head. 'Of course, old thing. There's nothing I'd like better. Let's have a picnic by the canal.'

Will dropped her off at Miss Moonshine's shop, with a rather chaste kiss – not least because Miss Moonshine was watching them through the window with beady eyes.

'It's really good of you to stay overnight so you can be up bright and early to help the old bird with the stocktaking,' he said.

'Isn't it? Goodnight, Will Travers,' she said, and watched him stroll off up the street to disappear into the darkness.

'Well,' said Miss Moonshine eagerly. 'I take it you haven't destroyed the world?'

'No. But I hear Will has a new career ahead of him.'

Miss Moonshine had the grace to blush.

Mark

Mark glared at the guy in the leather jacket.

'Don't get your knickers in a twist,' the man said, rising lazily to his feet. 'I wasn't poaching. The lady saw me light up and she was obviously gasping, so being a gent, I offered, didn't I?' He grinned down at Lily. 'Nice meeting you, darlin'. They don't make 'em like you any more and that's a fact.'

Mark waited till the biker had rejoined his friends before he relaxed and sat down.

'I'm sorry,' said Lily. 'I wanted a cigarette and there are none in Nicola's bag. Are you very cross with me?'

'For smoking? No.' Though he probably shouldn't tell Nic.

'For talking to him?'

'You can talk to anyone you like, Lily. Just as you're equally free not to.'

She didn't look as if she believed him. 'Can I ask you something?'

'Of course. As long as it's not the winner of the Grand National.'

'What is that thing everyone has in their hands or pressed to their ear?'

'What? Oh, that. It's a mobile phone.'

He tried to explain but she got cross, especially when he started on the uses of the internet.

'Now you're making fun of me.' She stood up. 'Excuse me, I need to use the powder room.'

Mark told her where it was, but she was gone so long he began to worry she'd been waylaid by her biker friend. He was just about to go looking when she reappeared in the doorway, chatting to the women who had glared at him earlier. Lily was wearing a happy smile and some bright red lipstick.

'Look what a lovely woman gave me!' she said, sitting down. 'I was sooo jealous of her make-up and I told her I didn't have any of my own so she gave me this and said I could keep it. Wasn't that nice of her?'

Nice? Mark was pretty sure it was downright peculiar. The woman was still looking at him as though he kicked puppies.

'She gave me this too.' Lily showed him a business card which said, '*Abuse comes in many forms. Talk to us. We're listening.*' It was followed by a phone number.

Mark felt his cheeks burn. 'Listen, maybe we've been out too long. Why don't we go home for a bit? Order a pizza?'

'Pizza?'

'You're in for a treat. Trust me.'

'All right. I'd like to see where Nicola lives.'

The streets of Haven Bridge were quiet as they walked home, Lily admiring the shapes and colours of all the cars, surprised to learn that almost everyone owned one of their very own. She pointed out the various shops and told him what they were in her time.

'That's Jackson the baker's. That one's a haberdasher and over there on the corner is the gentleman's outfitter where my father buys his handkerchiefs.' She turned to Mark with a frown. 'Why do you have so many shops selling candles? Is there a shortage of gas?'

'We use electricity now and no, no shortage.' But Mark

had never understood the need for so many candles either, so couldn't explain them.

The house where they lived belonged to Nicola. It was a little end-of-terrace cottage not far from the home of a famous writer and her growing family. It had a tiny front garden filled with tubs of flowers.

Lily was looking flushed from the exertion of walking up the hill. 'My parents would have kittens if they found out I was alone in a house with a strange man. The whole town would be talking about me.'

She exclaimed in delight over the lampshade in the hall that had taken Nicola at least a month to decide on, and admired the comfortable sitting room, stopping for a moment to look at Nic's books and notebooks piled on the table. Her laptop was there too, but it was closed, and Lily didn't ask about it. She did pick up a picture of Nicola aged about six on a picnic with her grandmother. Mark held his breath, but she put it back again without a word.

When she peeked into the kitchen, her nose wrinkled.

'Sorry.' He opened the window. 'I've been painting.'

Lily looked slowly around the room. 'So I see.'

'What do you think?'

She waited a beat too long before answering. 'It's lovely.'

'You don't like it.' He was annoyed. Neither had Nic. In fact it had sparked a huge row. Whereas Mark couldn't see anything wrong with it. The green walls looked fine with the cream cabinets and wooden worktops. Didn't they?

'Surely what matters is that you like it,' said Lily.

He sighed. 'Lily, you're allowed to have an opinion. Women have an equal voice these days, remember? Go on, tell me what you really think.'

'Well… it's too dark, for one thing. It's going to be really gloomy in the winter. The other room is so warm and welcoming, but this isn't a room I'd like to spend a lot of time in.'

'Don't hold back,' he said wryly.

'Sorry. You're angry. What does Nicola think?'

'She hates it,' he admitted. He pictured Nic coming home after her training course, tired and muttering about a hot bath and a glass of chilled wine. He'd been excited, eager to see her reaction. The green was a heritage colour. He hadn't just chosen something at random. The shop assistant had assured him it was in keeping with the age of the house. 'I suppose I should have waited, but to be honest I was just really eager to get started,' he told Lily defensively. 'A few days before we'd been talking about getting married, moving, having a baby. If I left it to her, we'd still be talking about it in ten years' time.'

'I see.'

'What does that mean?' He was already picking up her nuances. In fact he was beginning to see Nic in some of her mannerisms, too.

'Nothing.'

'Lily.'

'Well, you say she didn't like the colour, but that can easily be changed. Did you offer to repaint it?'

'Of course.' He'd been annoyed, though. That paint wasn't cheap.

'So it was some other aspect of what you did that she didn't like. I'd suggest it was a mixture of lack of consultation and the speed with which it was done. You say you only talked about it a few days ago? This house is loved,' she said softly. 'Everything in it has been chosen with care.'

'The house belongs to Nicola,' he said. 'I'm renting mine out. But the way the market is right now it makes sense to trade up.'

'It might make sense to you. But to Nicola? Is she ready?' Lily indicated the pile of textbooks. 'What is she studying?'

'Professional exams.' He didn't think he should tell her that Nic's ambition was to be a detective – that might stretch Lily's belief a bit too far. 'She's doing great,' he said proudly.

'It looks like a lot of work,' said Lily. 'It doesn't look like the life of someone who is ready to have a baby. And this course she was on, presumably that's to further her career too?'

He said nothing.

'I know you said women can do what they want in this time. But what if what they want conflicts with what the man they love wants? I think that will always be a problem, no matter how many laws are passed.'

'You don't think Nic wants to marry me?' he said dully.

'I have no idea,' said Lily. 'Have you actually asked her?'

'Of course. By which I mean, no, not in so many words.'

Nicola was so very bad at making her mind up about anything. Her indecision drove him crazy at times. But did that give him the right to make plans of this magnitude for both of them?

He looked at Lily. 'You are a very wise woman.'

'I know. Now what about this pizza thing you were talking about? And I thought you said you had a television set?'

He glanced at the flat screen on the wall. 'We do.' Though maybe he'd hide the remote, in case her head exploded. 'What's your favourite TV programme?' he asked, thinking of the two hundred channels of repeats he had access to.

'*Come Dancing*,' she said promptly and he laughed.

'Then it's lucky Nic has recorded every episode of *Strictly* ever made. Sit down, make yourself at home. I'll order the food. Do you want some tea while we're waiting?'

'I'd love some, but since I didn't see a teapot in your kitchen I've no idea how you're going to make it.'

The box of teabags in the cupboard might be the biggest shock yet. 'Magic.'

Nicola and Mark

'So how was Lily?' asked Nicola.

She and Mark were curled on the settee together sharing a bottle of wine – and their adventures – before bed.

'She was sweet but also shrewd and very practical.' Mark smiled. 'I liked her. It's a shame I didn't get to meet your gran when she was alive.'

'I barely remember her.' Nicola fingered her necklace, which she'd dug out of her jewellery box as soon as she got home.

'How was your grandpa?' asked Mark.

'I thought he was a bit wet at first, but he wasn't really. In fact he was ambitious and full of ideas.'

'Presumably you didn't give away any secrets, since the world is still here,' he said.

She mock-glared at him. 'Me? Do you know what my grandfather did for a living?'

'Something in development?'

'He worked for a subsidiary of the company that invented mobile phones. He would never say where he got the idea.'

'Oh,' said Mark, colouring slightly.

'Yes, oh. I think you and Miss M have a lot to answer for.' She snuggled closer.

'Lily hated the colour of the kitchen,' he said.

'Fine woman.'

'She said maybe it wasn't about the colour. That maybe I was rushing you into something you're not ready for. Is that true?'

Nicola looked up at him with a soft smile. 'What's true is that I love you. But, yes, we need to talk.' She thought of Lily and Will picnicking by the canal tomorrow, having a conversation about their future. 'Tell you what. Let's do it tomorrow. Take a picnic along the canal.'

Mark stroked her hair and smiled. 'I know just the bench to sit on.'

*

In her darkened shop, Miss Moonshine entered the changing room. The dress was on a hanger by the mirror. She scooped it up and, with Napoleon trotting at her heels, climbed to the attic and the large chest which housed some of her more 'troublesome' items.

Napoleon whuffed approvingly as she carefully laid the dress inside the chest and turned the key.

'I know. Better late than never,' murmured Miss Moonshine.

With a sigh of satisfaction and the knowledge that all was once more right with her world, she pocketed the key and went to bed.

Living on the edge of the Yorkshire moors, Jacqui Cooper doesn't have to look far for inspiration for her writing. Her short stories regularly appear in popular women's magazines, including *Woman's Weekly*, *The People's Friend* **and** *Take a Break*. **Writing has always been her dream and she is thrilled to now be able to do it full time.**

Caught Red-Handed

By Sophie Claire

Ruby moved furtively around the shop. By the window a young man with his back to her was browsing, a tiny chihuahua was curled up asleep in a basket, and the shopkeeper, Miss Moonshine, was in the back doing what looked like ballet exercises at a barre. Weird, thought Ruby, glancing twice. And Miss Moonshine was surprisingly flexible for her age. Ruby had heard she was well into her eighties, although no one in Haven Bridge was sure. Gramps said she'd been running this shop when he was a boy, but that didn't stack up, because he was in his eighties too; Ruby figured he must have got mixed up.

She swept her gaze over the display of felt birds in a basket, and an antique sewing machine labelled 'In perfect working order'. But she couldn't see the fountain pen. Her skin prickled with panic. She searched for it frantically. It had been on this shelf when she'd come in a couple of days ago, nestled in an open case that bore the name of an exclusive brand. She'd been surprised Miss Moonshine had left it out and not kept it in a glass cabinet.

Her spirits dipped. Perhaps it had been sold.

Then she spotted it. The gold lettering shone out against the sleek black pen. Her heart jumped with excitement that it was still here. Then slugged heavily at the price.

Ruby bit her lip. On her first day in Haven Bridge, she'd been casually browsing Miss Moonshine's emporium when she'd seen it and instantly recognised it. But the price had made her eyes water, so she'd walked away. She had no money left – not a penny – after the gap year she'd just spent travelling around the world, and her parents were both financially stretched following their divorce.

But the pen had played on her mind ever since. It would mean so much to Gramps to be reunited with it. She could picture his face and how his eyes would light up. Like they used to – before Gran died. He could really do with an injection of happiness.

What should she do? Her fingers twitched and she glanced at the back room. Perhaps if she talked to Miss Moonshine.

But it was risky. She'd been visiting her grandparents in Haven Bridge since she was a girl and although she'd heard of people who'd negotiated with the eccentric shopkeeper, she also knew Miss Moonshine could be stubborn. If she didn't want you to have an object, that was the end of it. What if she turned Ruby away? What if someone else bought the pen? She was only here for a week. No, there was only one option. Her fingers tingled. Her gaze fixed on the pen and fiery desperation gripped her. She *had* to have it.

Glancing left and right, she picked up the pen and slipped it into her denim jacket pocket. Her face flushed with violent heat as she headed for the door. This made her a thief. A criminal! She had to get out fast. The shop bell jingled behind her, but she didn't look back.

Outside, a bitter wind swept down the street and slapped her burning cheeks. She set off at a brisk pace towards her grandad's house, trying to look purposeful rather than guilty. She couldn't quite believe what she'd done. She'd never stolen anything before. Her hands dug deep into her pockets and curled around the pen. It felt solid and warm in her fingers. It was comforting, actually.

At Gramps' house, she let herself in. He was in the kitchen. 'Ruby! There you are. I've just put the kettle on.'

'How are you feeling today, Gramps?'

'Oh, I'm fine. You know, keeping on. Mustn't grumble.'

She smiled. He never grumbled. Despite his arthritis and the gout that sometimes laid him up for days and meant he couldn't get out into his beloved garden.

Which reminded her. She glanced out of the kitchen window. 'Got any jobs you want me to do? I can mow the lawn if you like.' Conscious that he was on his own, she wanted to make herself as useful as possible while she was here.

He waved a hand. 'Later. Let's have a cuppa first. I've got ginger snaps.'

'Here, let me.' She took the heavy kettle out of his hands and poured hot water into the chipped teapot that he refused to replace because it reminded him of Gran. Ruby got a spoon out of the drawer to stir it as he always told her to.

'There's something I want to talk to you about, Ruby.' He handed her the packet of biscuits and lowered himself stiffly into a chair.

She looked up, surprised by his serious tone, and carried their mugs of tea over to the table. 'What is it?'

'I've booked to see a solicitor. I'm going to change my will.'

His will? She didn't like to think about that. She broke a biscuit in half and ate it hungrily.

He continued, 'I'm going to sign this place over to you.' He gave a slight nod to indicate his modest terraced house. 'I don't want her to have any of it.'

Her face fell. 'Oh Gramps –'

He shook his head resolutely. 'Not a penny.'

The taste of ginger on her tongue suddenly lost its sweetness. Mum wouldn't care about the house or its value, but she'd be really upset. 'That's a bit harsh, don't you think?' she said carefully.

'No. Your mother made her bed.' His lips pressed together.

Ruby loved her grandfather, but oh, how he could be stubborn. And old-fashioned. 'She fell in love, Gramps. It's not a crime.'

His face flushed with dark colour and she felt a jab of alarm. At his age, with his heart condition, a spike in blood pressure could be dangerous. 'She committed adultery,' he ground out. 'In my book that is very much a crime.'

'Dad's moved on.' She couldn't say he'd forgiven her, but he'd moved to the South, met someone and started a new life. He was happy.

And Ruby was relieved to see her parents both making new lives for themselves. They'd been so unhappy together. None of this had been easy, but it had been clear for a long time that their marriage wasn't working.

'Yes, well – your dad always was a pushover.'

Ruby gazed sadly at her grandad. He hadn't always been grouchy and sour like this. She remembered when she was little he used to take her out into the garden with him and give her simple tasks: raking leaves in the autumn or sieving compost for stones and twigs. He used to chuckle at her squeals when she found a worm, and he'd been so patient with her. Even the time when she accidentally pulled out all his lupin seedlings, mistaking them for weeds. They'd taken twelve months to cultivate from seed, she later discovered.

No, it was only since Gran died two years ago that he'd become short-tempered, and then last year when he'd learned about Mum and Nick, he'd completely lost it. And things hadn't improved since. In fact, by cutting his daughter out of his life he'd isolated himself, and the loneliness was only making him more bitter. Ruby could see how much worse he'd got while she'd been away and wished she could help.

'Gramps, will you think about it again? Please? I don't

want you to regret it.' She didn't even want his inheritance anyway.

'My mind's made up. I'm going to see the solicitor next week.'

*

'How's Gramps?' was the first thing Ruby's mum asked when she called her that evening. Ruby was sitting cross-legged on the bed, gazing out of the window at her grandad's back garden. It looked beautiful now at the height of summer. There was colour everywhere, the bushes and lawn were neatly trimmed, and the fruit trees at the top of the hill were studded with tiny apples and pears that would swell and ripen in the autumn.

'He's fine. I dead-headed the roses for him under his careful instruction.'

'You mean, he sat on the bench with his stick and barked orders at you?'

Ruby laughed. 'Exactly that.'

'Remember how you used to love to help spread his "special fertiliser" around the roses when you were little?'

Ruby grinned as she remembered. 'Yeah – until the day I slipped and landed in it.'

Her mum's laughter was like tiny bells. 'Then he told you what it was. You refused to go near the manure or even the roses after that.'

'Once bitten, twice shy,' she murmured.

Mum asked quietly, 'Did he get my birthday card?'

'Yes.' Ruby didn't say he'd taken one look at it and tossed it aside. There was a short pause before she mustered the courage to say, 'Mum, he said something I think you should know.'

'What is it?' her mum said quickly. 'He's not ill, is he?'

'No.' She sucked in air. 'He's going to see a solicitor. He's planning to change his will.' She gripped the phone, bracing herself and feeling the pain her mum must be feeling.

A long silence followed, then her mum said sadly, 'I thought he might.'

Ruby didn't know what to say.

'Is he going to leave it to you, love?'

'Yes,' she said heavily.

'Well, that's good. At least he's not giving it to a donkey sanctuary.'

Ruby laughed, but it sounded forced. 'I'm sorry, Mum.'

'Don't be. It's not your fault.'

'I don't know why he won't see you. I've tried talking to him, tried to persuade him, but…'

'Don't worry, love. This is between me and him. I don't want it to spoil your relationship with him too.'

Ruby clenched her fist in frustration. Her mum was only half an hour away, but she might as well be on the other side of the world now Gramps refused to see her. 'He's so stubborn and – and old-fashioned.'

'He is.'

'I don't know why he won't move on. I thought by coming here and talking to him… But he won't listen.' She glanced at her rucksack and thought of the pen she'd secreted away inside it.

She still couldn't believe she'd stolen it, and it had been keeping her awake at night. Several times she'd considered taking it back to the shop. But she couldn't let go of the hope that it might bring Gramps a spark of joy. Change him, help him soften a little. More than anything, she wanted him and Mum to be reunited and, irrational as it might seem, she'd felt certain when she'd seen the pen that it held the key.

Mum said, 'I never told you about your gran and Nick's father, did I?'

Ruby frowned. 'What do you mean?'

'He was her first love. Alfie Wright.'

What? Ruby sank back against the pillow. Her grandparents had been the most solid and loving couple she'd known. She couldn't imagine Gran with anyone else. But she supposed this must have been a long time ago. 'Did Gramps know?'

'Yes. He was extremely jealous of Alfie. Always held a grudge. If I'd met anyone else but Nick, your grandad might have forgiven me, but because he's a Wright…'

She didn't need to finish the sentence. Ruby understood. 'What happened? With Nick's dad and Gran, I mean. Did she – were they…' she tried to think of the word Gramps would use, '… sweethearts?'

'For a short while. But when his family saw he was getting serious about her, they put a stop to it immediately. They were mill owners, you see, and she was just a local girl. Considered beneath him.'

'How awful.'

'Not for Gramps. She went on to marry him instead.'

'But he was her second choice?' Ruby asked.

'Only in his mind. Your gran really loved him. But he always saw Alfie Wright as a rival. Couldn't even be civil to him when they met. He was always bitter.'

'That sounds like Gramps.' She sighed.

'Yes. Quick to anger, slow to forgive.' She added sadly, 'If he forgives at all.'

'He'll come round, Mum, I'm sure he will.'

The silence on the line suggested her mum disagreed, but Ruby couldn't bear to lose hope for her small family. She desperately wanted to see Mum and Gramps reunited.

'Well, anyway,' Mum said. 'Are you still coming to the garden party on Saturday? Nick and I are looking forward to seeing you.'

'Of course I am.' It was more than a garden party. Her mum and Nick were celebrating their engagement, and they'd invited all their close friends and family – Gramps included, although he'd refused of course. 'I wouldn't miss it for the world.'

*

'Happy birthday, Gramps!'

Ruby gave him the small package she'd carefully wrapped in tissue paper, hoping it would be easier for his arthritic fingers to unwrap. She held her breath as he tore the paper back, revealing the black fountain pen. The gold letters caught the light as he held it up and squinted to read it.

Then his eyes widened with shock. 'Where did you find this?'

'I spotted it by chance… in a vintage place.' Guilt corkscrewed through her, but she couldn't tell him the truth. He'd be livid if he knew she'd taken it from Miss Moonshine's.

'I can't believe it,' he said, staring at the engraving: *To Betty, with all my love.* 'Betty's pen.'

Ruby smiled fondly as she remembered watching her gran write letters with it when she was small. Gran's sister lived in America and they used to write to each other every week: long handwritten letters on thin lightweight paper and posted in airmail envelopes. Ruby used to sit next to her right here in the front room and pretend to write her own letters, although as an only child she didn't have a sibling to send them to.

'I know Gran lost it before she died, and when I saw it I thought you might like to have it back. To remember her by.' But her fond nostalgia vanished when she looked up.

Gramps was staring at the pen.

'Gramps? What's wrong?'

'Nothing.' He put it down on the table hastily, as if he couldn't bear to touch it. 'I hope you didn't pay much for it.'

Her cheeks burned with guilt. 'No.'

He didn't say anything. Just kept on glowering at it. This

wasn't the reaction she'd expected. She'd taken it thinking it would mean the world to him. Perhaps he was a little overwhelmed. Perhaps his emotions and love for Gran were choking him up. After all, he'd adored her, and when she'd died he'd taken it hard.

Yet he didn't seem choked up. He seemed… furious.

Ruby tried to fill the silence. 'It should come in handy. And every time you use it, you'll think of Gran.'

Was it her imagination or did a look of pain make his features momentarily crumple? But it was gone in an instant. 'Not much use for these things nowadays, is there? Not with all this technology.' He gestured to his iPad nearby.

Ruby didn't know what to say. She swallowed her disappointment, and berated herself. This was only what she deserved after stealing a pen then passing it off as a gift she'd paid for.

He cleared his throat and said stiffly, 'Well, anyway – thank you, Ruby.' He crossed the room to put her card on the mantelpiece. It joined one other solitary card from his cleaner, and she wondered what he'd done with Mum's card. He must have binned it. 'I mean it. It's been lovely having you here on my birthday, pet,' he said. 'Thanks.'

'Don't be soft. You know I love coming to stay, Gramps.'

'Yeah, well. I'm sure a young girl like you has got better things to do with her summer holidays. I feel… privileged.' He blinked hard and his grey eyes gleamed in the dark hallway.

Ruby's heart folded. Everything about his empty kitchen and quiet life screamed loneliness. If only he wasn't so stubborn. 'Gramps,' she said carefully, 'you know Mum misses you loads. She'd have loved to come over today too.'

Immediately, his expression changed. His eyes became icy slits. 'That's enough of that.'

'Gramps, I really –'

He opened the door to go. 'It's been a good day. Let's not spoil it.'

*

Day had drifted into evening, and now it was almost night the beautiful gardens took on a whole new appearance as Ruby looked around admiringly. The grand country home had belonged to the Wright family for over a hundred and fifty years and was now an upmarket hotel, which made it perfect for events such as this: Nick and her mum's engagement party. As the bulging, colourful borders were swallowed up by darkness, rows of golden spotlights sprang to life around the edges of the neat lawn. Uplighters made the stately house and old oak trees glow, and thousands of sparkling fairy lights had been strung all around, illuminating the guests' smiling faces.

Ruby had been here since four o'clock, though, and she was beginning to tire of making small talk with people she didn't know. But it was a little early to leave, so she found a quiet spot on the fringes of the crowd where, in the shadows, she could gather her thoughts for a few moments. Her mum and Nick were busy threading their way through their guests, trying to speak to everyone, welcoming the late arrivals and being accosted by people congratulating them on their engagement. Ruby watched as Nick said something which made everyone laugh, then wrapped his arm around her mum and they smiled into each other's eyes. Ruby smiled too. It was good to see her mum so happy. Since she'd met Nick, she'd changed. She was more relaxed, and seemed younger. If only Gramps was here to see it.

As her gaze swept over the unfamiliar faces in the crowd, she spotted a guy around her own age, or perhaps a little older, twenty or so. He had glossy brown hair that flopped over his eyes. She'd seen him before, but couldn't think where.

A waiter passed carrying a tray of empty glasses and Ruby shifted from one foot to the other, wondering how long she needed to stay before she could politely leave. She didn't want to upset her mum and Nick, but she was getting cold and there was only so much champagne you could drink on your own.

'It *is* you. I saw you in Miss Moonshine's.'

The deep, accusing voice made her whirl round. It was him – the guy with the gorgeous hair. As his words sank in, she felt the buzz of fear. It came back to her now: he'd been in Miss Moonshine's the day she'd stolen the pen. She swallowed.

But he'd been on the other side of the shop with his back to her – he couldn't have seen what she'd done. Could he?

She tried to calm herself, but her heart had picked up in panic and wouldn't listen. 'Did you?' She smiled. 'Great place, isn't it? A real treasure trove.'

He was really good-looking. In the darkness she couldn't make out the colour of his eyes, but she could see how well-structured his features were. She wondered who he was and how he knew Mum and Nick.

'Except it's not, is it?' he said. 'A treasure trove, that is. It's a shop and you're supposed to pay for what's on sale.' His tone was clipped, his eyes cool.

Mortified, her gaze slid away from his. He'd *seen* her! He knew what she'd done. 'It – it used to be my gran's,' she mumbled. Her mouth was papery dry.

'What did?'

'The pen.' How to explain? She couldn't. The feeling, the compulsion she'd had to take it. Electricity crackled in her head and words began to spill from her mouth. 'The price tag was steep, I don't have that kind of money – neither does my grandad – but I thought he'd be so pleased to have it back because it was lost years ago when my gran was alive – and now she's dead and...' She broke off, blinking fast.

Gramps hadn't even seemed happy to see the pen, and the heavy weight of disappointment only added to her guilt. It had all been for nothing.

The stranger's eyes narrowed. 'So you thought you'd steal it and that would be OK?' he said, astonished.

She lowered her gaze. The champagne glass in her hand felt thin and fragile. Shame swirled through her – and resentment, too. This stranger had written her off as a thief, but she wasn't, not normally, and she hated that he'd caught her in the act.

'How do you even know it was the same pen?'

She lifted her head and met his gaze. 'It's engraved with her name.'

His eyes widened with surprise. Then his expression softened. Perhaps he understood now. 'Yeah, well. It's still no excuse for stealing. Especially from an old lady like Miss Moonshine.'

OK, maybe he didn't understand, then. She felt a flush of anger as she watched him walk away, and her hand curled into a tight fist.

But he was right.

She'd done a bad thing, and although she'd done it for Gramps, that didn't justify it.

*

The stranger's accusation played on Ruby's mind and kept her awake all night. Next morning she got up early and slipped out before Gramps was even out of bed. Wearing her smartest clothes, she walked down the hill into the town centre. The sun had only just risen above the hills, but the sky was ink-blue and it promised to be a beautiful day.

She'd decided she couldn't live with her guilty conscience any longer, which left her with two options. Either she returned the pen to Miss Moonshine – but how would she explain that to

Gramps? Or she found a job and repaid her debt. She'd planned to spend this month visiting her dad and going camping with friends, but perhaps she could rethink. Haven Bridge was popular with tourists, after all; there was bound to be casual work going.

She paused outside the first café and breathed in the smell of freshly baked bread, feeling confident she'd find something, and once she'd saved enough money she'd repay Miss Moonshine.

Drawing her shoulders back, she put on her brightest smile and went in.

*

'Where have you been all day?' Gramps asked, when Ruby got back.

The clock in the front room chimed six-thirty. He was sitting at the table with a notebook open. Her heart gave a tiny leap when she spotted the fountain pen in his hand.

'Just doing a spot of job-hunting.'

'Job-hunting? I thought you had a holiday planned.'

'It won't be the end of the world if I cancel.'

'Are you short of money?' He reached for his wallet. ''Cause if you are –'

'No!' She held her hand up, horrified. 'I mean, thanks Gramps, but I'm fine. Would you mind if I stayed with you a bit longer?'

He beamed. 'Mind? Why would I mind?'

That was a relief.

'What kind of work are you looking for?'

She shrugged. 'Bar work. Waitressing.' She'd done both while she'd been travelling. She wasn't afraid of getting her hands dirty.

'Did you find anything?'

'Not really.' Every pub, café and restaurant had told her

they didn't need anyone. There'd only been one place with a vacancy: a small museum that needed an 'actor' to stand outside in the pillory and have rotten fruit thrown at them. In bygone times it had been a punishment for petty criminals, and now it was a great way of drawing in customers, apparently. Ruby held out hope that she'd find something more suitable tomorrow.

'What about you?' she said, sitting down opposite him. 'What are you up to?'

Her grandad wasn't the kind to blush, but she was sure she detected a spot of colour in his cheeks as he smoothed out the pages of the notebook. She made out the words *Dear Betty* at the top of the page.

'Thought I'd see if the pen worked, that's all.' He held it up. 'Still does, I'm glad to say.'

'That's good.'

He cleared his throat and ran a finger across the gold engraving. 'Your gran loved this pen.'

'I remember.'

'Used to pour her heart out to her sister each week, she did. Pages and pages telling her every little detail of what she'd been up to.'

Ruby nodded, smiling. She felt the sudden bite of tears. Her gran had been such a warm, loving woman. Losing her had changed her grandad. She didn't remember him being so angry before and she was sure the argument with Mum would never have happened if Gran had still been here.

'Thank you,' he said unexpectedly.

'What for?'

'For finding this pen and bringing it home.' He held it up and gazed at it. There was a faraway look in his eyes, as if he was watching scenes from the past play out in his mind.

Ruby's gaze fell to the words he'd written:

Can you believe Ruby found your pen? After all these years. I always wondered what happened to it…

Gramps turned back and his lips curved. 'Feels like I've got a tiny part of her back.'

*

'You OK there?'

Ruby closed her eyes as yet another tomato flew towards her. Thankfully, it hit the wooden board a few inches away from her left ear, but she felt the spray of seeds and juice hit her cheek. 'I'm fine,' she said stoically and licked her lips.

Then wished she hadn't. They were *rotten* tomatoes, remember?

'Good,' said Penny, her new boss. She was the matronly type and very efficient at converting curious passers-by into ticket buyers for the museum. Ruby appreciated that she never strayed far and kept an eye open in case anyone got too close or too enthusiastic about hurling soft fruit at her. So far, only very young children had taken part – and they were mostly terrible aims – but it would only take a group of teenagers or drunken adults to spoil the fun. She could lift the wooden block and free herself at any time, but Ruby still felt a little vulnerable like this.

'You're doing really well,' Penny told her. 'The longest anyone's lasted has been forty-eight hours. We were beginning to despair about the whole idea, but it's a fantastic way to draw the crowds. Really gets the tourists' attention.'

Ruby tried to nod, but found she couldn't. 'Yes, I can imagine,' she said instead, and braced herself as another family approached. Their little boy snatched a handful of grapes and looked a little too eager to throw them at her. She closed her eyes. Damn, he was a good shot. Right on the nose.

Penny approached and wiped her eyes for her. 'There, that's better,' she muttered, then resumed the conversation as if nothing had happened. The boy, meanwhile, was reloading with fruit. 'We thought it would appeal to would-be actors, but I suspect the role isn't challenging enough.'

Ruby side-eyed her. She couldn't tell if this was dry Yorkshire humour or a serious observation. 'Well, I'm no actress. I just need the money. And I'm not from round here so there's no danger of anyone I know recognising me.'

'Ah, yes. Although with all that tomato juice, they probably wouldn't know it was you anyway.'

Ruby laughed – just as another tomato hit her.

'I got her in the mouth!' the boy yelled, delighted, and squeals of laughter rang around the busy square to excited chants of 'Can I have a go? Can I?'

Ruby could have kicked herself. What a rookie mistake. 'Keep your mouth shut' was rule number one. Reminding herself of how well this job paid, she opened her eyes to see lots more children excitedly crowding round the bucket of fruit, and Penny scooting towards their parents with her ticket book.

It was the figure beyond that caught Ruby's eye – the one that suddenly stopped and turned to look twice.

He'd been skirting the crowd, head down, hurrying past when he abruptly halted. Ruby closed her eyes because a rainstorm of grapes flew her way, and when she reopened them he was staring directly at her.

It was him. From the party.

Later, she wondered if her cheeks really had glowed tomato red. At the time, all she could think was *please carry on walking*. There were more fruit missiles, then Penny herded the now enormous group of families into the museum and suddenly the square fell quiet.

His shoes tapped lightly on the cobblestones as he approached. He looked a little wary – and very concerned. 'Are you – erm – OK?' he asked.

'Never better,' she said with bright sarcasm. Her toes curled with embarrassment. Of all the people…

'Were they –' He ran a hand through his hair, clearly perplexed, 'I mean, are you being paid to do this?'

'No. I just fancied absorbing my five-a-day for a change. A fruit facial.' She tried to lift the wooden board up and free herself, but it was stuck. Panicking, she glanced left then right, and spotted that a catch had been knocked and the contraption was jammed.

She hesitated, wondering if she should ask him to free her, then decided no. She couldn't bring herself to ask for his help, not after the last time they'd met.

He shifted his weight from one foot to the other, clearly perplexed by the situation, and it would have been quite comical – if it wasn't so utterly humiliating.

Just then, the doors of the museum opened and Penny flew out. 'Right, off you go, Ruby,' she said. 'You're due a break. Take as long as you need, but don't clean up too much. We need them to see a bit of tomato juice so they understand what they're aiming for.'

'I think the catch has stuck,' Ruby said.

Penny peered closer. 'Ah. So it has. There you are.'

The wooden beam lifted, and Ruby straightened up, a little stiff, and reached for the face cloth in her back pocket. Penny turned to the young man. 'Were you waiting to buy a ticket? You've just missed the guided tour, I'm afraid, but there'll be another one as soon as I can drum up a few more takers.'

'Oh – no,' he said. 'I just – I was just passing when I saw… Ruby. That's all.'

Penny shot Ruby a quizzical look, no doubt remembering how she'd said she didn't know anyone round here. She opened her mouth to explain, but a family approached and Penny rushed off towards them brandishing tickets.

Ruby was caught between wanting to dash inside and make the most of her break, but also desperately curious to know something.

In the end, curiosity won out. 'I'm Juliette's daughter,' she said. 'Are you a friend of Nick's?'

He shook his head. 'I'm his nephew. My name's Paul.'

Ah. So they were practically family.

This was not good. Not good at all.

*

Ruby went straight to the bathroom to shower the minute she got home, while Gramps prepared tea. His cleaner had made lamb hotpot earlier and left it on the stove, and when Ruby came downstairs she could hear him moving about the kitchen. The clink of crockery, the chunner of the radio.

As she passed the front room, she glanced in – then did a double take. The notebook and pen had been left on the table, and it seemed like Gramps had been writing in it again.

She hesitated, then went to take a closer look. Her eyes skimmed the words on the page. Like letters, the entries each began *Dear Betty,* and to start with they were short and hesitant.

You'd call me an old fool for writing this, but I miss you…

…

I always hated seeing you using this pen, but you flat out refused to get rid of it. You said it was given with love and there wasn't enough love in the world that a single drop should be wasted. Perhaps it's a sign that it's turned up again now…

…

This may sound daft but writing this is making me feel closer to you. Almost like your pen is helping me find the words I wish I could say to you if only you were here…

Not wanting to pry any more, Ruby closed the book, her head full of questions. Why had he hated seeing Gran use the pen?

Just then the kitchen door opened. 'Ruby!' Gramps called. 'Tea's ready.'

She left the room, feeling a burst of joy that he was using the pen after all.

*

'I really don't think we should do this,' Mum said, as she paced up and down in the back garden.

Ruby had given up trying to persuade her to sit next to her on the wooden bench. It might be best if her mum worked off her nervous energy. Keeping an eye on the back door, she willed Gramps to hurry home from the pub.

'It'll be fine, Mum,' she said, crossing her fingers. 'He's always in a good mood after seeing Harry, and I promise he's been missing you as much as you miss him.'

'No.' Her mum stopped. 'No,' she said again. 'I can't do it. I'm sorry, Ruby, but I can't take any more of his criticism.'

'Don't go!' Ruby shot to her feet, but her mum had already disappeared inside the house. She chased after her. 'Mum, wait!'

Mum stopped, reluctantly, in the hall. 'I know you mean well, love, but I know him better than you, and this is not a good idea.'

'It is. It is! He just needs to see you and he'll –' Her mum was staring at something. 'What is it?'

Mum stepped in the front room. 'Is that –'

Ruby followed as she hurried over to the table.

'Your gran's pen?' Mum gasped. She picked it up, wide-eyed.

Ruby avoided her gaze and crumpled with shame.

Mum seemed too astounded to notice. 'She lost that years ago. Where did he find it?'

'Actually, I found it.' Ruby pushed the toe of her Doc Marten boot into the thick carpet. 'Someone was selling it and I recognised it straight away, so I – I got it for him. For his birthday.' She hated herself for lying, but she was so scared her mum would look at her the same way that guy Paul had.

Although she knew she'd have to confess eventually. She just hoped Paul wouldn't spill the beans first.

'You gave it to Gramps?' Her mum looked astonished.

She nodded. 'I thought he'd like it, but he was a bit weird about it at first.'

'I'm not surprised.' Mum put the pen back beside the notebook.

'What do you mean? I thought he'd be thrilled to have it back. He gave it to her, after all.'

Mum frowned. 'No, love. Alfie Wright, Nick's dad, gave it to her.'

The clock on the mantelpiece ticked loudly. A short riff of birdsong drifted in through the open window. 'What?' Ruby's mouth became dry. 'But the inscription – *To Betty with all my love...*'

Mum shook her head sadly. 'It's an expensive pen. Gramps could never have afforded it.'

'Oh, God. I'm surprised he didn't throw it in the bin.' No wonder he'd looked horrified when he'd unwrapped it. Then she glanced at the notebook. 'But you know, he seems to have come round since. He's started writing a diary and it's like letters to Gran.'

'Really?' Mum's eyes lit up. 'That's so sweet.'

'That's what made me think –'

The metallic scrape of the key in the door made them both turn. Ruby squeezed her mum's hand. 'Don't worry,' she whispered, then went into the hall to greet him.

'Hello, love,' he said. 'I thought I heard voices.'

She drew her shoulders back and bravely met his eye. 'Hi, Gramps. Yes, Mum's here. I invited her.'

He stopped. His benign expression turned thunderous. 'Juliette? Here – in my house?'

Ruby stepped back as he barrelled past into the front room. 'Gramps, wait. I was hoping you'd just talk to each other and –'

'Talk? We have nothing to say.' He glared at her mum.

'Please, Gramps. It's really upsetting me that you two aren't speaking, and I know it's upsetting you too –'

'What's upsetting me is her being in my house!' His face had turned red and his eyes were huge in their sockets. He pointed to the front door. 'Go! Get out!'

'Gramps!' Genuinely shocked, Ruby stepped forward.

'It's OK, love,' Mum said. 'I'll go. I knew this was a bad idea.'

'No. Mum, don't go! Gramps, think about what you're doing. We're your family. The only family you have left. Are you really going to throw that away for the sake of an old grudge for a man who isn't even alive any more?'

He stared at her. He seemed shocked by her words. Ruby rarely lost her temper, but this was heartfelt. She desperately wanted this rift to be over, and the more she learned about what had happened in the past, the angrier it made her that those events were casting such a black shadow over the present day.

Tears pricked her eyes. 'Gran would never have wanted you two to fall out like this. She'd be –' She stopped. 'Gramps?'

He clutched a hand to his chest and she realised belatedly that he wasn't staring in shock. He was having some kind of–

'Dad!' Her mum rushed forward to catch him, but his weight must have been too much because the two of them tumbled to the floor. 'Call an ambulance, Ruby, quick!'

*

Gramps was in hospital for six days, but it seemed like weeks to

Ruby. She felt totally responsible for his heart attack, no matter what her mum or the doctors said.

'He's had high blood pressure for months but wasn't taking his medication, apparently,' her mum said. 'Don't blame yourself, Ruby. You're young and you see the best in people. I've known your grandad much longer. He's always been headstrong. Only your gran could soften his hard edges.'

Ruby was still thinking about that when she got back from the hospital to Gramps' dark house. She'd been naïve to hope he'd change, her plan had been foolishly optimistic – and dangerous. She wished she could roll back time.

Too worried to sleep, she tidied the kitchen instead, then picked up a duster and went into the hall. When she'd removed a thin layer of dust from the pictures on the wall and the shelf above the radiator, she moved on into the front room. The brass clock ticked steadily as she wiped around it, and the framed photo of her gran smiled solemnly at her.

Ruby picked it up. 'I'm sorry, Gran,' she whispered. 'I really messed up this time. But I just wanted to help. I thought if he saw Mum he'd realise how stupid this whole argument is, and – oh, I don't know what I thought. But I'll never meddle again, I promise.'

And she meant it. She was so glad he was all right, and would hopefully be home again in a couple of days. From now on she'd do everything she could to make sure he took his medication and led a quiet, completely uneventful life. Even if Mum couldn't be part of it.

Ruby blinked hard as she replaced the photograph, then turned around. She stopped, her attention snagged. The notebook had been left open on the table again.

Dear Betty...

Ruby turned the pages. Each entry was longer than the last, as if his confidence was growing with the act of writing.

But she mustn't read it. It was none of her business. A private conversation between Gramps and Gran.

She went to close the book, but a line caught her eye – *I think you sold this pen because of me.*

Puzzled, she couldn't help herself and had to read on:

You thought I was jealous of Alfie, and that the pen was a reminder of him, so you got rid of it, didn't you?

Well, I hate to admit it, but you were right. I saw Alfie, rich and handsome, and I felt – well, intimidated. I knew you had *loved him once, and it seemed logical to me then that you must still love him.*

But now the years have passed and I've had to learn to live without you, I realise I was wrong, Betty. You did love me, didn't you? You must have, to put up with a jealous fool like me all those years.

And you didn't have to marry at all, did you? You could have stayed single and been happy that way. You always were an independent spirit. And beautiful. You could have had your pick of men, but you chose me.

Betty, I'm sorry. I know it's too late, but going over all this in my mind has helped me see the mistakes I've made. I wasted all that time being jealous when I should have been treasuring every moment with you. But there's one thing that's never changed. I love you, Betty. Always have, always will. Goodnight.

Your Fred.

Blinking hard, Ruby put the notebook down. She rubbed at her eyes, and her throat felt tight. Wow, Gramps. What a long and heartfelt letter. Perhaps giving him the pen hadn't been a mistake after all. Perhaps it had helped him in a small way.

The clock chimed, reminding her that it was midnight. She had work in the morning. She left the notebook and pen as she'd found them, and took herself off to bed.

*

'He'll be fine,' Mum said, when they met outside the ward. Ruby had left Gramps sleeping. He'd looked peaceful in his hospital bed, but pale and vulnerable too. Mum patted Ruby's hand. 'Stop blaming yourself. It wasn't your fault. And the doctor told me he can go home tomorrow.' Mum picked up her handbag. 'Come on. Let's go back to my place and eat. Nick's making curry and I bet you're hungry.'

Ruby forced a smile. She was hungry, this was true. Visiting Gramps each night after work meant she'd hardly had time for anything else this week so she'd grabbed quick snacks.

But when they got to Mum and Nick's, he already had a visitor.

Ruby stopped in the doorway of the lounge. He was sitting on the sofa with his long, jeans-clad legs stretched out in front of him. His glossy brown fringe flopped over his eyes and he pushed it back, then stilled when he recognised her.

Nick smiled. 'Ruby, have you met my nephew Paul?'

She nodded politely and sat down a safe distance away from him, while her mum and Nick disappeared into the kitchen to finish preparing dinner. Her heart drummed. She was wary of another confrontation, but worse than that – what if he let slip what she'd done?

'Hi,' she said awkwardly. 'Again.'

At least he didn't seem so angry this time. In fact, he was staring at the bottle of beer in his hand looking distinctly uncomfortable too. Finally, he lifted his head and said, 'Listen, Ruby, I –'

'It's OK,' she cut in quickly. 'I know what you're going to

say, and I'm going to pay Miss Moonshine back. All of it. That's why I took the job. And when I've done that I'll tell Mum what I did. But please don't say anything until then. Please? She has enough on her plate.'

He looked appalled. 'I wouldn't do that. I wasn't going to tell your mum – or anyone.'

'You'd have every right to. What I did was wrong.' She gave a nervous laugh. 'I don't really know what came over me in that shop. I had the weirdest feeling…'

He met her gaze square on, and she felt a jolt. 'I'm sure you had your reasons. And maybe I was quick to judge. I – ah – was a bit worried after I saw you at the museum the other day. That job looks… dangerous.'

'Oh, it's really not,' she said, relieved at the neutral topic and his conciliatory tone. 'Just…' she searched for the word, 'humbling. No room for an ego when five-year-olds are pelting blueberries at you.'

'They seemed very enthusiastic.' He had a gorgeous smile.

'Yes. It's a real draw. And the museum's good too. Have you been in?'

'Yeah. Years ago.' He shifted in his seat. 'I'm sorry about your grandad, by the way.'

'Thanks,' she said with a shy smile.

'How is he?'

'Better. Should be home tomorrow.'

He nodded. 'Nick told me he and your mum are estranged.' His blue eyes were warm with sympathy. 'It can't be easy for you – what with your parents' divorce and everything, too.'

She didn't know what to say. The last two years had been awful. Gran had died, her parents had separated, then there'd been the falling out between Mum and Gramps – it was a wonder Ruby had managed to get through her 'A' levels. Knowing she'd scraped into university, she'd taken off for a year of travelling, but being far from home hadn't really helped. She cared about her family too much. And it made a lump form in her throat that Paul was watching her with such… understanding. And sympathy.

'Listen,' he said quietly. 'I think we got off to a bad start the first time we met.'

'You could say that.'

'How about we meet for a drink sometime – in town? We could… start again?'

She thought of the last few dark days culminating in Gramps' heart attack, and this felt like a tiny glimmer of sunshine. She smiled and said, 'That sounds like a great idea.'

*

Two weeks later, Ruby parked up outside the solicitor's office. 'Are you sure you want to do this, Gramps?'

'I am,' he said. The appointment had been delayed due to his health, but as soon as he was well enough he'd called to rearrange it.

Ruby nodded sadly, but didn't say anything. It was up to him what he wrote in his will, but it still tore through her that he wouldn't let Mum back into his life. His stay in hospital had been a brutal reminder that things could change in the blink of an eye.

Inside, the solicitor, Ray Chalmers, made sure they were comfortable, and asked Gramps to check through the will a final time. Ruby watched as her grandad waved a hand impatiently. 'I've already read it, Ray. You know that.'

'In that case, providing you're happy, you can sign and date it here… and here.' Ray offered him a pen.

But Gramps was reaching into his jacket pocket. 'It's all right. I have one.'

Ruby raised a brow as he produced the black fountain pen.

He drew the papers towards him and scrawled his name on both copies of the will. A sad weight settled in the pit of her stomach, and she thought of what he'd written in the notebook. She was certain Gran wouldn't have approved of him writing his daughter out of his will.

Just then a knock at the door made them all turn. The secretary smiled as she ushered in Ruby's mum.

'Sorry I'm late.' Juliette beamed. She was breathless, as if she'd run here, and her cheeks were pink.

Ruby glanced anxiously at her grandad and frowned. Why was Mum here? And why did she look so… cheerful?

Strangely, Gramps didn't look angry – or surprised. 'Just in time,' he told his daughter. 'You can take a copy if you like.'

Mum wrapped her arms around his neck and hugged him fiercely. 'I don't care about the inheritance, and you know that. It's you I've missed, Dad.'

Ruby frowned again. 'Hold on a minute. Have I missed something here?'

The pair of them turned to face her. 'Gramps called me yesterday,' said Mum.

He had the grace to look a little sheepish as he added, 'I had time to think in hospital, and I – I realised I might have made a few mistakes.'

'What do you mean?' Ruby asked.

His mouth worked as if he'd rather not have this conversation. 'You were right, young lady. I was holding a grudge against a man – a family – and allowing that to come between me and Juliette. I should never have let that happen.' His eyes gleamed and Ruby stared because he looked almost tearful. He lifted the pen and the gold lettering winked in the light. 'Finding this pen again has got me thinking of your gran, what she would – and what she definitely *wouldn't* – have wanted me to do. It's made me see what a fool I was being.'

'You said it, Gramps.' They laughed, and Mum hugged him again. 'So this will leaves your house to Mum, then?'

He nodded. 'And you, Ruby. The two of you. My girls.'

So Mum was back in his life again. Thrilled, Ruby had to blink hard.

'Well, how about we go for a celebratory drink, then?' she suggested, adding quickly, 'A non-alcoholic one for you, Gramps.' She'd been saving all her earnings from the museum job, but she could afford a round of drinks in The Packhorse Inn. And how wonderful it would be to see her small family reunited again.

*

Ruby waited outside the emporium until the last customer had left, then she went in.

Miss Moonshine was crouching down, petting the chihuahua and talking to him. 'There, there, Napoleon. Just another ten minutes and we'll close up shop, then I'll make us something nice for tea…'

Ruby cleared her throat. The shopkeeper turned around, and was it Ruby's imagination or did her surprise seem a little… fake?

'Hello, dear,' she said, her hazel eyes sparkling almost as much as the tiara in her hair. She really did have an unusual fashion sense.

'I – ah –' Ruby had rehearsed what she was going to say over and over, but now it came to saying it her cheeks filled with heat and her tongue tied. She pulled the wodge of money out of her pocket and placed it on the till.

Miss Moonshine arched a thin white brow.

Ruby cleared her throat. 'A few weeks ago I stole something from your shop and it was really wrong of me. I feel terrible. So this is the money to pay for it. It's all here. I'm really sorry, Miss Moonshine.' Confessing to it was harder than she'd expected.

A chunky purple ring caught the light as Miss Moonshine waved away her apology. 'There's no need,' she said kindly. 'That pen was meant to be yours all along, dear.'

Ruby frowned. She hadn't said what she'd stolen so how did the old lady know it was a pen?

'I insist. It's a lot of money,' Ruby said, pushing the pile of notes towards her. Then, 'What do you mean, it was meant to be mine?'

All the stories she'd heard about Miss Moonshine rushed into her head and she felt a prickle of unease. Were the whisperings about magic true?

'I'm a firm believer that everything happens for a reason.' The shopkeeper picked up a pile of greetings cards and shuffled them into a neat pile. Her tiara had slipped a little.

'I'm not a thief. Honestly. I've never stolen anything before, but when I saw that pen…' She still couldn't put into words what had taken hold of her. 'It used to be my gran's, you see, but she lost it and I thought if I got it back my grandad might… well, I thought it would make him happy.'

'You don't need to explain yourself to me.' Miss Moonshine smiled kindly. 'I understand.'

Ruby frowned. The shopkeeper didn't seem angry at all. In fact, it was almost as if she'd expected it. *That pen was meant to be yours all along.* What had she meant by that?

'You know, if the price tag had been cheaper, I would have bought it.'

'Ah, yes, but then he wouldn't have noticed you.'

'What? Who?'

Miss Moonshine gave the merest shake of her head as if she'd let slip something she shouldn't have. 'It was expensive to deter other buyers, of course.' She straightened her tiara as she crossed the shop and flipped the 'Open' sign to 'Closed'. When she turned back, Ruby blinked. She was certain she hadn't been wearing those thick-framed glasses before. Yet her figure-hugging knitted dress didn't appear to have any pockets.

Deciding she hadn't been paying attention, she made herself refocus. 'But who else would want a pen that's personally engraved?' She'd only thought of this the other day, but it had been bothering her ever since.

Miss Moonshine shrugged. 'You never know,' she said, her gaze sliding away.

'There aren't many Bettys out there these days,' Ruby persisted.

'Well *you* wanted it, didn't you? Very badly, it seems.' The old lady reached down to scoop up the dog and Ruby thought she heard her mutter quietly, 'And that fool Fred was never going to come in here, was he?'

'Well, I insist on repaying what I owe,' she said, and nodded at the money. 'Please take it.'

Miss Moonshine glanced at the notes then sniffed, and Ruby wondered how profitable was this shop if its owner had such disregard for money?

She said goodbye and left, pausing in the street to look back at the shop. It was empty; Miss Moonshine and her dog had already vanished. Ruby chewed her lip, replaying their conversation. Something didn't add up, but she couldn't put her finger on what it was. It had seemed as if Miss Moonshine had almost *wanted* her to steal the pen.

But of course that was ridiculous.

*

'Cheers!' Ruby said, and chinked her pint against his.

'Cheers,' Paul said. 'What are we celebrating?'

'I finished working at the museum and I repaid Miss Moonshine.'

'Ah. I'll drink to that.'

They clinked glasses and sipped their cider. The weather was unexpectedly warm and sunny for September, and the beer garden behind The Packhorse was buzzing, every table filled. Paul had managed to get a table in the shade of a willow tree, but the cool air wasn't the reason why Ruby's skin was tingling. She glanced at him, noticing how his eyes creased when he smiled.

'I still can't believe you took such a terrible job. Being pelted with rotten tomatoes can't have been fun. I've never known a thief go to such lengths to repay their debt.'

She grinned. 'You know a lot of thieves, then?'

'You're the first.'

'What I did was wrong. I still don't know what possessed me.'

He eyed her a short while before saying, 'You know what they say about Miss Moonshine, don't you?'

'What?'

'She comes from Pendle.' His voice lifted, and he watched her reaction as if this should mean something.

Ruby stared at him blankly. 'So?'

'Put it this way, they say that everyone who goes into her shop finds what they need, even if they don't know it at the time.'

She frowned, remembering her strange conversation with Miss Moonshine, but it didn't make any more sense than it had at the time. 'Well, it was my first and definitely my last attempt at shoplifting. And don't feel bad about the job. It was fun in a way, seeing the kids get so excited.' She paused. 'But you know, Miss Moonshine reacted a bit strangely when I owned up.'

'Angry strange?'

'Not at all. She kind of waved it off. And when I offered

to repay her, she didn't seem to care. I had to leave it on the counter in the end.'

'Wow.'

'I know. And it was almost as if she'd been… expecting me. She said the pen was "meant to be mine", whatever that means.'

'Cryptic.'

'Very.'

'So what's next for you?' he asked. 'A career in acting with a speciality in playing medieval criminals?'

'Haha, very funny. Actually, I'm starting uni next week.'

'Where?'

'Manchester.'

He paused, his pint midway to his lips. 'I'm at uni in Manchester.'

Her heart did a tiny somersault. 'Really?'

'Yeah. Third year.' A beat passed. 'Maybe I could show you round.'

She tried to quash the fireworks she felt inside. Tried to sound casual. 'I'd like that.'

*

Later that night, when she let herself into Gramps' house, Ruby was still fizzing with excitement.

She hung her jacket up in the hall, and as she passed the front room she noticed Gramps had left the notebook out again. She stopped in the doorway, her gaze resting on the fountain pen, and wondered about Miss Moonshine.

What was it Paul had said? *Everyone who goes into her shop finds what they need…*

The clouds must have shifted because a beam of moonlight suddenly slid into the room, making the gold inscription shine.

Ruby smiled. Then, shaking her head, she went to bed.

Sophie Claire writes emotional stories set in England and in sunny Provence, where she spent her summers as a child. Previously, she worked in marketing and proofreading academic papers, but now she's delighted to spend her days dreaming up heartwarming contemporary romance stories set in beautiful places.

sophieclaire.co.uk

Three Butterflies

By Marie Laval

Chapter One

Olivier pulled up the collar of his coat and mumbled an oath as his shoes squelched in a patch of thick mud. Cold rain slid down his face and onto his neck. He could hardly see where he was going but taking his glasses off to wipe them would be pointless, as the rain showed no sign of easing.

The air smelled of slimy canal, wet soil and soggy vegetation, with a hint of smoke from some of the narrowboats' wood-burning stoves. If this was Haven Bridge in June, Olivier daren't think what it must be like in winter…

The boat he was looking for was moored on a quiet stretch of canal. 'Fork left after the bridge for the old branch of the canal. The *Elysia* is big and blue with clouds painted all over. You can't miss it,' Tamsin Sheridan had assured him.

He reached the bridge, dutifully forked left, and carried on walking on the muddy towpath. What was he even doing here? He was being exiled to deepest, wettest Yorkshire because Uncle George believed he could save Maison Dumas from bankruptcy, but Uncle George was wrong. Nothing short of a miracle could save the perfume house their ancestor had founded almost two centuries before. No matter how hard Olivier worked to chase deals and negotiate contracts, sales had slumped as new competitors emerged. He'd put his life on hold and had forgotten what fun or a good night's sleep felt like. His only contact with his friends was on social media, when they posted photos of their cute children or their exotic holidays.

An exotic holiday this trip certainly wasn't. It was Amelia's ridiculous idea that he come here. Uncle George's new girlfriend had been meddling again…

Irritation simmered inside him as he recalled the conversation he'd had in his uncle's office in Maison Dumas's elegant, if old-fashioned, Avenue Foch headquarters.

'Times have changed, Olivier,' Uncle George had said. 'Tradition is very much last century… People want fresh artisan perfumes produced with organic ingredients. If Maison Dumas is to survive, we need a range aimed at younger, environmentally conscious customers. I want you to come up with a niche concept. You have two weeks.'

Olivier had nodded, even though he was cringing internally. As far as he was concerned, tradition *was* everything. Maison Dumas already used the best organic essences on the market; that's why their production costs were so high. What's more, it was over eight years since he'd created his last fragrance. What if he couldn't come up with anything new – niche or not?

However, he could see his uncle's mind was made up. 'All right, I'll plan an itinerary,' he'd said, already mentally rearranging his schedule. 'Where do you suggest I start? Bali, Fiji, or perhaps Bulgaria for the Damascus rose harvest…?'

His uncle had shaken his head and dropped the bombshell. 'You're going to Haven Bridge in Yorkshire… and don't pull that face… Amelia has a niece there who is very much involved in all that return-to-earth, community thing. Exactly the type of customer we need to appeal to. Forget about contracts and balance sheets for a while; use that nose of yours and come back with a mood board and a unique selling point. I need you, Olivier. Maison Dumas needs you. You are our last chance.'

No pressure, then. Olivier rolled his eyes. What about rain, mud, dirty canals and shivering ducks for a mood board? And 'Eau de Yorkshire: Not for the Faint-Hearted' or 'Haven Bridge

Summer Cologne: Rain and Mist in a Bottle' for unique selling points?

A strident honking brought him to a sudden halt. A massive goose flapped its wings in the middle of the towpath, blocking his way.

He moved to the left, but the goose stepped to the side, too, and stared at him with mean, round eyes. Olivier's margin of manoeuvre was limited by the canal and he had no intention of joining the ducks in the murky green water.

'Don't worry about Frieda,' a woman said behind him. 'She has a bit of a temper but that's because she takes her job as guard goose very seriously.'

Surprised, Olivier glanced around. A woman's silhouette emerged from the mist. Trotting next to her was the tiniest chihuahua he'd ever seen, wearing a padded camouflage coat.

His curiosity was piqued. 'Guard goose? Haven Bridge looks like a quiet town to me.' What he really wanted to say was that it was completely dead. He'd hardly seen ten people since getting off the train.

The woman shook her head. 'Don't you believe it, young man. There are dark forces at play, and we need our Frieda more than ever.' She paused and cocked her head to one side. 'Are you going to Heaven?'

Great. First a mad goose, then a mad woman…

'It rather feels like I'm in hell,' he muttered, as more cold rain slid down his neck.

The woman stepped closer and Olivier had the weirdest sensation she knew exactly who he was and what he was thinking right now. She seemed middle-aged – or perhaps even older, he couldn't say – but there was certainly a lot of energy in those hazel eyes, and a twinkle of humour too. Like the dog, she wore some kind of camouflage gear – khaki boiler suit and wellies, a green-and-brown anorak and one of those waxed fishermen's hats on her white curls.

Beware, he thought, here comes Commando Granny and her chihuahua…

'I meant, are you going to Tamsin's boat – the *Elysia*?' the woman said. 'We call it Heaven around here because of the exterior paint. You'll understand what I mean when you see it.'

That fitted the description Amelia's niece had given him of her boat, and it was called *Elysia*– wasn't that a kind of heaven for Greek gods?

'I am indeed looking for Tamsin Sheridan's boat,' he said, conscious of sounding terribly formal.

The woman nodded. 'I'm going that way too. Walk with me, and Frieda will let you through.'

He cast a dubious look towards the chihuahua. 'What about your dog? Are you not afraid the goose will attack him?'

She chuckled. 'Oh no. She wouldn't dare upset me. And anyway, Napoleon and Frieda are friends.'

'Napoleon.' He repressed a smile and arched his eyebrows as he looked at the tiny dog trotting round the puddles.

The woman was right about Frieda the goose. As soon as they came closer it waddled to the side of the path with a honk and let them through. They walked side by side in silence. Then the woman pointed to the side of the path.

'What do you think of the garden?'

'What garden?' All Olivier could see were trees dripping with rain and an abundance of overgrown greenery. Then again the lenses of his glasses were smeared with rain… He took them off and was about to give them a hasty wipe and put them back on when a riot of scents hit his senses.

The herbs first – basil, chive, clary sage and lemon balm. Mint and wild garlic. He took another breath and smelled wet grass and rain on tree barks, then the sweetness of fruit and flowers: lilac, roses, stocks… Mauve, pink and white. And green, lots and lots of green.

'It's… surprising.' He put his glasses back on and examined the side of the canal. There *was* a garden there, and it ran all along the towpath. How could he not have seen it before? It looked like some kind of allotment, with fruit and vegetables growing in pots and planters, and flowers. A sign painted in garish colours, featuring a weird-looking carrot-man with googly eyes, invited passers-by to help themselves.

Olivier read the name aloud. 'The People's Garden.' Turning to the woman, he asked, 'Does that mean anybody can pick what they want?'

'Pick what they need, dear, yes, that's the idea. Isn't it marvellous?'

She pointed at a canal boat that looked like a piece of summer sky fallen to earth. 'Here is Heaven – I mean, the *Elysia.* Well, my dear, it was a pleasure to meet you. Napoleon and I need to get some work done in the garden but we shall meet again very soon.' And after a last smile, she walked into the garden, followed by the chihuahua.

'Er… goodbye, Mrs…' he started.

She glanced over her shoulder. 'Miss Moonshine. Bye for now.'

*

'What are we going to do with our guest, Josephine? Aunt Amelia said he was a stuffy snob, obsessed with work, designer suits and Italian shoes. I bet he's used to boutique hotels and posh restaurants too. He's bound to hate it here.' Tamsin tucked a strand of hair behind her ear. Ocean had cut it in a very short bob and dyed it a lovely soft pink the day before and it cheered her up every time she glanced in the mirror.

Josephine yawned and stretched on the sofa.

'I don't mind showing him the gardens, but does he have to stay here too? You know I love having friends round, but the last thing I need is to explain to a stuck-up French guy how the composting toilet works, and ask him not to use all the hot water when he showers, or leave his dirty socks and wet towels on the floor. What's more, you know how thin the partitions are… What if he snores and I can't get to sleep at night? Or worse still, what if *I* snore?'

Sharing the boat with a strange man – with any man – was bound to end in disaster. Aunt Amelia said Tamsin lived like an old spinster and she was right, but the People's Garden took all her time and she simply didn't have the energy, or the inclination, for boyfriends.

Josephine's blue gaze was unfathomable. Tamsin sighed and wagged a finger at her. 'You may not care about him now, but Amelia said he was awfully fastidious, so you won't be so chilled when he shoos you off the sofa, complains about the smell of your fishy food or steps on your tail as he goes to the loo in the middle of the night.'

She hadn't even met the man, but she already knew their cohabiting wouldn't work. Not only would they have nothing in common, but the timing of his visit wasn't ideal, with the vandalism to the gardens, the nasty graffiti around town and the attacks in the press against the association…

Sounds of honking in the distance made her pause. 'That may be him. Should I rescue him from Frieda?' She listened again, but the noise stopped. Whoever had been on the towpath had passed safely… or had turned round and headed back to town.

A man's voice with a slight French accent called from the path. 'Hello? Miss Sheridan? Tamsin Sheridan?'

She let out a sigh. So neither the rain nor Frieda had put Olivier Dumas off… She opened the cabin door and peered outside. A tall, dark and thoroughly drenched man stood on the towpath, holding an expensive-looking leather holdall and looking very elegant and completely out of place in his smart coat, suit and tie, and tortoiseshell glasses.

'Olivier? Good afternoon. Come in, quickly.'

He stepped onboard and ducked down into the galley kitchen which immediately felt tiny. His glasses steamed up so he took them off and blinked at her with gorgeous chocolate-brown eyes.

'Why don't you put your bag down and take off your coat?' she said. 'I was just about to make a cup of tea. Would you like one?'

He nodded. 'Yes… Yes, thank you.' He sneezed a couple of times.

'Bless you… That will be our Yorkshire summer.' She ripped off a couple of pieces of kitchen roll and handed them to him. Having a cold might stop him from doing the job Amelia had mentioned. How would he be able to create a new perfume if he had a blocked nose?

Tamsin didn't want anything to cause Olivier Dumas to stay any longer than planned. She'd make him a mug of thyme, lavender and rosemary tea with a blob of honey to clear his airways.

'Thank you.' He blew his nose, wiped his lenses and slid his glasses back on.

A worrying thought crossed Tamsin's mind. 'I hope you're not allergic to cats.' She pointed at Josephine, who was still stretched out on the sofa.

He frowned. 'Not usually, but that is some cat…'

'She's a Maine Coone. She's beautiful, isn't she?'

'She's… big,' he replied, as he divested himself of his coat, which was so wet it was dripping onto the floorboards.

Tamsin reached out for it and hung it next to her anorak, on which she'd embroidered the 'People's Garden' logo.

'I recognise that ugly carrot from the sign outside,' Olivier Dumas remarked with a tight smile.

'Ugly? Jack's carrot isn't ugly!' She curled her fists on her hips. 'You mustn't say that again or poor Jack will be heartbroken.'

This time he gave her a real smile – a smile that made her feel a bit funny inside. 'I'm very sorry if I offended you – and Jack, whoever he is – and I promise I'll never say his carrot is ugly ever again.'

'Good.' She smiled back. It was true Jack's carrot was a little wonky. Perhaps she had overreacted…

She looked at Olivier's shoes, which were caked in mud. 'You'd better take them off too.'

He glanced down and winced. 'Of course. Sorry.' He quickly removed them and she stared in surprise at his red-and-yellow socks with cartoon characters on them. 'These are very jazzy,' she said.

A slight flush coloured his cheeks. 'Well… yes. My niece bought them for my birthday. In fact, Veronica bought me a dozen, and gave me strict instructions to wear them every day.'

That was seriously cute. Perhaps Aunt Amelia was wrong, and there was more to Olivier Dumas than business suits and fancy Italian shoes…

Tamsin stepped behind the kitchen counter and put the kettle on the gas ring. 'I'll show you where you'll be sleeping whilst the kettle boils,' she said. 'This way, please.'

She led the way through the lounge area. 'The bathroom is through here,' she said, sliding open the door. She'd tidied her soaps and lotions as best as she could, but the bathroom still looked cramped and messy. Should she mention the toilet, the leaky shower, the hot water tank? Judging from the look on his face, perhaps not just yet…

She carried on down the narrow corridor and into the spare

cabin. 'This is your berth. The one at the back is mine. I made some space for you in the cupboard.'

Once again there was dismay on his face. The colourful South American throw and cushions were obviously not to his taste.

'I'll leave you to unpack and call you when the tea is ready.'

They performed an awkward ballet so she could step out whilst he walked in, and brushed against each other. They both said sorry at the same time. Tamsin walked back to the galley kitchen, her heart beating a little too fast. The rain tapping on the roof made calming, soothing sounds, and with uptight Olivier Dumas onboard, she needed all the calm and soothing she could get.

Chapter Two

Olivier was trailing through an enchanted forest with birds and butterflies fluttering around him. The forest moved and swayed in the warm breeze as giant frangipani, gardenia and hibiscus flowers released heavenly scents. A giant carrot with a human face waved at him, and Olivier waved back.

Suddenly his nose twitched as a new smell wafted towards him… Bacon. The singing of the birds was replaced by the sound of people laughing and talking; the giant carrot disappeared amongst the vegetation…

And Olivier opened his eyes.

His gaze swept from the low wooden ceiling to the tapestries hanging on the walls and then to the porthole, just as a duck swam past, followed by four ducklings. No wonder he'd felt the world was swaying under his feet. He was on a boat, his body cocooned in warmth and softness, and he'd just had the best sleep in weeks.

He remembered pushing his holdall against the wall, sitting on the bed to loosen his tie and undo a couple of buttons on his shirt, listening to the rain pattering against the roof of the boat… and then nothing. He'd fallen asleep so quickly he hadn't even taken his glasses off.

He glanced at his watch. He'd been asleep for two hours! What would Tamsin Sheridan think of him? She'd already laughed at his socks; no doubt she'd now find him rude or a complete oddball, far removed from the professional image he'd strived so hard to project these past few years, and definitely not what she must have been expecting.

On the other hand, Tamsin was exactly what Olivier had expected – and more. She was a rainbow of colours with her baby-pink hair, oversized green jumper, red corduroy trousers and purple trainers. She may lack fashion sense but she had the prettiest blue eyes he'd ever seen and a beaming smile that dug cute dimples into her cheeks.

He sighed and sat up on the bed. He didn't want to offend the young woman, especially after she'd obviously gone to the trouble of tidying the place up for his benefit, but he couldn't think of anything worse than being stuck on this canal boat. He'd stay tonight then make up an excuse and find a hotel in the morning. This trip was doomed to failure anyway. Uncle George was deluded if he believed that he, or anyone, could find inspiration for a new fragrance in this wet and miserable part of England.

His cabin didn't have a door and the curtain was too flimsy to stop the sound of the conversation between Tamsin and her guests from reaching him. A few words caught his attention.

'Let's dig everything up tonight, and never mind the police or the CCTV,' a man was saying.

'I agree. Rain or no rain, it's time for more guerrilla action,' a woman added.

'Napoleon and I will keep watch, of course,' another woman said.

This must be the Miss Moonshine he had met earlier… but what on earth were they talking about? Guerrilla action sounded serious – more importantly, it sounded illegal! He couldn't afford for Maison Dumas to be mixed up in any dodgy business. Slightly alarmed, he stepped out of the cabin and in three strides was in the lounge area. A group of half a dozen people were sitting on pouffes, rickety chairs and on the rug, whilst tiny Napoleon and Tamsin's grey cat stretched out on either end of the sofa, oblivious to the humans' discomfort.

'Ah! Here he is.' Tamsin jumped down from a bar stool behind the kitchen counter. 'Everybody, this is Olivier Dumas, my house guest for the next few weeks – or should I say boat guest? Olivier is the nephew of Amelia's boyfriend – George Dumas. You all remember my aunt Amelia, don't you? She stayed with me last summer for a few days.'

There was a chorus of 'ayes', 'of course', 'lovely woman…'

'Olivier and I have already met,' Miss Moonshine said with a smile. 'I rescued him from Frieda earlier.' She was still wearing her gardening dungarees but had taken her coat and wellies off, and her feet were clad in shocking pink fluffy socks decorated with flamingos.

Tamsin smiled at him. 'Then let me introduce you to the rest of my friends. Here is Ocean…' She gestured towards a woman who, like the others, wore some kind of combat clothing, contrasting with her elaborate hairstyle and make-up.

'And here is Reef.'

A youngish man with dreadlocks and nose piercings nodded. 'Evening.'

Tamsin pointed at two women sitting on the rug. 'Here are India and Sky…'

Olivier's lips twitched. Moonshine, Ocean, Reef, India and Sky… It sounded like a geography lesson. He couldn't help himself. Turning to the friend Tamsin hadn't introduced yet – a man with grey hair in a ponytail, and a long plaited beard – Olivier said in a dry voice, 'I suppose you're Rock or Pebble.'

The man chuckled and raised his bottle. 'You're not far off, mate. Actually, I'm Cliff. Cheers.' He took a sip of beer, and the others laughed too.

'Please sit down.' Tamsin pointed at the bar stool next to her. 'Would you like a beer? Cliff brought some of his dandelion homebrew… Or perhaps you'd prefer that tea I promised you earlier? I'm sorry I didn't wake you up but you looked so exhausted when I checked on you, I thought I'd let you have a nap.'

He frowned. So she'd checked on him? He could only hope he hadn't been snoring, dribbling or muttering stupid things in his sleep…

'I'll have some tea, please.' Although what he really wanted was a double espresso and to be back in his own Paris apartment, far away from this motley crew who were planning… what, exactly? As he perched on the bar stool, he felt a fool again for falling asleep, and for not changing his suit into something less formal, especially since he was still wearing Veronica's red-and-yellow cartoon socks.

'I'm afraid we have to leave you after tea tonight,' Tamsin said, handing him a mug filled with bright green liquid that smelled particularly unappetising. 'We have some… ahem… business to attend to, and things could turn nasty.'

Olivier looked at each of the people sitting in the lounge. He couldn't imagine a more unlikely bunch of criminals. 'What exactly are you doing?'

'Reclaiming disused or abandoned plots so we can grow fruit and vegetables,' Tamsin answered. 'You saw the garden on the other side of the towpath, didn't you?'

He nodded, remembering the wonderful fresh scents that had assailed him earlier. The garden would smell even more incredible after the rain…

'Over the past two years we've reclaimed quite a bit of land and set up Haven Bridge's People's Garden,' Tamsin carried on. 'Wherever there's a piece of land that's derelict or unused we move in, dig it up and plant crops and flowers. Then we invite volunteers to help with the maintenance, and the community is welcome to help themselves to any fresh fruit and veg… and everybody is happy.'

'Not everybody, unfortunately,' Miss Moonshine said in a gloomy voice. As if to echo her mood, the chihuahua growled and the monster cat let out a sinister meow.

Tamsin smiled. 'Napoleon, Josephine, ssh.'

Napoleon and Josephine? Seriously? To hide yet another cynical smile, Olivier drank a sip of tea and almost choked. This was no Darjeeling or Earl Grey. He forced down a few sips, trying very hard not to grimace, but then gave up and put the mug back down.

'For the past few weeks our gardens have been vandalised,' Tamsin continued, 'and our association threatened with legal action.'

'All this hostility is mind-boggling when all we want is to help people,' the woman called Ocean said. 'It's not only the free, organic and wholesome food we provide for the community. Tamsin also set up a training scheme to help people who are out of work, or people who have disabilities or health problems, get qualifications in gardening.'

'More than that, it makes everybody feel valued,' Reef added.

'I can't imagine why some people would object to what we do,' Cliff mused, taking a gulp of beer. Olivier wondered what the man's homebrew tasted like. Surely it couldn't be any worse than the tea.

'That's where Frieda comes in… and you too.' Miss Moonshine looked at Olivier with an unfathomable expression.

Olivier started. 'Me?'

'We've been worried about Tamsin being on her own out here for a while. It will be good for her to have company, especially at night. That stretch of canal is isolated, and no other boat ever moors there.'

'And for good reason,' India said, running her fingers through her short blonde hair. 'I don't mind coming to tend the garden during the day, but you couldn't pay me to stay here at night… not when there are so many tales of lost souls wandering on the path and white hands rising from the water to grab unsuspecting passers-by.'

'Nonsense!' Tamsin interrupted. 'There are no ghosts or evil spirits. At least, I've never seen or heard any in the two years I've moored here. And you all know the only reason British Waterways let us use the land for our garden is that this stretch of canal is disused and we're keeping an eye on it on their behalf.'

'Perhaps, but ghosts aren't the only problem, are they?' the woman next to India said. Sky, was it? She, too, had short hair, and with her glasses and serious expression she looked like a headmistress scolding a naughty child. 'There are real men causing trouble too.'

'Please, Sky, I don't want to talk about it.' Then Tamsin added in a more cheerful tone, 'Come on everybody, we'd better eat if we're to tackle the roundabout later.'

They all stood at once and the boat swayed from side to side. Olivier felt the blood drain from his face and held his breath for a few seconds to fight sudden queasiness. Surely he wasn't going to be sick on a canal boat?

The group of friends must be used to eating together on board because they all worked together and it took less than five minutes to set the table and bring the food over.

*

Tamsin loved her friends dearly but why did they always have to bring up the topics of the haunted stretch of canal and her safety onboard the *Elysia*… and mention the disgruntled locals who were making her life a misery? Their ringleader, loutish greengrocer Mitch Flynn, had a nasty temper, and his very public outbursts had embarrassed her enough over the past two years.

Next to her, Olivier tucked into his potato, cheese and bacon pie and she let out a relieved sigh. Her friends might be happy with her plain and stodgy food, but she was no cordon bleu and, being French, Olivier must be used to fine cuisine. He didn't talk much but looked at everybody in turn, and every time his chocolate-brown gaze met hers, she felt tingly all over. He was still wearing his suit, but his jacket was a little creased and his dark brown hair ruffled from his nap, and he looked very handsome.

She looked away. It was a bad idea – a very bad idea – to find the Frenchman attractive.

The rain stopped, dusk turned the evening blue and grey, and mist rose from the canal. It was time to go out. They put their coats and wellies back on, bade Olivier goodnight and left to retrieve the gardening tools from the shed and put Frieda in her pen.

Miss Moonshine scooped up Napoleon from the sofa and turned to Olivier. 'Come and visit me tomorrow. I believe I have just the thing to inspire you.'

He frowned. 'Visit you? But… where?'

'You will find me, dear. People always do,' Miss Moonshine replied.

If Olivier was baffled by the woman's comment, he was too polite to say anything.

Tamsin was the last to leave. 'I really am sorry to leave you, but please make yourself at home,' she said, shoving her feet into rubber boots.

'Can I be of any assistance?' he asked in a rather formal voice.

She laughed. 'Thanks for asking, but no. Technically, what we're doing is illegal, and I don't want to have to phone my aunt and your uncle and tell them you've been arrested for trespassing or for public disorder.'

He pulled a face. 'If you put it like that…'

He followed her out onto the deck. Her friends had retrieved the gardening equipment – the wheelbarrow, shovels and pickaxes, as well as buckets and compost bags – and had their headlamps on.

'Come on, gang,' she said, slipping her own head torch on. With a last wave to Olivier, she stepped off the boat and onto the path.

Chapter Three

Olivier might not want to be involved in anything unlawful, but he still felt rather sad and left out when Tamsin and her little troop walked away. Reef pushed a wheelbarrow filled with plant cuttings, along with Napoleon perched on top of a compost bag. With their torches, they looked like they were going on an adventure… which he supposed digging up a roundabout at night was.

He went back in to get some clothes from his holdall and a towel from the cupboard, before stepping into the minuscule bathroom. Five minutes of fiddling with the shower dial later, lukewarm water trickled out of the showerhead. Still, it was better than nothing.

After changing into a T-shirt and jeans, he took his laptop into the lounge. He wasn't brave enough to disturb Josephine, so he sat on one of the bar stools at the kitchen counter. It was time he collected his thoughts for the mood board his uncle had requested. Two weeks wasn't long to come up with a new concept, especially when he didn't think he had any creativity left in him, but he owed it to his uncle, and to Maison Dumas' staff, to try.

His grandfather, Henri Dumas, had once told him that to be a successful '*nez*' – or perfume creator – he should travel, live life to the full, and love. But Olivier hadn't done much living, or loving, these past few years, and the colours and scents in his world had become bland and elusive.

He sketched a few ideas, wrote random thoughts, growing more and more frustrated as nothing caught his imagination. As he worked he grew accustomed to the deep and silent darkness enveloping the boat, broken only by the rustling of water against the hull, the odd owl hooting or dog barking in the distance, and the soft snoring of the cat on the sofa. From time to time he wondered how Frieda the goose was faring in her pen and how the commando gardening operation was going.

Suddenly the cat lifted its head and hissed. The silence was shattered by frantic honking from Frieda as the sound of hurried footsteps came from outside, followed by a sloshing noise, as if someone had thrown something on the side of the boat. Olivier rushed out but by the time he stepped onto the deck whoever had been there was gone, leaving only an empty plastic bucket on the path and dark red paint dripping from the roof onto the deck.

What was going on? Who had vandalised Tamsin's boat?

Two things were certain: whoever had done this wasn't one of the ghosts Tamsin's friend had mentioned – ghosts didn't carry buckets or run away – and whether he liked it or not, he now had to stay on the *Elysia*. There was no way he could leave as long as Tamsin was in danger…

*

'Of course I can stay here on my own while you explore Haven Bridge,' Tamsin said for the umpteenth time the following morning, as she served Olivier's breakfast – another vile herbal concoction, some sort of dock pudding, and thick slabs of coarse brown bread lathered with lumpy strawberry jam. 'I have lots of work to do and I'm perfectly fine on my own. Whoever threw the paint last night won't be back, and certainly not in broad daylight. Besides, I have Frieda and Josephine.'

'A cat and a goose are no protection against vandals,' Olivier objected before forcing down a mouthful of gritty bread. What was in that loaf – gravel? 'Are you sure you still don't want to call the police?'

'Positive. There's nothing they can do. Like I told you last night, it would be a waste of their time.'

He'd stayed up to wait for her, concerned she was walking alone on the towpath at night, and when she finally came back, she'd resisted his advice to call the police. Olivier wasn't happy, but there was nothing he could do. Tamsin might say she was fine but her pink hair emphasised the paleness of her skin, and there were dark circles under her eyes. She probably hadn't slept much, whereas he was ashamed to admit he'd dozed off the second his head touched his pillow, and had only woken when the sun's rays poked his eyes though the curtains.

He promised to be back for lunch and stepped out into the morning sunshine. The red paint made a garish and sinister bloodlike stain on the *Elysia*. He wondered if the reason why Tamsin was reluctant to report the incident was because she would have to say where she'd been the night before…

The towpath was still muddy. Olivier stepped over the puddles to get to the garden, relieved to see that Frieda was still safely enclosed in her pen. At least he wouldn't have to worry about being pecked to death. It was a shame the goose hadn't been out during the night, as she would probably have deterred whoever had been lurking.

As the vegetal scents hummed and danced in the air in a

farandole of delicate greens and pinks, an idea for a fragrance flitted into his mind, fragile like the wings of a butterfly. What about a garden after the rain, basking in morning sunshine? But the images vanished as quickly as they had appeared. Disappointed, Olivier made his way along the towpath towards the town centre.

Haven Bridge was a lot busier that day than when he'd arrived. He mooched about at the market, and bought a takeaway coffee and a croissant, which he ate sitting on a bench in the square, before stocking up on cheese, luxury crackers, Darjeeling tea and Columbian coffee at a delicatessen. He might have to stay on Tamsin's boat for the next two weeks, but he didn't have to put up with her horrid herbal teas, gritty bread or stodgy pies. It was safer for his stomach if he did the shopping from now on. Besides, it wasn't fair to expect Tamsin to feed him when it was obvious she didn't have much money.

He walked past an attractive building of honey-coloured stone hiding behind an archway of sweet-scented roses. It looked like an old chapel, or a Sunday school, which had been turned into a bric-a-brac shop. At the front were two large planters overflowing with a riot of vegetation, and a People's Garden sign invited passers-by to help themselves to fruit and vegetables. So that was what Tamsin and her friends did around town, as well as turning a derelict canal-side into a miniature Eden and reclaiming roundabouts…

''Scuse me, mister.' A teenager pushed past him to get to the planters. He was carrying secateurs, a garden trowel and a large refuse bag, which he dropped on the ground as he knelt to begin snipping at the plants, talking and humming to himself.

Smiling at the youngster's obvious enjoyment of his little patch of garden, Olivier glanced at the shop window, just as the sun's rays glinted on the wind chime displayed inside. It was made up of three delicate glass butterflies, their wings shimmering with colour. Charmed, Olivier stepped closer to the window. He'd seen a very similar piece at a René Lalique exhibition in Paris the year before. It was no doubt only a copy, but he wanted to take a closer look, so he pushed the shop door open.

After the bright sunshine it took him a few seconds to get accustomed to the darkness. The smell of patchouli and beeswax wood polish tickled his nose, and something else too – something that reminded him of someone…

'I knew you'd find your way here sooner or later,' a familiar voice said behind him, making him jump.

He turned and opened his eyes wide. 'Miss Moonshine?'

She smiled. 'Welcome to my emporium, my dear.'

Today she wore a kilt with black tights, black biker boots and a frilly white shirt, which was tied with a large bow under the chin. Gold hoops dangled from her ears and her hair was piled up in an elaborate chignon. She looked very different from the woman in the khaki boiler suit he'd met the day before, but just as extravagant.

'Er… Thank you, and good morning. So this is your shop?'

She nodded. Now his eyes were used to the relative darkness he could see all kinds of junk on display – everything from tea services to old typewriters, from porcelain figurines to second-hand books, to vintage clothing, posters and jewellery.

'That wind chime in the window… The butterfly one… I was wondering if I could have a look at it.'

'Of course.' Miss Moonshine removed the glass butterflies from the display and handed it to him. 'Isn't it exquisite?'

He took his glasses off to examine it more closely. The workmanship was stunning. Each butterfly was a different colour – one was pale pink and green, another deep fuchsia and sunny yellow with a hint of azure blue, and the last one a dark, iridescent ultramarine tipped with gold. Art Nouveau pieces by Lalique were sold at auction houses all over the world for extortionate amounts, yet the price tag showed this piece could be his for a mere ten pounds. He turned the largest butterfly over but the signature was scratched and unrecognisable where there should have been the distinctive 'L' for Lalique.

'It looks like a Lalique, but it must be a copy,' he said in a disappointed voice. 'Anyway, copy or not, it's a very nice piece.'

She gave him an impenetrable smile. 'Indeed. Many lovely things find their way to my little shop.'

He looked at the wind chime again, stroked the butterflies' delicate glass wings, and made up his mind. The pink and green one reminded him of Tamsin's hair and of her garden in the early morning sunshine. 'I'll take it… but it's worth a lot more than ten pounds.'

Miss Moonshine tutted. 'Ten pounds is the only price I will accept. Now let me wrap it for you.'

As she slipped behind the counter and the old-fashioned till, some shouting erupted at the front of the shop. Alarm flashed on Miss Moonshine's face and she rushed outside, followed by Olivier. Three heavy-built youths were shoving the teenager who'd been tending the planter earlier. The boy was crying, which the others seemed to find hilarious. Flowers, as well as carrots and runner beans, lay trampled on the pavement amongst piles of soil and discarded tools.

'Let go of him immediately,' Olivier warned. The lads ignored him so he strode towards them, grabbed the biggest one by the arm and yanked him off the poor boy, who was now crying so hard he couldn't breathe.

'Hey, don't touch me!' the youth protested, but he must have seen the threat in Olivier's eyes because he clamped his mouth shut.

Olivier let go of him. 'What do you think you're playing at, three of you ganging up against one boy?'

The trio stepped back. 'It's not our fault Jack can't take a joke.'

'Yeah, it's not our fault he's a weirdo.' The boys laughed.

'You should all be ashamed of yourselves – and especially you, Reece Flynn,' Miss Moonshine said to the big, beefy boy with sandy hair whom Olivier had tackled. 'I shall have a word with your father about this.'

The boy smirked but took another step back. 'My dad won't say anything. He hates those fruit and veg planters. He's fed up that people don't come to our shop any more because they can get stuff for free.'

Miss Moonshine glared at him. 'That doesn't give you the right to vandalise them or be mean to Jack. Now go away.'

The three teenagers turned round and took to their heels.

'Don't worry, Jack,' she told the boy, who was wiping his eyes on a corner of his T-shirt. 'Olivier is a friend of Tamsin's. He'll help you sort the planter out.' She looked at Olivier. 'You will, won't you?'

Olivier nodded. 'Of course.'

He didn't have much choice, but he didn't mind. He didn't like to see the boy upset, his flowers trampled on, his vegetables all ruined by some louts playing a cruel prank.

Jack gave him a shy smile. 'Thank you.' He pointed at the People's Garden's sign and his smile widened. 'It's my carrot, you know. I drew it and Tamsin said it was so good she'd put it on all the signs.'

Olivier remembered how annoyed Tamsin had been when he'd called the carrot ugly. 'You should be very proud that it's all over town. Now, Jack, I've never done any gardening before. What do you want me to do?'

The boy's beaming smile warmed his heart. 'Don't worry, I'll show you.'

Chapter Four

Tamsin glanced outside, where Olivier was sitting on an old

rickety chair in the garden, looking totally absorbed in his work as he scribbled notes and drew sketches on a notepad. From time to time he cast a worried glance at Frieda, who was grazing and waddling around the plot, happy to be out of her pen at last. Sundays were the garden's busiest day and it was better for the goose to be out of the way so as not to scare people.

Contrary to what she'd expected, Olivier hadn't been put off by Friday night's paint incident, and Tamsin may not want to admit it, but it was comforting to have him on board. So far he was proving a thoughtful housemate who didn't leave dirty socks lying around or stubble in the sink after shaving. He hadn't baulked when she'd explained about the composting toilet and didn't complain about Josephine taking all the space on the sofa.

The oven pinged, announcing the spinach and goat cheese tart he'd made was ready. He'd offered to cook every day in exchange for Tamsin putting him up on the boat, and as well as the savoury tart he'd made a salad, set up a cheese board, sliced a baguette and uncorked a bottle of red wine, now standing on the worktop, ready for their evening meal. Tamsin's only contribution was a bowl of freshly picked strawberries from the garden and a jug of cream.

Josephine jumped from the sofa and rubbed her body against Tamsin's calves in a not very subtle reminder that it was time for her tea too. Tamsin filled her bowl with cat food then brought a tablecloth, plates and cutlery and two wine glasses outside to set the table on the deck. It was a tight squeeze, but it would be a shame not to make the most of the glorious summer evening.

As soon as he saw her, Olivier checked his watch and got up, holding on to his pens and notepad. 'Is it ready? I'm sorry. I lost track of time.'

He climbed on board, took the savoury tart out of the oven, then whisked up a vinaigrette with olive oil, vinegar and mustard, which he sprinkled over the salad, together with freshly chopped basil, chives and coriander. As he slipped the tea towel over his shoulder, he gave her one of his shy, heart-melting smiles. 'I hope you'll like it.'

'It smells delicious.' She tried to ignore the heat creeping on her face, and once again reminded herself that being attracted to Olivier was a very bad idea. She carried the salad bowl outside while he took the tart and the wine.

'Aunt Amelia said you were working on a new fragrance. What a magical job you have! I hope it's going well,' she said.

Olivier poured the red wine into their glasses. 'It's going surprisingly well. I thought this trip would be a complete waste of time but it seems I was wrong. It's quite extraordinary.' His voice was thoughtful as he lifted his glass, swirled the wine and looked at its deep burgundy colour before taking a sip.

Tamsin ate a bite of tart and almost groaned with delight at the flaky pastry and the filling's rich flavours. 'You should be a chef. In a way, cooking must be a bit like mixing ingredients to create a fragrance. I would love to know how you come up with the ideas, if it's not a secret, of course.'

He smiled. 'You'd be disappointed if I told you that after the first burst of creativity, the rest of the process is rather boring and repetitive and takes place in a lab.'

'Oh… I always thought there was magic involved. Did you see anything here that inspired you?'

He gave her a strange look, and didn't answer straight away. 'Well… er… yes, your garden…and Miss Moonshine,' he said at last. 'I bought something in her shop yesterday before the kerfuffle between Jack and those boys.'

Olivier pulled a small wind chime out of his shirt pocket

and dangled it from his index finger so that the three tiny glass butterflies caught the evening sun's rays. 'The idea still needs work,' he said, 'but I was thinking of having three vials of perfume – the main one would be fresh and vegetal, like dew in a summer garden at dawn… I'm thinking mint, basil and lavender with a hint of lemon and grapefruit for the top notes, geranium and lemongrass for heart, with moss and musk for base notes. I'm aiming for light pink and green, like this small butterfly here.'

'Why are you talking about colours?'

He gave her a shy smile. 'It may sound crazy but when I think about scents, I see colours.'

'Really? That's incredible. What about the other two perfumes?'

Olivier looked at the butterflies again. 'They would come in smaller vials and have deeper, warmer notes. People could mix them together to achieve the perfect individual blend according to the weather, the time of day, or their mood.' He glanced at her. 'Do you think it could work or is it a completely rubbish idea?'

She smiled, happy that he cared about her opinion. 'I think it's a brilliant idea. You're turning people into mini-alchemists, and thanks to you they'll have the chance to create their very own unique perfume every single day… You should call the new fragrance "Three Butterflies".'

'"Three Butterflies",' he repeated in a thoughtful voice. 'Of course! *Papillon du Matin* for the pink and green fresh morning scent; *Papillon du Soir*, filled with warmth, sunshine and a hint of blue sky; and for the deepest, most potent and mysterious one, *Papillon de Nuit*. Yes, this would work…What a wonderful suggestion. Thank you, Tamsin.'

Her cheeks heated up and she drank a quick sip of wine to hide her embarrassment. After eating the strawberries and cream, Tamsin put Frieda in her pen for the night and did a bit of tidying up in the garden. Olivier brought their glasses and the bottle of wine over.

'Tell me about the People's Garden,' he said. 'When did you get the idea for it?'

'A friend of mine set up something similar in a neighbouring town and it was so successful, I decided to do the same here. At first people were a little unsure, but we had some gardening sessions and food-tasting events and the idea caught on. We got more and more volunteers to help us, and now we have planters all over the town. And of course, there's the gardening apprenticeship scheme for the association. Jack is one of our most dedicated students.'

A mix of anger and sorrow tightened her chest. Reece Flynn and his gang deserved to be taught a lesson.

'Jack's a good teacher too. He told me exactly what I had to do yesterday.' Olivier frowned and gestured towards the towpath. Two police officers were walking towards the *Elysia*. 'I wonder if they're here because of what happened to your boat on Friday night.'

Frieda clucked and flapped her wings, and Tamsin quickly shut the gate to the pen. It wouldn't be a good idea to have the goose flying at the police.

'It's more likely they came because Mitch Flynn complained about us again.'

'Good evening, Miss Sheridan,' one of the officers said as they stopped in front of the garden. 'I'm afraid there's been a report of assault against a minor by a gentleman who is staying with you.' He turned to Olivier and took out his notebook and pen. 'Are you the gentleman in question, sir?'

Olivier nodded. 'Well, I am staying here, yes that's true, but I didn't assault anybody –'

The police officer interrupted. 'I need your name, address of residence and phone number, sir, and I'll ask you to come with us to the station to make a statement.'

Chapter Five

'Olivier did nothing wrong! Reece Flynn was picking on Jack Bradshaw again.' Tamsin's face was flushed with anger and frustration, but Olivier put a calming hand on her arm.

'It's all right. I'll take care of it,' he said, before giving the policeman his personal details. 'I will of course help you with your enquiries. There was a witness to yesterday's incident. Miss Moonshine. Did you ask her what happened?'

The policeman shrugged. 'Not yet, but we will.'

What a rotten end to what had been a very pleasant evening, and a wonderfully productive day, Olivier thought, as he followed the police officers to town. He made his statement and Miss Moonshine came to the station and corroborated his version of events. She also mentioned a security camera outside the shop which would have captured the full incident. It took another two hours for an officer to check the recording, but at last Olivier was free to leave.

Tamsin was waiting for him outside the police station. 'I'm so sorry you got caught in the dispute between us and Mitch Flynn,' she said, slipping her arm under his. 'Let's go to the pub. I owe you a drink.'

They found Tamsin's friends sitting at a table in the beer garden of The Packhorse Inn.

'How are you, mate? What happened?' Cliff asked, shuffling on the bench to make room.

Olivier told them about the incident in front of Miss Moonshine's Emporium the day before and the allegation made against him as a result. Ocean, Sky and India shook their heads, appalled.

'It was lucky Miss M was a witness and even luckier the whole thing was captured on CCTV,' India remarked.

'Mitch Flynn is a bully,' Cliff said. 'He runs a chain of upmarket greengrocers in town and in the valley and claims we're taking his livelihood away by enabling people to get fruit and veg for free.'

'He's talking rubbish. The people who come to our garden can't afford to buy stuff in his shops,' Reef said.

'Trying to shut the association down is one thing,' Tamsin added in a gloomy voice. 'But accusing you of assaulting his son is something else entirely. I can't believe he stooped that low. I bet you can't wait to leave Haven Bridge and go back to Paris now.'

As he looked at Tamsin, her eyes shining in the evening light, he was startled to realise he didn't want to leave at all – not now, not at the end of the two weeks… not ever.

*

For the next two weeks the weather remained glorious and Olivier sat in the garden most of the time, surrounded by buzzing bees and multicoloured butterflies as he worked. Tamsin often joined him, chatting away as she weeded, snipped and trimmed the plants, or picked up fruit and vegetables to take to the food bank or the People's Gardens stall for the Midsummer Market at the weekend.

Olivier loved listening to her as he worked, and often asked for feedback as he refined the mood board and the list of ingredients for the new fragrance. He was getting more and more excited by the project and dutifully reported his progress to his uncle, who congratulated him on his innovative idea. For some reason, however, Uncle George seemed more interested in finding out how he was getting on with Tamsin than his blend of natural essences.

'We're getting along fine,' Olivier replied, aware his cheeks had gone pink and relieved his uncle couldn't see him. What he should have said was that he loved staying on the *Elysia* – loved cooking every day, loved the quiet evenings with just the two of them, or the impromptu parties with Cliff, Reef and their friends either on the boat or at The Packhorse Inn.

Olivier had accompanied them on a couple of occasions as they reclaimed yet another roundabout and once as they mounted a stakeout one night to catch whoever was trampling all over the planters in town. Unfortunately the only thing he'd caught was a runny nose, which had prompted Tamsin to brew another batch of the concoction she'd given him the day he arrived.

He hadn't worn a suit, checked his emails or indeed worried about the company's accounts and sales projections for two weeks. It felt like he was on holiday – a holiday that was unfortunately coming to an end.

The day of the Midsummer Market, he got up at dawn, showered and dressed. He poured a splash of milk into Josephine's bowl and spent an hour stacking up crates of fresh produce on the boat. They were taking the *Elysia* to Haven Bridge Marina, where they would unload the fruit and vegetables and take them to the market.

There was a real party atmosphere in town that day, with buskers and street food. The People's Garden stall was at the heart of the market, between Cliff's pop-up kitchen and Ocean and Reef's organic hair and beauty products. Miss Moonshine was selling jewellery, vintage postcards and second-hand books. All had agreed that the proceeds from the day would be put back into the association, as every penny was needed.

Everything was going well until late afternoon, when a sandy-haired man with florid cheeks and a beer belly stopped in front of the People's Garden stall. Behind him was the boy Olivier had been accused of assaulting.

'I want a word with you lot,' the man started in a loud voice. 'You were seen digging up the verge along the road on Thursday evening. You were there too, Miss Moonshine, even though you should know better at your age than to be out and about at night with your wheezy, scrappy, ratty dog.'

Miss Moonshine stepped out from behind her stall. 'Watch your language, Mitch Flynn. Never mind talking about my age, how dare you refer to my darling Napoleon in such an insulting manner?' A strange trick of the light made her suddenly look taller and quite menacing.

The man paled. 'Well…erm… Anyway, I have news for you. I lodged another complaint with the council and this time I hope they put a stop to your activities and the conspiracy against me and my business.'

Tamsin sighed. 'There is no conspiracy, Mitch. Why don't you work with us instead of against us? You could even sponsor one of our planters, or perhaps fund a place for an apprentice on our scheme. It would be great publicity for you.'

'Work with you? Never! I'll get your stupid association shut down one way or another.' Mitch Flynn turned to his son. 'Come on, lad. It's time we showed these losers we mean business.'

The mood was somewhat dampened after that. It took Olivier and Tamsin a while to tidy up after the market closed, and to bring the empty crates back to the *Elysia*. Cliff and the others were going to The Packhorse to celebrate Midsummer, but Tamsin and Olivier said they were too tired to join them.

Olivier didn't feel like celebrating anyway. It was his last evening on the boat – his last evening in Haven Bridge, and he wanted to enjoy every minute he had left with Tamsin. He was flying back to Paris the following day, with his mood board and his new fragrance concept, but what he really wanted was to stop time. Perhaps he should tell Tamsin how he felt, he thought, as she steered the *Elysia* back, with the late afternoon sunshine glowing on her pink hair. Or perhaps he would just make a fool of himself…

'What's going on over there?' Tamsin called to him once the

Elysia had passed the stone bridge. 'Frieda is running loose and I can see people messing about in the garden.'

Olivier climbed onto the roof and ran to the front of the boat.

'It's Jack… and Reece Flynn and his friends.'

Tamsin let out an anguished sigh. 'I hope they're not pestering him again. And why is Frieda out of her pen?'

The boat was still a few yards from its mooring when Frieda suddenly charged towards Reece, honking and flapping her wings. As she launched herself at him he tried to run away, tripped and fell backwards into the canal. His friends looked at one another and took to their heels.

'Help! I can't swim!' Reece shouted, waving his arms frantically.

Although the canal wasn't that deep and the teenager could have stood up and got out by himself, it was clear he was panicking, leaving Olivier no other choice than to jump into the slimy water. There was a splash next to him. Glancing round, he saw Jack had jumped in too, and together they pulled a coughing, crying and spluttering Reece Flynn out onto the towpath.

'Are you hurt?' Olivier asked, checking the teenager's face for injuries. Reece shook his head but carried on crying.

Tamsin had moored the boat and now came running, holding several towels in her arms.

'How are you all?' she asked, handing them out.

'Reece seems all right,' Olivier replied, as he draped a towel onto Reece's shoulders. He did the same for Jack, and rubbed his own face and hair with another.

Tamsin let out a relieved sigh. 'Jack, you were a true hero to jump in,' she told the youngster, who flushed with pleasure.

Reece looked up. 'Thanks, Jack. I'm very sorry I was mean to you.'

Jack held out his hand to pull Reece up. 'It's all right.'

Reece bit his lower lip and looked at Tamsin. 'And I'm sorry I messed up your boat the other night.'

Tamsin's eyes widened. 'It was you who threw the red paint?'

He nodded.

'Did you leave graffiti and wreck the planters in town too?'

The teenager looked down at his soggy trainers and let out a despondent sigh. 'Will you tell my dad… or the police?'

Tamsin shrugged. 'No, but you're going to have to help us fix things, and don't tell any more lies about Olivier. Understood?'

Reece's phone was completely soaked and so Tamsin lent him hers so he could call his mum and ask her to pick him up and bring dry clothes and shoes. Mrs Flynn came quickly and gave her son a thorough telling-off for being so careless. She thanked Jack and Olivier, suggesting that they could come to any of their shops and choose whatever they wanted as a reward for fishing Reece out of the canal. She also offered to take Jack home.

'She seemed very reasonable, especially compared to her husband,' Olivier remarked as they stepped onto the boat. He couldn't wait to peel his wet and smelly clothes off and take a shower.

'She's a nice woman,' Tamsin agreed. 'I hope Reece realises the harm he's done and changes his attitude. And who knows, perhaps he'll be a good influence on his father. You were a true hero too, you know. Now you go and get changed and I'll look after you and make you a nice cup of tea. I'll put extra honey in it too,' she offered, as Olivier sneezed again, and again.

Olivier managed not to pull a face. A mug of Tamsin's horrid herbal concoction was a small price to pay if it made her happy.

Later that evening they sat side by side on the sofa that, for once, Josephine had vacated of her own free will. Despite the hot drinks, Olivier was still cold and shivering and he kept sneezing.

'This isn't how I envisaged our last evening together,' he said.

She smiled. 'Oh? What did you have in mind?'

Would he dare? His grandfather's words about living and loving came back to him. If he didn't try, he'd never know if things could have worked between Tamsin and him.

He looked at her. 'Something more romantic… A glass of wine and a nice meal, or perhaps something like this…' And he put the tea down, leant towards her and kissed her.

Chapter Six

It rained as hard on Olivier's last day as on the day he'd arrived, and as on the first day he wore his suit, shirt and tie, and his coat. They'd had lunch at The Packhorse, where Olivier said goodbye to Tamsin's friends before walking to the station.

They now stood on the platform, waiting for the train for Leeds.

'I want to thank you for welcoming me on your boat, in your garden… and in your life.' Olivier took an envelope out of his pocket. 'I believe this could be quite valuable. Miss Moonshine may be able to get it valued and sell it for you, and then you can use the money for the People's Garden.'

She knew what it was before she opened the envelope and looked inside. The three butterflies. She shook her head. 'I can't sell them. You said they were the inspiration for your new perfume.'

He smiled, and his eyes became warm and soft behind his glasses. 'It wasn't completely true. *You* were my inspiration. In fact, I've been thinking my Uncle George and your Aunt Amelia knew exactly what they were doing when they sent me here.'

The station tannoy announced that the next train would be to Leeds.

'What did they know?' Tamsin asked, her heart beating fast and hard as the train rumbled into the station and screeched to a halt.

'That I would fall in love with you,' Olivier said, gazing at her.

'And I with you,' Tamsin whispered, as he bent down and caressed her lips with the gentlest, lightest kiss.

For a few seconds it felt like they were alone in the bustling crowd of passengers pushing past them to get to the train as the doors slid open. Then Olivier stepped back. 'I'll come back very soon. I promise.'

He walked down the compartment, waved at her through the window, and the train started moving. Tamsin had promised herself she wouldn't cry in front of him, and she managed to hold the tears until she left the station, but as she walked back to the *Elysia*, pulling her hood down against the driving rain, she realised they weren't tears of sadness. They were tears of joy. Olivier would be back, and they had many, many happy days to look forward to together…

Originally from Lyon in France, Marie now lives in the Rossendale Valley in Lancashire. Her bestselling novels include *Escape to the Little Chateau*, **shortlisted for the 2021 RNA Jackie Collins Romantic Suspense Award, and her new romance** *Happy Dreams at Mermaid Cove* **is available from Amazon and various digital platforms.**

amazon.co.uk/Happy-Dreams-Mermaid-Cove-uplifting-ebook/dp/B094RBWWCJ/ref

GU 1909

By Angela Wren

May – Thursday

Maddie stood aghast. 'Wow!' Her eyes were wide and staring as she took in the sight before her. As her vision became accustomed to the gloom of the stone-built outhouse, she finally let her grip on the large tarpaulin cover loosen, and it slipped to the ground at her feet. 'You do know how important this might be, don't you?'

Miss Moonshine smiled and gave a slight shrug. 'I have some idea,' she said, as she rubbed her hands together against the early chill of what promised to be a bright spring day.

'If I'm right –' Maddie glanced down at the front grill and noticed that the expected manufacturer's decal was missing. 'If I'm right and it is genuine, and the chassis number matches the records in the archives, then this may have been one of the very last Wolseley E4s to leave the factory in the late 1920s.' She glanced at the black registration plate with its silver characters: GU 1909. *Definitely a London dealer*, she thought.

Miss Moonshine frowned and pulled her long charcoal-grey cardigan closer around herself. 'Perhaps,' she said. 'But what is of more importance to me is whether you can get it going again.'

Maddie was already scrutinising the bodywork as she made her way down the side of the car, the brick wall of the dim windowless storage space grazing her waxed coat. She peered inside it as best she could in the half-light. *That looks in reasonable condition.* Her hand automatically reached for the handle on the passenger's door.

'Ouch!' A momentary burning charge shot through her fingers and halfway up her arm.

'Everything all right, my dear?'

Maddie nodded. 'Just static, I expect,' she said, rubbing her palm. She moved around to the back and then continued her careful inspection along the driver's side of the vehicle. When she reached the front, she popped the fastenings on the bonnet and pulled it up. 'Four-cylinder engine,' she announced, with a wide grin on her face. 'I haven't worked on one of these since Dad –'

Something snatched at her heart, and she moved a little further into the light, keeping her gaze focused on the antique machine.

'Incredible,' she said after a moment. Turning to Miss Moonshine, she smiled. 'This is an incredible piece of mechanical engineering, and I'd be stoked to restore it for you.'

Miss Moonshine relaxed. 'Excellent,' she said.

'But there's a lot of work to do. The engine will need to be removed, cleaned and refitted. We may need to source replacement parts, and if we do, I would want them to be as close to authentic as possible.' She took a couple of steps back, her eyes never leaving the car. 'It's going to take time. There's some old damage to the bodywork that has had an inadequate repair, and that will need specialised handling. I will have to buy that expertise in.'

'And do you know someone who can do it?'

Maddie winced as she thought of Simon. It had been two weeks and three days since they'd last seen each other. Not that she was counting, or so she kept telling herself. She just knew so precisely because she had a good head for detail. That was her story, and she was sticking to it.

'Yes.' Maddie summoned up a smile and tried to bring her mind back to the important matter in hand. 'Simon and his dad are the best people for this job.' She turned aside as the picture of Simon walking away from her all those days ago flashed into her mind. She sniffed and folded her arms across her chest. *I can't think about that now*. 'But I'm not certain they will want to… umm… that they will have time to do the work,' she continued.

Miss Moonshine peered at her. 'Are you sure about that, my dear?'

Maddie nodded. 'Pretty sure.'

Miss Moonshine gave Maddie's arm a gentle squeeze. 'I think that when they see the car, they will make time,' she said, a broad smile on her face. 'Now, it might be spring, but that breeze is chilly, and we've been out here for long enough. Come inside, and I'll make us some tea.'

Unable to refuse, or even protest that she needed to load the vehicle onto the flatbed truck waiting for its cargo outside, Maddie found herself being led back into the emporium.

*

Under the bright lights of her workshop, Maddie circled the Wolseley. *Stunning. Absolutely stunning.*

'If Dad could see this, he'd be going ape right now.' A wave of sadness hit her as she uttered the words. She paused for a moment, trying to fight back the tears. The battle very quickly lost, she reached into the only clean pocket on the bib of her overalls and pulled out a large white handkerchief. She dabbed at her eyes and sniffed. 'Work,' she announced to the walls.

She strode across the workshop to the cramped office space where her father, grandfather and their ancestors had kept all the paperwork, magazine articles, manuals and anything else relevant to the cars they'd worked on since the garage was established. There were shelves of box files, all labelled and grubby from the generations of oily fingers that had handled them. The shelving occupied the majority of the space. The only other pieces of furniture were a small desk, and a chair wedged into one corner. The place was full without Maddie's presence; with her there, it was overcrowded. Long-time clients were used to standing at the doorway and discussing business. They took it as normal and never complained. Occasionally a new client would attempt to enter, only to find himself rebuffed and politely asked to wait outside. The office was of its time and of its predominantly male origin. The only nod to modernity was Maddie's laptop, which occupied the central space on the desk. A pair of old wooden trays of papers filled the flanking spaces; the one on the left marked 'In' and the one on the right marked 'Out'. With its sleek metallic lines, the laptop stood out as a slim grey anachronism amongst the scratched and dented surroundings, the only evidence of its belonging being the myriad of oily daubs that covered its surface. Maddie's device had been grudgingly accepted as a necessity when she joined the family business as a full-time mechanic.

She scanned the shelves until she found the box file she needed. After squeezing behind the desk, she plopped down on the hard wooden chair. As always, she balanced the laptop on top of the in-tray, shoved the out-tray on the floor under the desk and set the file in the newly created space. She tugged at the drawer in the plinth – it had always stuck – and grabbed a notebook and pen. She would need to make extensive notes before considering taking the engine out of the Wolseley.

Ollie and Pete, two employees at the workshop, popped their heads around the office door.

'We're off now,' said Ollie, his unruly blond hair flopping into his eyes as it always did.

Maddie looked up from her work. 'Is the Renault Alpine ready for collection tomorrow?'

'Yeah,' he said. 'I've already moved it out of the bay. I'll put it on the front forecourt first thing tomorrow morning.'

Maddie nodded. 'Good, we've got the…' She glanced at the constantly open diary on her laptop. 'The Mini Cooper S is coming in tomorrow morning, and I need you to start work on that as soon as possible.'

Ollie grinned. He drove a Mini himself and never tired of working on his favourite vehicle.

'And what about the Alvis, Pete?'

'On schedule, and it will be ready for pick-up next week as agreed.'

'Great, and thanks, guys.'

'It's well after six, Maddie, and we're just going to pop round to the Fox for a pint. Do you want to join us?'

A beer with the team seemed inviting. *How long is it since we all last did that?* she wondered. About two months ago. But her father had joined them on that occasion and that… No. Maddie stopped her thoughts and pushed her mind back to work.

'Thanks,' she said. 'But… um, I've got to get on top of the work to be done on the Wolseley.' She grabbed a heavy bunch of keys from the out-tray. 'I'll lock up,' she said, as she deftly extricated herself from the tiny space between her chair and the desk. Ollie and Pete stood aside and then followed as Maddie made her way the entire length of the workshop.

'You know where we are if you change your mind,' said Pete.

Maddie smiled, pulled the front shutters down and locked them.

On her way back to her desk, she checked the stated progress on the other two cars. All was as it should be. As she passed the Wolseley, her pace slowed, and she couldn't stop herself brushing her hand across the bonnet. The prickling feeling made her jump. She ran her thumb over the tops of her fingers. There was unexpected warmth, tenderness from irritation, and the skin smarted with a bit of redness.

'What the –' She shook her head in disbelief. 'A car can't have an electric charge.' She strode back to her desk and resumed her second level of research online. She moved the mouse to wake up the laptop, then froze. The hairs on the back of her neck began to bristle. She looked over the top of the screen out into the bit of the workshop that she could see. Nothing had changed. The Wolseley was still there, unpolished, worn and with the forlorn look of a discarded toy. Deciding she was imagining things, Maddie focused on the information on the screen. Some of the pages needed printing out, and she clicked on the ones she wanted. As she watched the printer, which was perched precariously on a pile of box files stacked on the floor between her chair and the wall, she began to feel uneasy. She folded her arms and sat up straight. To stretch her back, she convinced herself, not for any other reason. In her mind, she believed her explanation, but the shiver that ran down her spine told her something else. She glanced at the car. The two headlights seemed to be glaring at her, even though they weren't lit. Maddie shook away the uneasy feeling that the Wolseley had spirit of its own. She turned her attention to the printer. As the last sheet came off, she almost snatched it out of the tiny tray. In one sweeping move, she had the pages in the front of her laptop bag. She slapped the computer shut and shoved it in the back compartment, grabbed her jacket from the back of the chair and walked briskly out of the office towards the side door. The alarm set, she stepped outside and locked up for the night.

At her car, she stopped and looked back. 'Weird.' She tutted. 'All the years I've spent in there and never before has a car got me so rattled.' Keys in the ignition, she paused for a moment.

'Or so excited!' Putting the odd experience out of her thoughts, she set off for home. Her empty home – apart from the cat.

Friday

The workshop was full of noise, the radio blaring at the far end where Ollie and Pete worked. The early morning banter between the two mechanics was as raucous as usual. Maddie grinned as she walked across to her office, her insulated coffee cup in her hand and laptop slung across her shoulder.

'Morning. Anything I need to know?'

'Nah,' came the chorused reply.

Maddie smiled. 'So, yesterday was just plain weird then,' she said to herself. She dumped the bag on the floor and draped her jacket over the back of the chair. As she sat down, she couldn't help but look at the Wolseley. *Are you going to be just as weird today?* she wondered.

She let out a heavy sigh and gazed up at the grey ceiling with its harsh strip-lighting. 'I've got to make that call, haven't I?' She pulled out her phone and scrolled through her contacts list. As she stared at the name and the handsome smiling face in the icon, she paused for a moment. Her thumb hovered over the green receiver. 'Do it,' she commanded herself. The next thing she knew, the phone was on her desk, the speaker switched on, and the other end of the line was trilling shrilly in the metallic confines of her room.

'Walker's Workshop and Repairs. How can we help you today?'

Maddie stopped breathing. It was the wrong voice. It was supposed to be –

'Hello, how can we help you today?'

Maddie sat up straight. 'Hi, Simon.' Her voice sounded thin and forced to her ears. 'I have a car, a Wolseley E4 from 1928 or 1929, and I was wondering if you'd be able to help with the restoration of the panels.' *I've said it. This is just business. Keep calm.* The pause was now at the other end of the line. Maddie waited, her heart beginning to shift its rhythm.

'We're always willing to take on any work that we can handle, but of course we'll need to assess what has to be done. Where is the vehicle?'

'It's here in my workshop, and available for your inspection from today. The client isn't in a hurry, but she does want the car in perfect working order and is prepared to wait, no matter how long that takes.'

'OK.'

Maddie heard the shuffle of papers and then pages turning.

'I could come over on Tuesday of next week. Would that be convenient…? Maddie?'

At the sound of her name, she stopped breathing. Had there really been a slight pause between the rest of the sentence and her name? She squinched her eyes closed for a second or two. *Of course not.*

Mustering her brightest possible tone, she blurted out, 'Great. That's in my diary, and shall we say ten?'

'Yes, and I'll see you on Tue –'

Maddie thumped the red receiver button. The line cut out, and she sat back in her chair. She needed to breathe, and she needed her stomach to stop tying itself in knots.

'How am I going to get through next Tuesday?' She stood up and marched out into the workshop. 'Work! That's what I need.' She grabbed the clipboard from the peg on the wall just outside her office and crossed to the Wolseley. She circled it and reached out to open the door, but hesitated.

'OK car, just so you know, Simon is coming to look at you next week. He's the best in the business…' Maddie caught a glimpse of her own reflection in the glass of the door and let out a gasp. She looked up. 'Get a grip, Maddie, you're talking to a car!'

She stretched her hand out to grasp the door handle, but still she hesitated. 'You're not going to go all weird on me again, are you?' Gingerly she placed her hand on the handle and applied gentle pressure. She felt nothing but the metal's smooth coolness and heard the click of the mechanism. She pulled the door wide open, and a breath of air, faintly scented with lavender, moved past her. For some reason, Maddie felt the need to look to her left, but there was nothing there. Just the wall of grey metal shelves filled with boxes of this and that, the labels as grubby as everything else. But the air seemed to float, and the scent with it, until it dissipated. Maddie frowned. *Miss Moonshine?*

She pushed the madness of the last few moments to the back of her head. She had a job to do and she needed to get on with it. She moved around to the passenger door, opened it to get inside, and began assessing the work to be done on the interior, noting the various tasks on the form on her clipboard.

*

Half an hour later, Maddie had a clear idea of the extent of the work involved and several sheets completed with ticks, circles, crossings through and notes.

'This is a big project,' she said to herself, as she stepped off the running-board. 'Where are you, Dad, when I really need you?' She turned to pull the rear passenger door shut, and realised she hadn't checked the internal pockets. She flipped through to the last page on her clipboard for the extensive notes section and laid it down on the vehicle's floor. Holding the ancient leather pocket-flap open, she peered in. There was something in the corner – something small and metallic. She reached in but couldn't get a proper grip, so gave up and went in search of a torch.

With her right wrist pressed against the flap and keeping

the pocket open as best she could, Maddie slowly played the torch across the dark interior. In the far corner of the pouch, a glint of silver caught in the bright white light. Using her left hand, she began to tease the object from its hiding place. At first, there was little resistance. Then it wouldn't move. It was as though it was being deliberately held in place. Maddie checked the exterior of the pocket. It was obvious that a couple of the stitches on the leather had worn thin and a third had broken. She picked at it to loosen it further. A gentle pull on the object on the inside of the pocket, and this time it came away.

'Ah-ha!' Maddie pulled clear a silver chain with a small pendant containing what looked like a piece of shell. She held it up, and the bands of colour within the nacre became iridescent as the object gently swayed in the light.

'I wonder who this belonged to?'

She collected the clipboard from the floor pan with one hand and, with the chain dangling from the other, returned to her office.

'Right, estimate for the work first, and then I'll return this chain to Miss Moonshine.' She carefully dropped the necklace into the pocket of her jacket.

Saturday Morning

Haven Bridge was busy. It was market day, and parking was impossible. Maddie circled her usual spots but had to be content with leaving her car on the main road at the town's outskirts. It was a ten-minute walk into the centre and Miss Moonshine's Emporium on Market Street. The sun was warming the early morning air, and the few clouds that had been in the sky when she left the workshop had drifted away to almost nothing on the distant horizon. The bustle of the shoppers and market traders' stalls brought the sleepy Yorkshire town alive as the sellers shouted out their wares and prices.

''And of bananas, ladies. Right cheap. I'm undercuttin' Morrison's today,' shouted the fruiterer from behind his stall as she passed.

'Must remember to go to the butcher's to get Dad…' Maddie mumbled to herself and then realised such a trip was no longer required.

She reached the open door to Miss Moonshine's Emporium and went in. The shop was empty apart from Napoleon, Miss Moonshine's ageing chihuahua, who was asleep in his tiny basket beside the counter. Maddie smiled.

'What a surprise,' said Miss Moonshine, appearing apparently from nowhere.

Maddie started and took a breath. 'Hi, I've come to bring you the estimate for the work on the car. It's going to be quite expensive, and it'll take a few weeks to get everything done.'

Miss Moonshine smiled. 'Oh well, I didn't expect it to be easy,' she said. 'Take as long as you need, my dear.'

'There's also the matter of the work to the panels on the vehicle.' Maddie cleared her throat. 'That's highly specialist work, and I will have to hire in the expertise.'

Miss Moonshine leant on the counter, her long thin fingers intertwined, and propped up her narrow chin. Maddie stared at her. Was that a twinkle she caught in her eyes?

'That's likely to be the bulk of the work and the cost, Miss Moonshine.'

'Is it indeed, my dear?'

Maddie saw a knowing look cross Miss Moonshine's face and… there it was again – that glint in those hazel eyes.

Maddie, hands on her hips, stared at the ground for a moment. 'Miss M, why do I get the feeling that I'm telling you something you already know?'

Miss Moonshine stood up straight. 'I really couldn't say, Maddie, but I do know that I suspected you would be telling me something like this. I've had that car a very long time.' Napoleon looked up, staring at his owner with his big, dark brown eyes. Miss Moonshine bent to pick him up and sat down in the chair beside the counter.

'Tell me all about the repairs,' she said, indicating to Maddie to take the chair on the opposite side of the tiny round table.

Maddie sat down and pulled out an envelope. 'First, I need to show you this.' She tipped the contents onto the table.

'Oh, you found it!' Miss Moonshine grabbed the chain and held it up to the light. 'It's ormer, you know.'

'Sorry?' Maddie watched as the pendant swayed in the sunlight streaming through the windows, the colours shifting from pink to silver-grey to cream and back again.

'The shell in the centre of the pendant – it's an ormer from Jersey. I've often wondered what happened to this.'

'Glad I could return it to you. It was hidden in the corner of one of the pockets in the back of the car.'

Miss Moonshine placed the necklace on the table. 'I'd like you to have it, Maddie,' she said. 'It would suit someone of your age much better.'

Maddie hesitated. To refuse may seem churlish. But to accept was troubling too. She frowned. 'But if it's valuable, wouldn't you want to keep it? Or sell it?'

Miss Moonshine blinked. 'The man who gave me this died many years ago,' she said, straightening the chain with her fingers. 'I haven't missed it all this time whilst it's been lost, so there's no real value in my having it back. I have everything I need here,' she said, gently touching her heart. 'And the memories, of course. No matter how recent or how long ago, the happiest memories never leave us, Maddie. Those remembered moments are the ones that sustain us and enable us to move forward.'

Maddie fought back a tear as her own heart missed a beat or two. 'Of course,' she said. 'Thank you.' She forced a smile.

She needed to move her mind back into the field of work. 'The repairs,' she announced, a little more forcefully than she intended. She pulled the second set of papers out of her bag and laid them out flat on the table.

'The full estimated cost of the engineering and mechanical work is at the bottom.' She pointed to the figure in bold halfway down the first page. 'The cost of repairs to the panels will need to be added, and you can expect to pay around the same amount again. At least. I won't know the actual cost for that work until Si – until the expert has made a detailed assessment of the work to be done. That will be next week. Today, I just wanted to let you know roughly what you might need to pay and to return the necklace too.'

'Thank you,' said Miss Moonshine. 'And the expert for the work on the car – is it someone you know?'

Maddie felt Miss Moonshine was asking for the sake of asking, but she answered anyway. 'Yes, it's Simon Walker. He and his father run another place on the outskirts of Haven Bridge, and they're the best in the business in this area.'

Miss Moonshine nodded. 'Now, didn't I meet this young man two or three years ago?'

Maddie stared at the floor, her left foot swinging backwards and forwards, considering her answer. 'Hmm, yes, I think you did,' she said at last.

'Ah, yes. He was the tall young man with the dark hair who helped you, wasn't he?'

Maddie let out a deep sigh. 'Miss Moonshine, he was the guy I got engaged to at Christmas.'

Miss Moonshine gently touched Maddie's ringless left hand as it rested on the arm of the chair.

'What happened, my dear?'

Maddie fought back the tears as the recriminations she'd voiced echoed through her mind. 'We decided to…'

'Yes, my dear?'

'It was just too… difficult.' Maddie couldn't keep the swelling tide of emotion at bay any longer. She let out a heartfelt moan as the tears began to flow down her cheeks. Miss Moonshine reached onto the counter, grabbed the box of tissues she always kept there and placed it in front of her guest.

'Tea,' she said gently, as she placed Napoleon back on his blanket. 'What you need is some of my special camomile tea.'

In a moment, she was gone, and Maddie was alone with Napoleon. She sniffed and wiped a tissue across her face, and then screwed it up. The dog, seeming to understand her distress, moved around in his basket to rest his head on her feet. The small gesture brought a fresh fall of tears, and Maddie helped herself to a handful of tissues.

Tuesday

By the time Simon was due at the garage, the Wolseley was almost unrecognisable. The engine was on blocks; the interior seats had been removed, along with the steering wheel and the canvas roof. The shell was all that was left. The radio was blaring out as usual, and Maddie's two employees were each working on their own jobs.

As Simon walked in, the clank of metal against metal ceased and for the first time, it became possible to hear the presenter on the radio introducing the next record. Ollie and Pete came out from their bays and followed Simon's progress across the shop floor with their eyes until he reached Maddie's office. Just outside the door, Simon stopped. Ollie and Pete exchanged quizzical looks and then disappeared into their work areas.

Simon stepped forward and stood in the doorway. 'Hello.'

Maddie started and sent half the coffee in her hand splashing out of the cup all over her overalls.

'Damn it!' She slammed the receptacle down on her desk and

started patting the damp patch with the nearest oily rag. 'You just had to make an entrance, didn't you?' She swiped at her trouser legs and threw the rag in the out-tray. Standing up and finally looking Simon in the eye, she felt a pang of regret. He stood so tall and smart in his suit. An urge to run and hug him was beginning to take hold of her. She looked away and moved out from behind her cramped desk.

'You have remembered that you're here to give me an estimate for the work on the Wolseley, haven't you?'

'Yes, of course. Sorry about the coffee,' he said. 'And these are for you.' He brought out a bunch of roses from behind his back.

Maddie didn't know where to look. 'We need to... I thought...'

'I'll just leave them here.' He edged forward and set the flowers on top of the in-tray.

'Yup,' said Maddie, the relief and the command in her voice struggling for supremacy. 'Right, let's, umm, look at the car, shall we?'

Simon stepped back into the main body of the garage. From his canvas bag, he pulled out a portfolio and a pristine pair of white overalls. He removed his jacket and hung it on the nearest peg. He pulled the overalls on over his suit trousers and shirt, retrieved his jacket, carefully folded it and put it in his bag. 'So what have we got?'

Maddie indicated the body of the car behind him. Simon took a stroll around the vehicle, his gaze drifting over it from top to bottom, occasionally getting up close to examine something in more detail. Maddie remained where she was, watching and waiting. As he moved along the far side, he squatted down for a while.

'That'll be the strange unevenness in the side panels,' she muttered to herself. A moment later Simon's tall figure appeared above the top of the car. She gave the slightest of nods in response to his smile. When he didn't break eye contact with her or speak, she turned and went back to her desk.

At the door to the office, she stopped. 'What on earth am I going to do with those?' She desperately looked around for something to put the flowers in. A rusty tin sat on a shelf, but when she lifted it, she realised it was full of washers.

'Nope, that won't do.' An empty can of paint propping up a series of box files caught her eye but was immediately dismissed. The files and the shelves were all so precariously arranged that Maddie deemed it too risky to dislodge it. She cast her eye over the flowers, the sumptuous burgundy of the petals so out of place and yet brightening up the many shades of grey and gunge that surrounded her.

She snapped her fingers and raced out of the office and to the far end of the workshop. She knew exactly what she could use. In a corner under the sink they used to clean the oil and grease from their hands was an old jerry can that had had the top section cut off.

Maddie grabbed it and began to fill it with water. 'Perfect!' She carried it back to her office, placed it in a cleared space on the desk and put the flowers in. The makeshift vase, a harsh vermillion in colour, and dotted with rust spots, jarred with the luxurious hue of the roses. The bunch of flowers was so full that Maddie could barely fit it into her workspace.

'Oh, for heaven's sake, what am I supposed to do now?' She glanced around the room. Every shelf and spare inch of space seemed to be occupied. Even the deep windowsill was obliterated by boxes of documents and papers – the black of the files merging with the decades of dust and muck that had accumulated on the glass behind.

'I really ought to clean those windows,' she said to herself. In sheer desperation, she moved the vase to the floor by the door.

It was the only space she could see, and she consoled herself with the fact that they were unlikely to be forgotten when she finally left that evening.

*

'I've got everything I need,' said Simon when he came to the doorway an hour or so later. Maddie looked up from her work on the accounts. Simon's blue eyes looked sad, and his usual smile was absent. As he stood there leaning against the door jamb, she half expected to hear her father's voice from somewhere within the workshop, reprimanding her for wasting time talking to business rivals. Not that their respective parents had ever really considered each other a rival. It was just her dad's way of letting Simon know… *Well, what exactly? Being protective of his little girl, I suppose.*

She shook the thoughts from her mind. 'OK, thanks. When can you book the vehicle in for your refurbishment?'

'I can fit it in on the 17th. We'll need about a month to get everything restored and refitted. But then you can come and collect the vehicle, or I can deliver, or…'

Maddie pulled up the calendar on her laptop. 'The 17th fits nicely with some other work we have scheduled, and it means we can get the car back to Miss Moonshine in the middle of June.'

'Great.'

Maddie forced a smile. Simon seemed to dither in the doorway. 'Was there anything else?'

Hands in his pockets, he shook his head. Yet he remained looking into her workspace.

Maddie focused on the computer screen and kept her head down. In her peripheral vision, she could see a pair of shoes moving as he shifted from one foot to the other.

'Maddie…'

Her head whipped up. 'Yup?'

He edged a little further through the doorway. 'Can we talk?'

'Mm.' She slapped the laptop closed.

'I just think we need to, umm…'

'Agree collection and delivery times for the vehicle,' she offered, the words leaving her mouth and hitting the air like a volley of bullets.

'Well, yes we do, but I wanted to talk –'

'It's OK, Simon. I'll understand if you don't want to be around to work on the Wolseley. That's OK. It's just that you are the best firm in Yorkshire, and it is Miss Moonshine's vehicle. But don't feel obligated.'

'*Maddie*!' Simon crossed the small space to the desk. 'It's not the car. It's you I want to talk to. There's a lot that's been left unsaid. And I…'

Maddie opened her mouth to speak, but the words wouldn't come.

'It's not my fault your father died,' said Simon. 'And it's not yours, either. It's nobody's fault. It just happened.'

'Yes, I know.' Maddie felt her chin beginning to quiver. She took a couple of deep breaths to try and still the broiling emotions. She could feel a prickle behind her eyes. With a great effort of will, she widened them, holding them open to prevent the welling tears from falling.

Simon hesitated. 'Well, I've said it. It needed to be said.' He turned to go. 'And… I mean it,' he added, as he collected his bag. 'Estimate with collection and delivery details will be in the post this afternoon.'

The next moment, he was gone. Maddie released the breath she was holding and let her head drop into her hands. Within seconds a long-held waterfall of tears flooded between her fingers.

*

Maddie woke with a start. Her back ached, and her right hand had no feeling in it. As she lifted her head, she realised she was still in the workshop. Pricking her ears, she listened for the familiar workaday sounds: the radio, the clank of spanners, the purr of engines being tested. There was nothing – just the eerie silence of an empty workplace. Sitting up, she put her hand behind her neck and slowly moved her head in a circle to stretch the joints.

'Long time since I've fallen asleep at the desk,' she said. She took in a breath of air. Instead of the usual oily engine tint, she picked up the smell of flowers. The vase by the doorway caught her eye. 'Oh yes, those.' She looked at the arrangement and wondered why it was lavender she could smell and not roses.

Thursday, late evening

'Now, my dear,' said Miss Moonshine, seemingly appearing from nowhere. 'I believe there is a bit of a problem with the estimate for the work on the car.'

Maddie stared wide-eyed. 'Where did –?'

'I thought it would make more sense for me to come and sort it out personally,' she continued, before Maddie had a chance to gather her thoughts.

Maddie wiped her overall sleeve across her face. 'Right, but I don't think I've seen Simon's –'

'Oh, I think so.' Miss Moonshine crossed to the desk and produced a piece of paper from the in-tray. 'I think this is what you need, isn't it?' She held up three stapled sheets with the name 'Williams and Son, Bodywork and Repair Shop' emblazoned across the top of the first page.

Maddie grabbed the papers and checked each sheet. 'How did you –'

'Don't worry about that, Maddie dear. I just need to let you know that the work costs are acceptable, and as soon as you can get the car back to me in full working order, the better.'

'Right.' Maddie stared at her visitor. 'There are just a couple of things that might slow us down,' she said. 'The decal for the front grill is missing, and I'd like to keep the car as authentic as possible. So, it will mean trawling specialist car collectors' sites and such like.'

'A decal? Is that the name thing on the front?'

'Yes, it attaches to the front grill.'

Miss Moonshine thought for a moment. 'I think I know exactly where I can find one,' she said, a knowing smile on her face. 'Now, you're looking tired, Maddie. Are you sure you're all right?'

'I'm fine. We've just got quite a lot of work on at the moment… and I –'

'Could do with some support?' suggested Miss Moonshine. 'It can't be easy running this place all by yourself.'

Maddie nodded. 'It's not,' she said. 'Especially now I seem to have lost my reference point.'

Miss Moonshine lifted her chin and thought for a moment. 'Perhaps it does feel like that at the moment. But you know all the right answers, Maddie. You're just not looking for them in the right place. Now, get yourself home, relax and get some rest, and come and see me the day after tomorrow.'

She moved to the door. 'Saturday, the day after tomorrow at two,' she said. Making an elegant turn, she strode away, leaving a waft of lavender behind her.

Maddie attempted to stand, only to realise she'd been so busy with her admin that her left foot had gone to sleep. Hanging onto the desk, she stretched her leg and waggled her toes as best she could inside her shoes. Once fully upright, she pulled her back straight and took a deep breath. *Miss M's right. It's time I went home.*

Saturday Afternoon

Saturdays in Haven Bridge were often busy, and the traffic usually snarled. Maddie was pleased she'd set off early. She hated being late for appointments. Not that a visit to Miss Moonshine's was an appointment – an appointment was something that had to be done, like seeing the dentist or the doctor. This was an agreed arrangement, and Maddie always looked forward to seeing her.

For a while, there had been a time when Maddie had wondered if Miss Moonshine and her father might become a little more than old friends. But just when it seemed her dad was considering suggesting that Miss Moonshine allow him to take her out to dinner, his health began to decline. His recovery from the massive heart attack three years previously had taken much longer than either he or Maddie had anticipated. When he eventually attempted to take up the reins of the business again, his enthusiasm had waned, and his interest was intermittent.

'I should have involved him more,' Maddie muttered to herself, as she sat waiting for the traffic lights on the edge of town to change. A tear dribbled down her cheek, just as the lights changed to green.

'I should have been there sooner,' she said, shifting into gear. A toot from the car behind brought a glare in the rearview mirror in response. She took her time releasing the handbrake and setting off.

Another ten minutes, and she was finally parked and walking along Market Street to Miss Moonshine's Emporium. The shoppers were out in droves in the bright afternoon sun. Maddie decided she'd take a walk along the canal after she left the shop. Some me time, she told herself.

The heavy wooden door to the emporium was open. Maddie stepped inside. As always, the place was empty. Napoleon was asleep in his basket at the foot of the counter. Maddie grinned.

Miss Moonshine appeared with a tray of tea and biscuits in her hands. 'There you are, my dear. Come and sit down.' She moved out from behind the counter and placed the tray on the table.

'Hi.' Maddie took off her jacket, threw it over the back of her chair. 'This is very nice.' She glanced at the tray and wondered why there were more cups and saucers than necessary.

'Is this what you need for the Wolseley?' Miss Moonshine placed a small silver-coloured oval of metal with two extensions at each side face down in front of her.

'It's the right shape.' Maddie picked up the decal and examined the front. The hard white material of the background was grubby. 'That needs a good clean and polish,' she said, more to herself than anyone else. She held it up to the light and scanned the red lettering. 'But everything looks in good order.'

'So it is what you need, then.'

Maddie nodded and added sugar to the tea that had been placed on the table for her. 'It's perfect.' She smiled at her companion.

'That's what I said.' The voice came from behind, and Maddie froze. She knew who was there. She willed herself not to look.

'Oh dear,' said Miss Moonshine. 'I seem to have forgotten the serviettes.' When Maddie looked up, the shop owner had disappeared.

Simon drew level with the table. 'Hello.' He pulled out a chair. 'May I?'

Maddie nodded.

'We need to talk,' he said. 'And… I miss you.'

'Mm.' Maddie looked around the shop. She couldn't seem to focus on any one thing. Not even Simon. *But he's right*, she thought. *We can't go on dancing around each other like this.* 'I'm sorry.'

Simon shook his head. 'No, I'm sorry. I should have been more understanding. Your dad was all you had left.'

Maddie nodded. Tears began to spill from her eyes. 'Not entirely. For a while, there was also you… But, now…' She looked up. Simon's forehead was deeply furrowed.

'Now?'

Maddie swiped her hand across her face.

Simon reached out, grabbed her hand and kissed it. 'You've still got me if that's what you want.'

'Yes, please.'

He reached into his jacket pocket. 'You might want this back then,' he said, placing a slim diamond ring on the table.

Maddie's eyes widened in disbelief. 'Where did you find that? After the… Well, I looked for it everywhere.' She picked it up and slipped it on her finger.

'It was buried at the bottom of the cat's basket.'

'Everything all right?' Miss Moonshine reappeared with a clutch of serviettes in her hand. 'Maddie, aren't you going to give Simon some tea?'

Without a second thought, Maddie grabbed a cup and saucer and began her task. 'We still need to talk about the workshop, though.' She added the milk and began to pour the tea. 'And your dad's idea, about merging the two businesses, well that's a –'

'Non-starter? Yes, I know, and I've told him that.'

Maddie shoved the tea towards him.

'I don't know why I let him carry me along with that idea.'

'No, Simon. He was pressuring you, and I think we both need to sit down to talk to him and let him know what our ideas are for our business future. Not the other way around.'

Simon smiled and sat back in his chair. 'I've got her back, Miss Moonshine. My fiercely independent Maddie is back.'

June 21st

Maddie sat at her sleek grey computer desk by the large

windows in her workshop office. The sunlight streamed in through the cleaned and polished panes of glass. The empty broad windowsill provided space for a straight four-cylinder engine block that had been refurbished and polished in Simon's workshop. It was a part of an engine her father had rescued from a scrap merchant's a few days after she was born. Now, carefully mounted in a specially manufactured fitting, it enabled Maddie to display flowers of all colours in the room throughout the year.

All of the old shelving had gone, too. The walls had been whitewashed for the first time in over forty years. The vast array of box files had been donated to the local motor museum, their contents being deemed a historical record of all the vehicles that been worked on over the decades. Maddie even had room for a chair for her visitors.

'My goodness! What a change,' said Miss Moonshine. Standing in the doorway, she gazed around the space. Napoleon, dressed in a small red-spotted neckerchief, stood nervously beside her at the end of his lead.

Maddie stood. 'It's the first of many, Miss M. Simon and I know what we want to achieve. Our respective businesses complement each other and, over the next few years, we want to build on that. We're going to do things gradually, and we're going to do things our way, too.'

Miss Moonshine grinned. 'Quite right, my dear. And my car?'

'This way.' Maddie strolled out of the office and along the entire length of the workshop. 'It's on the forecourt at the side,' she said, as they stepped out into the fresh summer air. 'We're going to put an opening in the back wall so that access is easier, and we want to make that side of the building the frontage. The road is the main thoroughfare, and that's where we should have our entrance and our primary forecourt. The forecourt is our selling space, Miss Moonshine.' Having traversed the pavement that followed the workshop's line, Maddie turned at the corner of the building. In the space in front was the Wolseley, its dark blue paintwork gleaming in the sunshine. The front grill dazzled as it caught the light. The hood was folded back, revealing the soft leather of the seats. In a navy suit and tie, Simon stood at the driver's door, holding it open for the owner.

'This looks magnificent.' Miss Moonshine scooped up Napoleon and took her seat.

'Thank you.'

'Summer is a glorious time of year,' she said as she deposited her dog on the passenger seat beside her. 'But I always think autumn is the best. So full of colour and perfect for weddings, don't you think?'

Simon closed the door behind her and a wide grin spread across his face.

Angela Wren is an actor and director at a theatre in Yorkshire, UK. She loves stories and reading and writes the Jacques Forêt crime novels set in France. Her short stories vary between romance, memoir, mystery and historical. Angela has had two one-act plays recorded for local radio.

angelawren.co.uk

The Secret of Greymoor Hall

By Kate Field

Prologue

Greymoor Hall, 1840

She handed the baby to his nurse and looked back at the house. The green saloon was ablaze, the flames a terrifying scar of colour against the dark night sky. Roderick sprawled on the grass nearby, pouring brandy down his neck while he placed bets with his friends on which room would burn next. A weary line of servants spilled from the house carrying paintings, chairs – anything of value they could salvage. There wasn't much left. Roderick had seen to that, secretly stripping the house of its treasures to satisfy his gambling debts until she had discovered what he was doing. She had vowed then to preserve what remained of her son's inheritance and she would keep that vow, no matter what the cost. She picked up her skirts and raced across the lawn, ignoring the warning cries of the footmen as she ran up the steps and into the burning house.

Haven Bridge, present day

'Libby dear, would you mind popping round?'

'What, now?' Libby tucked the phone between her ear and her shoulder, stirred a pan of soup with each hand, and peered through the glass wall that divided the kitchen from the café. Almost all the tables were full, and most were booked for the afternoon too. Miss Moonshine could hardly have picked a worse moment.

'If it's not too much trouble,' Miss Moonshine said. Libby stopped stirring the soup. She had never heard Miss Moonshine sound so frail – at all frail, in fact. For a woman of whatever age she was, she always seemed in robust health. Was she ill? What if she was lying on the floor of the emporium, writhing in agony from multiple broken bones, while Libby showed more concern about whether the soup might burn?

Libby tore off her apron, shouted an apology to the chef, and dashed out of the café, only narrowly avoiding broken bones herself as she tripped over one of the cats on her way. She ran along Market Street, weaving round the Saturday shoppers who were enjoying a leisurely afternoon in Haven Bridge, and burst into the emporium, gasping for breath.

Everything looked remarkably normal. Miss Moonshine was standing in front of the counter, all bones seemingly intact. Napoleon was curled in his basket, peering at Libby with the usual expression of distaste he seemed to save for her, presumably because she worked in a café full of cats and carried the odour of the enemy with her. There were only two things even slightly noteworthy. The first was the extraordinary hat Miss Moonshine was wearing: a fuchsia-pink concoction with a net covering half her face and a foot-high purple feather pinned to the crown. The second was the bizarre smell: an atomiser behind the counter was blowing out clouds of vapour that carried a strange, but not unpleasant, perfume.

Before Libby could ask what it was, Miss Moonshine dashed towards her and dusted her face with an old-fashioned powder puff.

'What on earth…?' Libby stepped back, choking on the face powder. What had got into Miss Moonshine? And then she noticed they weren't alone in the shop, and her suspicions were instantly roused. There was a customer loitering by the far wall, apparently engrossed in a display of hand-painted kitchenware. Not just any customer: a male customer, of a similar age to Libby. Libby sighed.

'I thought there was an emergency,' she whispered to Miss Moonshine. 'I hope you're not up to any of your tricks.'

'My tricks?' Miss Moonshine shook her head, but the one eye that wasn't obscured by netting twinkled with mischief. She reached out and tucked away a strand of hair that had come loose from Libby's bobble in her dash down the street. 'I have no idea what you mean. This is important. I called you over to meet this young man.'

'That's exactly what I mean. I've told you before, I don't need any of your matchmaking. I'm not looking for a date.'

Libby's words died away as she realised the man in question had crossed the shop and was standing right next to her. She couldn't deny Miss Moonshine had excellent taste. He was tall and muscular, with wavy brown hair that fell to his shoulders, sculpted cheek bones and hazel eyes that flickered with amusement.

'Thanks for sharing that.' He smiled, and for an instant Libby was aware of nothing but those laughing eyes, that wide smile and an odd feeling of recognition. 'I didn't come here looking for a date either,' he continued, breaking the spell. 'But I am looking for a rare eighteenth-century Julien salad bowl, and Miss Moonshine tells me you might have it.'

'A salad bowl?' Libby repeated. She was still feeling slightly dazed. Was she having a weird reaction to the perfume in the air? 'There are all sorts of bowls in the café, but none of them are valuable. Why would you think I have it?' she asked, peeling her gaze away from the man at last and turning to Miss Moonshine.

Miss Moonshine gave a tinkling laugh.

'Don't you remember, Libby dear, that you bought a dish a few months ago? The green one, with the flowers painted on the side.'

'Oh, that bowl.' Libby did remember now. That had been another strange visit to the emporium. She'd only popped into the shop to bring Miss Moonshine a leftover flapjack at the end of the day and, somehow, she had come away £10 poorer but the owner of a pretty green bowl. She still couldn't work out what had possessed her to buy it. 'Cyril took a shine to it. He uses it now.'

'Does it look like this?' The man held out his phone, showing a picture of what looked like a huge dinner service, consisting of plates, jugs and tureens all in green, decorated with panels of painted flowers.

'Vaguely…' Libby looked closer. 'Although maybe it's a paler shade of green? Sorry, it's hard to tell from a photo. Is it important?'

'Yes,' said the man. 'The bowl was stolen from my parents' house at New Year. I've been trying to find it ever since.'

He sounded desperate, and no wonder. Libby had a rough idea of what a Julien bowl might be worth from her previous job in an auction house. It wasn't one of the most famous porcelain brands, like Sèvres or Meissen, but it was still hugely collectable. His parents must be around pension age, and perhaps they had hoped the bowl would go towards their retirement nest egg. She turned to Miss Moonshine, unable to resist a grin.

'Have you been handling stolen goods, Miss Moonshine?'

'Maybe. Quite unwittingly. Isn't it thrilling?' Miss Moonshine glanced between Libby and the man. 'Why don't you both go to the café and look at the bowl now? I have high hopes that this search will have a happy ending.'

*

Seconds later, Libby found herself outside Miss Moonshine's Emporium, its solid, black door closed firmly behind her.

The man was waiting for her at the gate where the path from the shop opened to the street, standing under the ornamental arch that was currently decorated with pink and white flowers. Wedding flowers, Libby thought, and then immediately blamed Miss Moonshine and her mother-of-the-bride hat for putting such unwanted ideas in her head.

'She's a force of nature, isn't she?' the man said. He wore the air of faint bewilderment that Libby had often seen on customers emerging from the emporium. 'Are you sure it's no trouble to show me the bowl now? I could come back another time if you're busy.'

Libby thought of all the bookings in the diary for the afternoon. The timing wasn't great, but the desperation she'd detected in his voice earlier made her reluctant to put him off. This bowl was clearly important. She wanted to help him if she could.

'No, it's fine,' she said. 'You might as well come now.'

'Hang on.' He held out his hand. 'Were you never warned not to go off with strangers? I'm Gil.'

'Libby.' She smiled and shook his hand. A tingle of warmth ran through her fingers. She caught a flash of purple feather in the window of the Emporium and dropped his hand. 'Come on, it's this way.'

They wandered to the café on Ingleborough Lane. Gil stopped outside and looked up at the sign, a smile on his face.

'Feline Good Café? What is this place?'

'It's a cat café.' Libby pointed at the front window, where Hogarth, a ginger tom, lay curled up on the broad windowsill, sleeping in the sun. 'Come and see.'

She opened the outer door, which led to a narrow hall.

'You need to take your shoes off.' She pointed at a set of

shelves on one wall which already contained many pairs of shoes.

'What for?' Gil tugged off his boots.

'To reduce the risk of bringing dirt and germs in. This is the cats' home. We don't take any chances.' She peered through the glass door that led from the hall to the body of the café. 'OK, it's clear to go in.'

She opened the inner door and followed Gil inside. He took a few steps forward and stopped.

'Wow,' he said. 'I've never seen anything like it.'

Libby watched as he slowly circled, taking it all in. It was a common reaction for new customers, and seeing the wonder on people's faces was one of her favourite parts of her job. She'd been exactly the same on her first visit. As a café, it was a gorgeous, cosy place, with a wooden floor, bright painted walls, and comfy armchairs and sofas in rich jewel colours scattered around low coffee tables. There was everything to make human visitors happy. But then there were the elements to make the cats who lived here happy too. Tall scratching posts lined up along the walls, alongside platforms at varying heights so the cats could jump around for exercise or sit and look down on the customers. There were cat trees featuring a variety of boxes, baskets and hammocks spread around the room, and an open door in the corner that led to a 'cats only' area for when they wanted peace or privacy.

'This is incredible,' Gil said. Biffy, a short-haired British blue kitten, ran along a wooden bridge suspended over their heads, leading from one side of the room to the other. Gil laughed. 'You must really love cats.'

'A friend does. This is all her creation.' Libby waved her arm around. 'I'm looking after the business while she's on a mature gap year. I agreed to do it without even seeing the place, so didn't realise exactly what I was taking on.'

'You must be a very good friend.'

'More like a desperate one.' Libby smiled and shook her head when he looked at her with surprised interest. No need to bother him with all that history. 'The table in the corner should be free for the next half hour if you want to sit there. I'll get the bowl. Would you like a coffee too?'

She went through to the cats' private area, where a couple of snoozing cats greeted her with a lazy look before nodding off again. She picked up the bowl from the floor, emptied and dried it before taking it back to Gil with their coffees. His face fell as soon as she handed it to him.

'It isn't Julien, is it?' Libby said. 'I didn't think it could be. It's pretty, but the porcelain is too thick, and the green doesn't have the right depth or lustre. But you don't mind a copy, do you, Cyril?' she said, bending down to stroke the cat who had followed her.

'Cyril's a cat?' Gil laughed. 'I should have guessed.' He stretched his arm down and Cyril sniffed his fingers before arching his back so Gil could scratch it. 'No offence, mate, but the bowl I'm looking for would have been too precious even for a handsome fellow like you.'

'I should think so,' Libby agreed. 'Even a bowl this size must be worth a few thousand.'

Gil looked up. 'So I'm told. But how do you know about Julien porcelain? Not many people have heard of it.'

'I used to work in an auction house in London.' Libby hesitated. She didn't usually talk about those times; she'd happily left that Libby behind when she moved to Haven Bridge. 'We sold a Julien tureen a couple of years ago. There was quite a battle for it, and it sold for well over the reserve.'

'From auction house to cat café? That's an unusual career move.'

'Maybe. It was for the best.' Not that she'd had much choice in the matter. She tickled Cyril behind the ear as he scratched at her leg. 'These gorgeous creatures make much better colleagues.' She smiled, and ignored the curiosity evident on Gil's face. 'How did your parents come to own a Julien piece? They must be devastated to have lost it.'

'We all are. Apparently, there aren't many complete dinner services left, so it would make a huge difference to the value if we could find the one missing piece again.'

Libby almost choked on her coffee.

'You have a complete dinner service? You mean that photo you showed me – you own all that?'

'My parents do. All except the salad bowl.' He sighed. 'My brother held a house party at New Year, which was a wild affair from what I heard. He seems to have offered an open invitation, and barely knew half the people who turned up. A few weeks later we noticed some items missing here or there: a couple of miniatures, a silver snuff box, the salad bowl from the Julien service. It was cleverly done. The thief took a few random pieces so we wouldn't immediately notice the gaps.'

'Where do you live?' Libby asked. Her belongings would barely fill a suitcase. She'd know at once if anything was missing. 'Buckingham Palace?'

It was intended as a joke, but Gil took it seriously.

'Greymoor Hall. Have you heard of it?'

'No.' She was sure she hadn't, so why did she feel a sharp prickle of interest at the name? 'Is it in Haven Bridge?'

'About ten miles away. Close to Brontë Country, but with no known Brontë connections, so it's largely overlooked.' He put down his empty coffee cup. 'The Julien service is the only thing of significant value we have left. We've no choice but to sell it to pay for some urgent repairs. The house has been in the family for centuries. No one wants to be the generation that loses it.'

He stood up.

'I don't know why I'm bothering you with all this. I've taken up enough of your time. Thanks for showing me the bowl.'

'What will you do next?' Libby asked, following him to the door.

'Keep looking. Keep trying to raise money.' He smiled. 'The house and grounds are open on summer weekends and every day through August. If you're ever over that way, knock on the door and I'll return the favour and make you a coffee.'

*

Libby kept her curiosity in check for two whole days, but on the third she caved in and looked up Greymoor Hall on the internet. If she'd been asked to guess what it was like, she'd have suggested a modest stone manor house, with a few acres of garden. Instead, when she visited the website, she discovered a magnificent Jacobean mansion, whose walls were made of red brick decorated with a diamond pattern of blue bricks and stone facings. Although it was only two storeys high, it appeared larger because of the attic rooms set into the gables, the high mullioned windows and tall chimneys. Libby pored over the images, feeling the sparks of her old self rising from the ashes of her London life: the girl who had explored stately homes and art galleries while her friends had attended concerts and music festivals. Was it possible to fall in love at first sight with a house? Libby was lost. It was perfect – or almost perfect. One wing lay in ruins, apparently destroyed in a fire in 1840.

When she popped into Miss Moonshine's Emporium later that week, under the pretext of delivering a leftover brownie, she asked if Miss Moonshine had ever heard of Greymoor Hall.

'Oh yes, I know it well. It's an extremely fine house. It used to be famed throughout Yorkshire for the parties that were held there.' Miss Moonshine had a smile on her lips and a faraway look in her eyes. 'That was before the wars, of course. Everyone wanted to receive an invitation to a house party at Greymoor Hall. No expense was spared to entertain guests. There was exquisite food from the finest chefs, the best musicians and actors brought up from London, endless supplies of champagne, dancing throughout the night…'

Miss Moonshine's smile suddenly dimmed.

'Those were happy times for the house. It was a very different story a few generations before. Then, it was notorious for all the wrong reasons,' she continued with a shudder. 'The owner at that time, Roderick Lawrence, was a terrible character. Drinking, fighting, womanising, gambling away the family treasures… Those were his more innocent pastimes. It's a wonder the house and any of the contents survived his custodianship. It almost didn't. Part of the north wing burned down one night during one of his parties. His wife, Elizabeth, was lucky to survive the blaze.'

Libby felt goosebumps rising on her skin, despite the warmth of the day.

'The house is on the fringes of Brontë Country,' Miss Moonshine continued, 'but the Brontës would never go near the place. Not the sisters, at any rate. It's a shame, as it would have done much for Greymoor's fortunes now if they could have claimed a connection.'

'None of that information is on the website,' Libby replied, fascinated by Miss Moonshine's revelations. 'There are hardly any details other than the opening hours. You'd never know the house had such a scandalous past.'

'I believe the more recent owners have wished for a quieter life than their ancestors,' Miss Moonshine said. 'Although there's usually a rogue member of the family every generation or so…' She looked at Libby and smiled. 'It's the young man with the bowl that has sparked this interest, isn't it? I did wonder when I saw those cheekbones. So like his… now what would it be?

Great-grandfather? I lose track. He was an extraordinarily handsome man, too. Yes, I see it all now. You should go and look at the house, Libby dear. There used to be some interesting paintings, which would be just your thing with an art history degree, wouldn't it? The weather will be glorious on Sunday, so why don't you go then?'

*

Libby was woken early on Sunday morning by the sun streaming through the thin curtains in her bedroom above the café. It was her day off work; all she had to do was open up at ten, and then the whole day was hers to do as much or as little with as she pleased. She could lounge around in bed for a few more hours, catch up on some paperwork or household chores, join the tourists in Haven Bridge and wander round the shops before enjoying lunch out…

Who was she kidding? There was only one possible plan for the day. By half past ten she was in her car, heading north towards Brontë Country. Miss Moonshine had been right. The weather was glorious, and it was far too good a day to waste indoors. She'd loaded her rucksack with sandwiches and cake, put on her walking boots and plotted out an eight-mile circular hike from a hamlet nestled in the hollow of the moors.

By an extraordinary coincidence, the path she had chosen took her through the parkland surrounding Greymoor Hall. She caught her first glimpse of the house as she was descending a rocky trail down from the moors. It was even more stunning in real life, especially now she could see the full layout of the estate. A long, tree-lined drive led to a lawned turning circle in front of the main entrance of the hall. There were formal gardens on all sides, including a walled garden, and symmetrical outbuildings in the same red brick as the main house. The surrounding parkland seemed to have been left wild rather than landscaped, and a river snaked through a dense patch of woodland. It really was a hidden gem; even the ruins added to the romantic charm of the house.

A kissing gate led from the open moor into the estate, according to a small sign attached to a gatepost. Libby leant with her back against the gate as she checked her map. The public footpath definitely went straight ahead, through the park, but now she was here she was struck with a sudden dread that she would run into Gil and he might think she was pursuing him. Could she get away with it? Apparently not. As she was dithering, wondering if there was another route to get back to her car, she heard a familiar voice behind her.

'You are allowed in,' Gil said. 'We don't bite.' Libby turned round. Gil was right in front of her, on the other side of the kissing gate. 'We no longer insist on a kiss as the price to come through the gate either.' He grinned. 'That's entirely optional.'

'Do you spend all day lurking here, just in case?' she asked, torn between laughter and mortification at being caught snooping. He laughed.

'Not all day. I usually take a break for lunch.' He glanced at his watch. 'You just caught me. I was heading for a picnic now. Do you want to come?'

She noticed he had a bulging rucksack on his back.

'I've brought lunch. I was going to look for somewhere to have it later.'

'Great. We can pool supplies. And I promise you won't find a better place to have it than the one I can show you.' He opened the gate to let her through. 'Don't worry. We won't call this a date. You were quite clear you don't want one of those.'

She had to laugh at that, though it was embarrassing to be reminded of their first meeting.

'I'm glad I made such a lasting impression,' she said.

'You certainly did.'

Without another word, she went through the gate and followed him as he cut off the main path and through the trees, on a narrow trail that she would never have noticed on her own. After the heat of the open moor, it was deliciously cool under the shade of the trees. Deliciously peaceful too. Gil only spoke to point out the occasional bird high up in the branches, a rabbit darting through the undergrowth, or a snatched glimpse of the house, but it felt an easy silence, the sort that usually rewarded years of careful friendship.

Eventually they emerged from the wood and Libby looked round in delight. The trees had opened out into a clearing, with the river she had seen from the moors curving through the centre of it. The riverbank had eroded in one place and formed a pebbly beach. It was an idyllic picnic spot, with the peace broken only by birdsong and the gentle murmur of the river. It felt as if they had wandered into their own private world.

'This is amazing,' she said.

'Isn't it?' Gil was already unpacking his rucksack, taking out a book and a pair of binoculars before unloading a foil-wrapped package. 'Aren't you glad you ran into me? Not many people know of this place.'

Libby *was* glad, but his comment provided a timely reminder about who Gil actually was. He wasn't a weary walker, like her. He owned this place. She had a sudden vision of him lounging here with his family and friends, all dressed in linen and wearing straw boaters, enjoying champagne-fuelled picnics that had been carried here by an army of uniformed staff; the image may have owed something to a recent costume drama she had seen on television. She hesitated, fiddling with the zip on her rucksack. She'd been so adamant when they'd met in the emporium that she hadn't wanted a date. This wasn't a date. But what if Gil thought she'd changed her mind after seeing the size of his house? She couldn't bear him to think her so shallow.

'Perhaps I should go. I don't want to get in your way,' she said, indicating the book he'd brought with him. He had clearly anticipated a peaceful lunch on his own. 'And I don't think you'll want to share my sandwiches. They're not very sophisticated.'

'Unsophisticated sandwiches?' Gil laughed. 'Now I'm intrigued. What are they?'

'Cheese and pickle on granary. About as plain as you can get. It's probably not what you would call a picnic.'

'Interesting.' Gil unwrapped his foil package to reveal a pile of white bread rolls. 'I've brought cheese-slice-and-salt-and-vinegar-crisp sandwiches. Definitely the height of sophistication. But I'm still willing to share my bounty if you are.'

Libby thought he was joking until he lifted the top of one of the rolls to show her. She smiled, and sank down onto the grass beside him. She took one of his sandwiches and bit into it.

'Delicious?' he asked. She nodded, smiling. 'Don't be fooled by all this,' he said, leaning towards her and looking suddenly serious. 'It's an incredible privilege to call this place home. But it's a huge burden too.' His eyes met hers, a wary look hovering in his. 'We're dirt poor. I don't know how much longer we can hold on here. Does that make a difference?'

To this date that wasn't a date, but already felt like the most enjoyable date she'd had for years?

'Yes, it does,' Libby said. He leaned away from her, with no attempt to hide the disappointment on his face. She touched his arm and smiled as he looked at her again. 'I have cake too. How can I refuse to share it with you now?'

*

Lunch passed quickly and with remarkable pleasure. After finishing the sandwiches and cake, they lay side by side in the grass at the edge of the river and chatted, while bees and dragonflies hovered nearby. Gil was easy to talk to, didn't take himself too seriously and laughed often. He listened to what Libby said with genuine interest and without ever appearing to judge her. If it had been a date, it would have been a perfect one.

It ended too soon when Gil checked his watch and Libby realised that a couple of hours had slipped by in the sunshine.

'Sorry,' she said, gathering up the rubbish and stuffing it in her rucksack. 'I've taken up too much of your time.'

'Not at all,' he said. 'I wish I could stay, but I have to head back to the house. My shift starts soon.'

'Your shift?' Libby swung the rucksack onto her back. 'Do you give guided tours?'

Gil laughed.

'Definitely not. We have a team of loyal volunteers who would probably murder me if I tried to take over that role. I don't work at the house. I'm a firefighter.'

'Really?' Libby hadn't expected that. Despite his talk of being poor, it hadn't occurred to her that someone who lived here would have a real job. 'I assumed you would be busy managing this place.' She waved her arms around to encompass the estate as they took the path back through the woods. 'It must be a huge commitment.'

'It is. Roddy, my older brother, is supposed to be in charge of managing it. He enjoys all that lord of the manor stuff much more than I do. I wanted to do something useful, something to make a difference, and as I've grown up seeing the consequences of fire every day, the fire service was an obvious choice.'

'Your brother's called Roddy?' Libby remembered Miss Moonshine's story about the scandalous Roderick Lawrence. It seemed an unfortunate choice.

'We were both given family names. Roderick and Gilbert. Aren't we lucky?' Gil smiled. 'Mum loves a good tradition.

Although Roddy took the traditions a bit too far with the disastrous party at New Year. When we realised some things were missing, he disappeared off to London in disgrace, leaving me here on my own.'

'Don't your parents live here?'

'Not likely.' Gil laughed. 'They decamped to a compact bungalow with double-glazing and central heating as soon as they could. Don't get me wrong,' he added. 'We love Greymoor, but it takes a terrifying amount of money simply to keep it running, without factoring in the upgrades and maintenance it needs. I don't know how we'll meet the next major repair bill after the Julien dinner service is sold. We're that close to the brink. You're not a secret millionaire, are you?'

They stopped as they reached the lawn where their paths would separate. Gil smiled at Libby so warmly that she wished she could say yes and solve all his problems. She turned and looked back at the house. The red bricks blazed with colour in the afternoon sun, and the windows sparkled like diamonds. She felt inexplicably drawn to the house, as if it were trying to pull her closer. A baby's urgent cry broke into such fanciful thoughts, but when she looked round there was no one close by, only an elderly couple wandering across the grass.

'Could you not extend your opening hours?' she asked, wondering why there were so few visitors around on such a beautiful day. 'Most stately homes open for the full summer season, and then put on special events through the year, particularly around Christmas. I'm a bit of a buff,' she admitted, laughing. 'I love nothing more than wandering round old houses admiring the architecture and artwork.'

'You're out of luck here,' Gil said. 'Half the house is a ruin, and although records show there used to be an impressive art collection, the paintings of any value are long gone. Now we're stuck with the portraits of gloomy old ancestors, who watch our every move and frown with disapproval as the house falls into disrepair. They're a terrifyingly ugly bunch.'

It was hard to believe, if Gil took after them, but Libby distracted herself from that thought by surveying the garden and park. The estate made a perfect adventure playground, full of misshapen trees, mysterious statues and paths that snaked away through the woods with a promise of mystery.

'Have you ever held a scavenger hunt?' she asked. 'I attended one in Scotland, on an estate that was quite similar to this. Hundreds of people took part. We paid a fee to enter and there were prizes on offer. It could work brilliantly here.'

'I don't know,' Gil said, looking round. 'Is it interesting enough?'

'Of course it is. I suppose there are different ways to organise a hunt, so you would adapt it to suit the house and grounds. Perhaps you could run one with a nature theme, if you want the visitors to stay outside. The one I did was photo-based. We had to take a photograph of something that matched each clue.' She laughed. 'Extra points were awarded for imaginative answers. One of our challenges was to find something prickly, and so I took a photo of my future mother-in-law.'

Gil's smile dropped, and it felt like the sunshine had disappeared from the day.

'I didn't realise you were married,' he said.

'I'm not. The wedding didn't go ahead.'

'I'm sorry.' Although he didn't look it; a wide smile had returned to his face.

'It's fine. It was the right decision.' How many times had she said those words before, trying to ease an awkward conversation? She'd never felt them with such certainty as she did now.

'Did you change your mind?' he asked.

'Actually, I was dumped two days before the wedding. I

was having my nails done when he called to say he'd decided it was a mistake. The marriage, not the nails.' Libby felt a sudden compulsion to explain, even though she'd spent the last twelve months avoiding the subject. 'It *was* a mistake. We met at university and it was a classic case of opposites attracting. I was a quiet girl from rural Northumberland, with a head full of dreams about the exciting life that surely waited for me beyond my village. When I met Henry, I thought I'd found it. His family owned the auction house in London where I went on to work; his lifestyle seemed so glamorous and sophisticated compared to my ordinary one. I tried to fit in, to be who they expected me to be, but it was never good enough, and never real. Somewhere along the way I lost sight of me.'

It all seemed so obvious now. The real Libby was here, living in a friendly community, breathing the fresh northern air, and talking to a man who she knew instinctively would never expect her to be anything but herself.

'And so you took over a cat café and found yourself again. I'm glad.' Gil glanced at his watch. 'Sorry. Rubbish timing, but I really need to get to work. Take my number. Give me a call and we can talk more about this scavenger hunt idea.' She nodded and had walked a few steps away when he shouted after her. 'I don't think you're ordinary.' She turned and saw him smiling.

*

Should she call him? Libby spent the next week mulling it over, picking up her phone multiple times and then putting it back down again. Did she want to get involved with this? It wasn't just the scavenger hunt idea; it was Gil. She hadn't sworn off men since her broken engagement, and so it wasn't that holding her back. She was scared, not scarred. She'd only met Gil twice, and it sounded ridiculous to admit it even in the privacy of her own thoughts, but it felt like on a deeper level she had recognised him; as if her heart had suddenly said 'oh, there you are.' The strength of that feeling terrified her. How could she trust it, when she had made such a huge mistake before?

She was cleaning the café on Saturday evening, after the last customers had gone, when she heard a knock on the window. She looked up and saw Gil standing outside, smiling and waving. She met him at the front door.

'Hello,' he said. 'Should I pretend I was passing, or be hopelessly uncool and admit I came to Haven Bridge to see you? You didn't ring.'

'No. I wasn't sure…'

'Weren't you? I am.'

He accompanied this random comment with a disarming smile that made her wonder why she had wasted a week by dithering over whether to ring. Why had she been scared? She liked him. She wanted to know him better. She wanted to help him in whatever way she could. There was nothing more to think about.

'Are you free tonight?' he asked. 'I thought we could go out to eat and discuss the scavenger hunt idea.'

'I had lined up a hot date with Cyril and a frozen pizza.'

'Well, I can see why I would be second best to that, but will you take pity on me? Do it for Greymoor, at least. You said you were a history buff, so you must be keen to preserve our heritage for the nation.'

Libby laughed.

'OK, no need to lay it on so thick. I'll come. The chance to avoid more washing-up would have been temptation enough. Give me ten minutes to finish sweeping and settle the cats.'

She expected him to wait, but instead he took off his shoes and followed her into the café, where he helped clean the cats' bowls and fill them with fresh water while Libby finished the sweeping.

'Not bad,' she said, as they finally left. 'You could get a job in a cat café if you're ever looking to leave the fire service.'

'Don't joke,' he said, as she led him towards The Packhorse pub. 'I might need both jobs if things carry on as they are.'

'Is it really that bad?'

'Yes. On a day-to-day level we get by, just. But we've no reserves left for when the big maintenance bills come in, and the more of the contents we sell, the less there is to show the public. If visitor numbers fall any further, we won't survive. It's a vicious circle. We really need to use the house for big events – weddings, festivals, maybe even film locations – but to do that we need to fix the electrics, and the plumbing and numerous other things that will all cost money we don't have… And so it goes on.'

They found an empty table in the pub and ordered their food and drinks.

'Are there no grants you can apply for? Lottery money maybe?'

'Do you think I should buy a few tickets and hope we win?' Gil smiled. 'Roddy was supposed to be looking into all that. I need to chase him up. He's keeping a low profile after the New Year party disaster. Mum had a real go at him and swore he'd inherited the family bad blood. She's calmed down now, but it wasn't pretty.'

'Miss Moonshine told me about the family history.' Libby smiled. 'I believe one of your ancestors was a true hellraiser.'

'The original Roderick Lawrence.' Gil nodded. 'He almost burned the whole house down, so it was a little unfair to compare my brother Roddy to him for the loss of some bits and pieces, however valuable. We know of some of his exploits from letters his wife Elizabeth wrote to her sister. There's a box full of them at the house. Having read them, I'm not surprised she looks so stern and forbidding in her portrait. It's no wonder someone hid it in the darkest corner of the library. We were terrified of her as children.' He laughed. 'I can't thank Miss Moonshine for telling you all the family secrets. It's hardly a good advert, is it?'

'I think it's fascinating.' Libby sat back as the food arrived. 'I've always enjoyed finding out the stories behind paintings. I'd love to see the terrifying Elizabeth. You could do an exhibition about the history of the house, and show some of the letters. Visitors would love that.'

They chatted as they ate, and when they finally pushed their plates away, Gil mentioned the scavenger hunt idea again.

'I've done some research and I think it could work,' he said. 'It sounds perfect to have an event that's based wholly outside. We can manage to pull together some clues, can't we?'

That 'we', accompanied by Gil's easy smile, made Libby feel indescribably happy.

'You'll need prizes too,' she reminded him. His face fell.

'Nothing too expensive, or we won't make any money out of it.' He picked up his phone and started to make a note. 'What sort of thing were you thinking of?'

'Maybe some chocolate for the children who take part,' she said. 'But you could ask local businesses to offer the main prizes. I have a friend who's just set up an eco-friendly glamping site in Northumberland, and she would probably donate a weekend away. It's good advertising, isn't it? I'll give you an afternoon tea for four in the cat café.' She grinned. 'Miss Moonshine could offer a gift voucher for the emporium.'

Gil gave a mock grimace.

'Can you ask her about that?'

Libby laughed. 'You're a fireman. You can't be scared of Miss Moonshine.'

'I can. It's strange, but since I visited her shop, things have felt different. I can't explain it.'

'Not quite right?' Libby suggested. 'You wouldn't be the first to say that.'

'No, the opposite,' he said. His hand lay close to hers on the table, and he stretched so his fingertips brushed against hers. 'Things have felt exactly right.'

*

The scavenger hunt was fixed to take place on the August bank holiday weekend, and over the next few weeks, Libby and Gil met or spoke regularly to discuss it. She tried to tell him she wasn't an expert, having only attended one once – and her hen weekend was an occasion she'd rather forget. But he insisted on asking her opinion and involving her in the arrangements, and she soon stopped querying why. She liked spending time with him, and she felt a pull to help save the house that she couldn't explain.

The only disappointment was that Libby still hadn't managed to go inside Greymoor Hall. More often than not, Gil had visited her, and the few times she'd been to the house, something had always prevented her going in: there'd been a large party of pensioners clogging up the rooms on a guided tour; or Gil had been due on shift at the fire station by the time they'd finished exploring the grounds. Once she'd been about to step through the door when she was summonsed back to the café to look for a cat who was thought to be missing but was actually fast asleep under a chair. Even Miss Moonshine had got in the way, begging Libby's assistance at an auction on the first day off she'd had in a fortnight. Every attempt to visit seemed doomed to fail.

The August bank holiday arrived with a fanfare of sunshine and with a forecast that promised three perfect, dry days. They couldn't have wished for better. Libby was working over the weekend and so she'd teamed up with Miss Moonshine to take part in the scavenger hunt on the Bank Holiday Monday. They drove to Greymoor Hall just after lunch, and found the car park was full.

'This is incredible,' Libby said, squeezing her car into a space after circling round for five minutes. 'Look how busy it is. They've even had to open the extra field for parking. Gil will be thrilled.'

'It's an encouraging start,' Miss Moonshine agreed. 'Perhaps the house's fortunes are turning at last. Shall we begin the hunt? Napoleon is straining at the leash. He must be on the scent of a rabbit.'

Libby looked at Napoleon dubiously. She didn't rate his chances of catching one; even a small rabbit would be larger than him. They headed towards the park, paid their entrance fee for the scavenger hunt and were given a sheet of clues. Libby hadn't seen the final version and was impressed by how well it looked. The hunt started with easy challenges, to suit the younger members of the family, who had to find things including a feather, a pine cone and a patch of wildflowers, and to carry out activities such as taking a rubbing of a leaf or of tree bark. The list then went on to include some cryptic clues leading to a particular location such as an ornamental fountain or a stone bench, where participants would find a special code to include on the answer sheet. Libby spent an enjoyable couple of hours exploring the park and the formal gardens with Miss Moonshine as they worked their way through the list.

The last clue brought them to the rear façade of the house, where they found the secret code hidden in the ivy trailing over the ruined wing.

'I'm surprised no one ever rebuilt this,' Libby said, studying the ruins.

'I suppose it would have cost too much money,' Miss Moonshine said. 'Many of the family's most valuable pieces were said to have perished in the fire. Poor Elizabeth. She loved this house dearly, you know, despite the wickedness of the husband who brought her here. She would have done anything to preserve it for her children and future generations. She was a most resourceful lady.'

Libby shivered as a sudden draught swept across her bare legs. There was a hint of smoke in the air, and a rustle of skirts… She looked round in confusion and spotted Gil, watching her with a bemused look on his face.

'You were miles away,' he said. Libby smiled and shook her head. It was her imagination playing tricks on her, that was all. The smoke had probably been from a cigarette, and the draught nothing more than the breeze. Not that there was much breeze today.

'Have you seen the crowds?' he asked. 'This is incredible. It's been as busy as this all weekend. It just shows the potential if we can put on events more regularly. The teashop has almost run out of tea. The place is still packed.'

'Oh dear, and I was about to suggest we stop for a drink to celebrate completing our quest,' Miss Moonshine said. She gave a gentle cough. 'It's thirsty work walking round in the full sun.'

'Do you want some water now?' Libby asked. She'd brought bottles for both of them, but Miss Moonshine had declined hers last time she offered.

Miss Moonshine shook her head. 'No thank you, dear. I expect I can manage until we reach home, and I can make a cup of tea.'

She cleared her throat again and Gil grinned.

'There's no need to wait. The house has just closed for the day. Come inside and I'll make you both a cup.'

Libby didn't need to be asked twice. She'd been longing to go in the house for weeks, and she dashed up the steps to the door, almost overtaking Gil. Miss Moonshine and Napoleon followed behind at a more stately pace. Gil opened the door and stood back to allow Libby in first. She found herself in a magnificent hall lined with oak panelling and dominated by a grand wooden staircase. Several doors lay off the hall, some marked 'private' and others standing ajar. She noticed immediately that though the scale of the room was impressive, it was relatively bare, and there were darker patches on the wood panelling where paintings must once have hung. Gil followed her gaze.

'I suppose this is disappointing for an art historian,' he said, gesturing at a wall where one landscape painting hung amid a row of empty spaces. 'All that's left are the family portraits and the odd amateur painting like that one.'

'Family portraits can be interesting,' Libby said. 'I'd still love to see them. They can reveal so much about a character.'

Gil laughed. 'I think these will reveal that my ancestors were a miserable bunch. Come into the library and see for yourself. We can have our tea in there.'

He led them into a beautiful room, decorated with blue silk wallpaper and matching sofas and chairs. There were gaps on the walls here too, and patches of bright paper revealed the brilliant colour of the original wall covering. One wall held a row of glass-fronted display cabinets, whose shelves contained a familiar green dinner service.

'Is that…?' Libby asked.

'Yes, that's the Julien dinner service. Or what's left of it. We never did find the salad bowl.'

'I'm sorry we couldn't help you with that search,' Miss Moonshine said. She tugged at Napoleon's lead as the little dog strayed under the guide ropes preventing visitors from walking into the centre of the room. 'Behave, Napoleon, or I shall have to put you in my handbag.'

Gil exchanged a grin with Libby and then carried on through a set of double doors that opened into the library. There were no signs of missing items here. Huge bookcases were filled with leather-bound books, and the gold lettering on their spines glittered in the glow of the lamps that lit the room. There was an enormous fireplace at one end, and comfortable sofas and armchairs were gathered together in groups. Gil waved at one of them.

'Why don't you sit down, Miss Moonshine, while I make the tea?'

'Do you need any help?' Libby asked. She gazed round the room, hoping he would say no so she could explore. He must have guessed what she was thinking as he laughed and shook his head.

'I think I can manage three mugs of tea. Feel free to have a look round. See if you can find Elizabeth.'

Libby hardly waited for him to finish speaking before she was wandering round, browsing the bookshelves. She wasn't an expert in antiquarian books – they had been dealt with by a different department in the auction house where she'd worked – but it was still fascinating to see what subjects had captured the interest of previous generations. She couldn't resist the pull of the paintings for long, though. There were several portraits hanging on the walls in here, either full length or head and shoulders, and while they were competent pictures, there were none by names she recognised or that had any particular merit. Still, she pored over them, trying to find a likeness to Gil.

'I haven't found Elizabeth,' she said, as she turned away from the last painting. 'I thought Gil said she was in here.'

'I believe it was one of her favourite rooms,' Miss Moonshine said. 'I imagine her husband wasn't a reader.'

Miss Moonshine said this with such disapproval that Libby laughed. Glancing round again, she noticed for the first time a gloomy alcove tucked away between the door and the side of the fireplace. There was one more picture hanging there, almost invisible when the door was ajar as Gil had left it when he went to make the tea. She slipped into the gap behind the door. It was a portrait of a woman, several years younger than Libby, and the quality of the painting was far superior to any of the others in the room. The paint still glistened with colour and life, as if it had only been completed yesterday, and the woman's face was so expertly rendered that it was as clear as a photograph. She had a forbidding expression, as if warning people not to come too close, and yet as Libby studied the picture more carefully, she thought she read a silent appeal in the woman's eyes. Dismissing such a foolish idea, she peered forward to read the nameplate on the bottom of the frame: Elizabeth Lawrence 1818–1845.

Afterwards, Libby could only remember the next few moments as a series of fleeting images. The door she was standing behind was pushed further open… it slammed into her side and she stumbled… Gil shouted out… Miss Moonshine called for Napoleon… and then Libby lurched forward, crashing into the wall and knocking the portrait of Elizabeth to the ground. She fell to the floor beside it, banging her head against the solid wood of the fireplace.

Gil was at her side in an instant.

'Are you OK?' he asked, kneeling beside her. 'Let me look.' He cupped his hands around her face and looked into her eyes, and then tenderly began exploring her head. She winced as his fingers touched the spot where she'd banged it.

'It was only a bump,' she said. 'I'm fine, honestly.' As far as the effects of the fall were concerned, at least. The sudden giddy breathlessness had more to do with the way Gil was looking at her. Although perhaps she was hallucinating: glancing round, she could have sworn she saw Miss Moonshine pat Napoleon on the head and give him a treat.

'But look at Elizabeth,' she said, sitting up and reluctantly tearing herself away from Gil's attentions. 'I'm so sorry. The frame and the painting aren't damaged,' she said, inspecting the portrait. 'It's just the backing board that seems to have come loose. It looks like it wasn't attached very securely.'

She lifted off the backing board and froze when she saw what lay underneath.

'What's that?' Gil asked. 'A letter?' He brushed past her and picked up a folded piece of paper. 'And another painting? What's that doing there?'

Hidden between the portrait of Elizabeth and the backing board lay a smaller painting of what looked like an old-fashioned scene of the Grand Canal in Venice. Libby stared at it, transfixed, hardly able to believe what she was seeing.

'Is it something special, Libby?' Miss Moonshine asked, peering over her shoulder. 'Do you know?'

'I'm not sure,' she said. 'I think it might be a Mattarocci. The signature's right, the subject matter, the colours, the spirited brushstrokes… I wrote my dissertation on him at university,' she explained, marvelling at the coincidence. 'He was a student of Canaletto. But why would one of his paintings be hidden away behind Elizabeth's portrait?'

'It is a mystery, isn't it?' Miss Moonshine said. 'Would it be valuable, if it were a Mattarocci?'

Libby laughed. 'Yes! It would be worth a small fortune. But it can't be genuine, can it? It seems so impossible.' Impossible – and yet her whole being told her it was right. 'It would need to be checked by an expert and properly authenticated. What's in the letter? That might give an explanation and provide provenance.'

With shaking fingers, Gil unfolded the paper. He frowned.

'It's not a letter,' he said. 'It's a list. Or maybe a weird poem? It makes no sense. The first line says, "*Hearne might give an interesting speech about the origin of diamonds*". What does that mean?'

'It sounds like one of those fiendish cryptic clues we've been following all afternoon for the scavenger hunt,' Miss Moonshine said. 'You were better at them than me, Libby dear.'

Libby looked at the note and read the first line again. 'That name rings a bell,' she said. 'I'm sure I saw…' She wandered over to one of the library shelves she had studied earlier, scanning the rows. 'Here it is,' she said, excitement threading through her voice. 'There's a book here called *Hearne's Collection of Curious Discourses*. Do you think it's significant? An interesting speech could be another way of saying curious discourse. Am I reading too much into it?'

'There's only one way to find out,' Gil said. He pulled the book from the shelf, disturbing decades of dust as he withdrew it. He flicked through the pages.

'There's nothing here,' he said. 'I was hoping there might be another priceless painting hidden between the pages.'

'We don't know it's priceless,' Libby pointed out.

'But you believe it is, don't you? I can see it in your face. And I trust you.'

Libby wasn't ready to give up yet, especially when Gil looked at her the way he was doing, with absolute faith in her ability. She slipped her hand into the gap left by the book on the shelf and felt around, just in case, but there was nothing there. She stretched further, reaching behind the books on either side, and the tips of her fingers grazed something large and soft. Desperately hoping it wasn't a dead mouse or something equally horrible, she pulled at it and extracted a heavy velvet bag.

Miss Moonshine had joined Gil and they both looked at the bag.

'I can't bear the suspense,' Miss Moonshine said. 'Aren't you going to open it?'

Libby unfastened the tie and tipped the contents into Gil's waiting hands. No one spoke. An incredible set of jewellery lay in his hands: a tiara, a necklace, bracelets, rings, all heavily set in gold and sparkling with enormous diamonds.

'I believe you may have found the Lawrence diamonds,' Miss Moonshine said. 'I've heard about them but never seen them. They were thought to have been lost. Aren't they magnificent?'

'This is unbelievable,' Gil said. He placed the jewellery on the nearest table and picked up the list again. 'This is Elizabeth's writing. I recognise it from her letters. You don't think this whole list is a treasure hunt, do you? There must be twenty or thirty items on here.'

'Miss Moonshine said Elizabeth was resourceful and would do anything to save the house. Do you think she might have hidden some of the valuable items so Roderick couldn't gamble them away? And look,' Libby said, pointing at the list. 'Some lines have been crossed out, and the bottom three rows seem to have been added at a different time. They aren't cryptic clues at all. See, this last one says there's something in the secret drawer of the walnut bureau. I can't read it very well. It looks like it was written in a hurry.' She frowned. 'What if there was an emergency and Elizabeth had to move some of the things she'd previously hidden? Perhaps when the house was on fire?'

'So as well as the painting and the diamonds, there might be other treasure hidden in the house? This is fantastic. Elizabeth might have saved Greymoor after all.' He looked at Libby, and his smile grew. 'You might have saved Greymoor. You will help me look for the treasure, won't you?'

'Just try and stop me,' Libby said. But as she looked at Gil, she couldn't imagine finding anything more precious than the man standing in front of her. She glanced back at the painting of Elizabeth and for an instant she could have sworn the stern expression transformed into a smile. Then Gil stepped forward, put his arms round her and kissed her, and she forgot everything else.

Miss Moonshine picked up Napoleon, nodded at Elizabeth's portrait, and quietly slipped away.

Kate Field lives in Lancashire with her husband, daughter and cat. Her debut novel won the Romantic Novelists' Association Joan Hessayon Award for new writers. Kate writes heartwarming, uplifting love stories and her latest novel, *Finding Home*, **is available now from Amazon and other retailers.**

https://amzn.to/2EsWkBm

The Treasure Seekers

By Mary Jayne Baker

Chapter One

'Do you think Hugh wants us to lose?' Toby whispered to Joely as they waited outside Miss Moonshine's Emporium with the television crew. 'There's nothing in this place but tat.'

'Teams always start in their hometown, don't they? I guess there weren't many options in Haven Bridge.' Joely cast an underwhelmed glance at the porcelain spaniels and Charles and Di commemorative tea towel in the grimy front window. 'Let's hope there are better options inside.'

She reached up to pat her red curls, and Toby smiled.

'Jo, you look great. Stop fiddling.'

'I'm nervous, Tobes. I've never been on TV before, you might be surprised to learn.' She took out a pocket mirror and grimaced at her reflection. 'Ugh, look at me. I bet the viewers will laugh out loud when I say I'm only thirty-seven.'

'Rubbish. They'll be begging to know what your secret is.' Toby peered over the crew. 'What's the hold-up?'

The door of the shop swung open and Hugh Waverly – long-time host of *The Great British Antique Swap* and winner of the *Good Housekeeping* award for television's best-dressed man – stormed out with a filthy look on his deeply tanned face.

'That… that *harridan* is refusing to grant us entry,' he spluttered. 'You'd think a dive like this would be grateful for television exposure, but she's refusing to have cameras inside.'

'You mean you didn't check beforehand?' Joely asked.

'How? This place has no telephone number, no email address, no website: it might as well not exist.'

'Oh well, we tried,' Toby said brightly. 'Let's go to a proper antiques shop, with stuff that might actually win us twenty grand. This gaff's only one up from Oxfam.'

Hugh was still glowering. The crew glanced nervously at each other. Filming was evidently no picnic when their star got into a mood.

'It's not cheap, getting all these people here,' Hugh muttered. 'Why that mad bat wants to throw away free publicity I can't fathom.'

'Perhaps because that mad bat is closing early to attend her godson's wedding, Mr Waverly,' an amused voice observed. 'Or perhaps she just doesn't like your tone. I can quite see her point.'

Hugh turned to glare at the old lady who'd appeared in the doorway. She was wearing an emerald silk dress, with a cherry-pink fascinator clipped to her shock of white hair. In her arms, an elderly chihuahua in a matching bow tie watched the scene with a bored expression.

'You're throwing away the opportunity of a lifetime, you know.' Hugh curled his lip at the peeling paint on the black door. 'It's obvious this place is on its last legs. I'm giving you the chance to make it the biggest thing this side of the Pennines.'

'I'm sorry, Mr Waverly, but this isn't –' Miss Moonshine broke off, her attention caught by a movement. 'Well, well, well,' she said quietly. 'Joely Fox. I'd quite given up on you.'

Joely gave a feeble smile. 'Hello, Miss Moonshine.'

'Are you with these television people, dear?'

'Yes. Me and my friend Toby are contestants on the show.'

'You know, young lady, I was expecting you –' Miss

Moonshine looked at her watch '– two months ago. Where on earth have you been?'

Joely blinked. 'Expecting me?'

'Well, in you come. We don't have long.'

'But…' Joely gestured helplessly to the TV crew.

'Oh, all right,' Miss Moonshine said. 'Bring them in then.'

Hugh shot his team a triumphant look.

'I knew you'd see sense in the end,' he said, as he barged past her.

Miss Moonshine's hazel eyes sparkled. 'I usually do. In the end.'

Inside, the crew set up their equipment while Toby, Joely and Hugh examined the shelves.

'I told you, Jo. Tat, everywhere you look.' Toby picked up a dappled conch seashell with a large-bosomed clay lady reclining on it, inscribed with the words 'A souvenir from Blackpool'. 'We're done for if we can't get something better than this.'

'No, no,' Hugh said, in a hushed voice. 'It's not tat. Not all of it.'

Toby blinked. 'Why, is this a Fabergé smutty seashell?'

'Not that.' Hugh picked up a rosewood music box and eyed it greedily. 'This… I can't believe it.'

Toby hooked a dangling price tag. 'Seventy quid. That's a shame; we've only got fifty to spend. What do you reckon it's worth?'

'More than she's asking, that's certain.' Hugh's awestruck gaze drifted over the shelves. 'There are treasures here. Real treasures.'

Joely couldn't see anything that looked like a treasure. Maybe she just didn't have Hugh's eye for antiques. Still, there couldn't be anything truly valuable. Miss Moonshine's had been around forever, with a pretty unvarying collection of dusty, neglected junk. If the music box was worth real money, it had to be the only thing that was.

Please God, though, let Hugh be right. Winning *The Great British Antique Swap* was Joely's only hope of saving Bluebird Cottage. If they could just find one treasure among the rubbish…

Miss Moonshine called from across the shop. 'Your people look to be ready, Mr Waverly.'

'Yes. Right.' Hugh put the box he'd been admiring back on the shelf, then moved a shabby teddy embroidered with the words 'I wuv u' in front of it. His eyes had filled with a cold, piggy-like expression of avarice.

'That old witch has no idea what this stuff's worth,' he muttered. 'I could clean up in here.'

Joely shot Toby a worried look.

'So what do we do, Hugh?' Toby asked.

'Hmm?' Hugh faced him, his focus returning. 'Oh. We'll start with my intro, then it's straight into your interviews.'

One of the crew approached to put Hugh into position. The make-up woman made a valiant effort to tone down his tan before Kevin, the cameraman, counted him in.

As soon as the cameras rolled, the boorish, arrogant Hugh of behind the scenes vanished, becoming the charm-dripping silver fox who had nanas the country over swooning into their afternoon cuppas.

'Welcome to *The Great British Antique Swap* – where one man's trash becomes another man's cash!' he boomed. 'Our red team has been given a kitty of £50 with which to buy one item from this shop in the Yorkshire town of Haven Bridge: Miss Moonshine's Wonderful Emporium.' He flinched, as if the shop's florid name grated. 'They then have one week to swap their starter item for a series of different items, with each swap – they hope – giving them something of higher value than the one before. The piece each team is left with will be sold at auction, and whichever sells for the biggest sum will win its finders a prize of £20,000. Let's meet the reds.'

Joely felt sick as Hugh turned his white smile towards her. It hadn't felt fully real before. It was just Miss Moonshine's, after all. But now, with the boom mike hovering over her and Hugh in full gameshow-host mode, Joely suddenly understood that she was going to be on TV, with people all over the country watching her.

She hoped she wasn't going to throw up.

'Joely. I understand you grew up right here in Haven Bridge,' Hugh purred.

'Um, yes.'

Hugh waited expectantly, but Joely just blinked. What else was she supposed to say?

'I've lived here all my life,' she told Hugh in a trembling voice. It was the only detail she could think of to add.

'And what do you do?'

'I was my dad's carer until he passed away three months ago. Now, um, I work at the Co-op.'

Hugh, looking beyond bored at this summary of her career, turned to Toby.

'Joely's teammate Toby lives in the neighbouring village of Hepton,' Hugh read from his card. 'So, Toby. Are you on the tills as well?'

Toby bristled at Hugh's subtle sneer. 'Actually I'm a nurse, Hugh. I help care for people with Parkinson's Disease – people like Joely's dad, Ned. That's how we met.'

'And why did you want to come on *The Great British Antique Swap*?'

'Because *Cash in the Attic* turned us down?' Toby said brightly.

Hugh frowned. 'All right, Toby, less of the smart-arsery,' he muttered. 'We'll have to edit that out.'

He cleared his throat and eased back into host mode.

'Well, here's the million-dollar question – or the £20,000

question, I should say.' He gave an ingratiating grin to the camera. 'What would you spend the money on, folks?'

Joely flushed. 'I'm saving for the deposit on a house. My dream house, actually.'

'Ah. Newlyweds, are you?'

'No, just friends.' Joely felt her blush grow deeper. Toby looked pretty pink too. What had Hugh said that for? He knew they weren't a couple.

'I see,' Hugh said, winking at the camera. 'What will you spend your share on, Toby?'

Toby shrugged. 'Not sure yet. I'm sure if we win, I'll think of something.'

Hugh held his grin for a moment before making a throat-slashing gesture. When filming had stopped, he turned a look on Joely and Toby that clearly said they were the worst pair he'd ever had the misfortune to interview.

'We'd better get on with it,' he said in a bored voice. 'Just hunt around until you find something. Kevin will be following with the camera. You've got half an hour.'

'You've got twenty minutes,' Miss Moonshine called from behind her mahogany counter. 'I told you, I'm closing early.'

Chapter Two

Ten minutes later, Joely and Toby still hadn't found anything worth investing in.

The bell over the door jangled as a woman in a stylish white suit entered. Miss Moonshine pursed her lips.

'Scarlett, honestly,' she said to the new arrival. 'Trousers, on your wedding day! I could have found you the perfect dress.'

Scarlett laughed. 'You're the last person I'm taking fashion advice from, Aunty M. You look very chic today though.' She bent to stroke the chihuahua. 'You too, Nappy, you handsome devil. Loving the dicky bow.'

'Must you call me Aunty M, dear? I feel like I ought to move to Kansas and buy a farm.'

'With your reputation, you're just lucky no one's dropped a house on you. How much longer will you be? Lucas is waiting in the car.'

'Give me ten minutes to shoo these television people out.'

'Sounds like we'd better get a move on,' Toby whispered to Joely.

'We're never going to find anything.' Joely combed her fingers through her curls. 'It's doomed, Tobes. The cottage is as good as gone.'

'Now, come on.' Toby put an arm around her. 'Where's that bouncy ray of sunshine who made home visits to Bluebird Cottage the highlight of my week?'

'She's not in.'

'Then it's my turn to chivvy you up, isn't it? You heard what Hugh said: this place is full of treasures. Shame we can't afford that music box he was fondling, but there must be something else. We just need to trust our gut.'

Joely hooked a cheap-looking necklace from a stand. 'Well my gut's telling me this came out of a Christmas cracker.'

'I did have a good feeling about the Toby jug that looked like my Uncle George. If we can't find anything else, let's plump for that.'

Scarlett was alone behind the counter now, observing them. 'Looking for something in particular?' she asked.

'Yes. We just don't know what.' Joely nodded to Kevin, discreetly shooting footage of them a little distance away. 'It's for that TV programme, *The Great British Antique Swap*.'

'I know the one. Fifty-quid kitty to buy something you can trade up, right?'

'That's it.' Joely started to turn back to the shelf she'd been examining, then paused. 'What would you pick?'

'Oh, I'm hopeless at anything like that. You should ask Miss Moonshine.'

'Does she know about antiques?' Joely asked doubtfully.

'Are you kidding? She was probably there when they were minted.'

Joely couldn't help feeling sceptical. If Miss Moonshine knew about that stuff, why would her shop sell so much that was clearly worthless? Hugh must be right: if there were valuable pieces among the junk, then the shop's proprietor surely had no idea.

Sensing her hesitation, Scarlett approached her. 'Look – Joely, is it? Trust me, Aunty M knows her stuff. The first time I came in here, she…' Scarlett glanced at an old typewriter on the counter marked 'Not For Sale'. 'Well, never mind me. Just trust that whatever she advises you to buy, it'll nudge your life in the right direction.'

Toby looked unconvinced.

'This isn't just a game to us,' he told her. 'Joely's trying to raise the money for something very close to her heart.'

'Then believe me, Miss Moonshine's your best hope.'

The curtain behind the counter billowed and Miss Moonshine appeared, her handbag hooked over her arm.

'All right, Mr Waverly, your time's up,' she called. 'Everybody out, lickety-split.'

Joely shot Toby an uncertain look before approaching the counter. 'Um, Miss Moonshine?'

'Yes?'

'What would you buy? If you were us?'

Miss Moonshine regarded her with shrewd little magpie eyes. 'My dear, I thought you'd never ask.' She hobbled to a shelf of tatty books and drew one out. 'Here you go,' she said, putting it on the counter.

Toby frowned. 'A storybook? But this isn't even old: just

knackered. I doubt it's worth 50p, let alone £50.' He opened *100 Bedtime Tales* to look at the title page. 'And it's been written in. That'll decrease the value.'

Miss Moonshine shrugged. 'Nevertheless, it's what you need.'

'You really think we can win with this?'

'It's what you need,' Miss Moonshine repeated.

Toby glanced at Joely. 'What do you think, Jo? I reckon we'd be better off with the Toby jug.'

But Joely wasn't paying attention. Something behind the counter had caught her eye.

How had she not spotted it before? Hanging just above Miss Moonshine's head was the most wonderful wooden clock in the shape of a house, looking just like…

'I wouldn't bother if I were you,' observed Hugh, who'd approached with the music box he'd been admiring. 'Tourist rubbish. They flog those in souvenir shops all over Switzerland.'

'But it looks just like my house,' Joely whispered. 'Even the plaque Dad carved for the door…'

'Yes, it does rather, doesn't it?' Miss Moonshine said, turning to observe it. 'In fact, I feel it really ought to go home to the real Bluebird Cottage.'

Joely blinked. 'You think we should buy it as our starter item?'

'No. I told you, the book is what you need. Call the clock a gift.'

'Oh, I really couldn't –'

'Please, humour an old lady when she's feeling generous. It might bring you luck.'

'Trust me, Joely, it's easier to just agree.' Scarlett tapped her watch. 'Aunty, we need to go.'

Hugh pushed past Joely to put his music box on the counter.

'I might as well take this while I'm here,' he said airily. 'It's the sort of thing my old mum likes. Tell you what, as a gesture of goodwill for letting us film here, I'll give you £85 for it. That's fifteen over the asking price. Can't say fairer than that, can you, eh?'

'For that old thing?' Miss Moonshine shrugged. 'If you wish, but you're being robbed, Mr Waverly. I probably overpriced it at seventy.'

Joely plucked Scarlett's elbow as Miss Moonshine wrapped Hugh's item.

'I think he's trying to rip her off,' she whispered. 'We heard him say it was really valuable. Should we say something?'

'I wouldn't worry,' Scarlett whispered back. 'Aunty M knows what she's doing.'

When the music box was shrouded in tissue paper, Hugh marched off with it, looking smug.

'So?' Miss Moonshine said, nodding to the tatty storybook.

Joely hesitated, exchanging a doubtful look with Toby.

'All right,' she said. 'We'll take it.'

*

'Well, there goes our shot,' Toby said, when he and Joely were walking back towards Bluebird Cottage.

Joely felt her cheeks heat. 'I'm sorry, Tobes. Miss Moonshine sounded so certain, I was sure… I mean, you hear so many stories.'

'What stories?'

'That shop… People say some funny things about it. It felt like the right thing to do – in my gut, like you said.'

'Then I guess we shouldn't give up hope.'

'No.' She was silent for a moment. 'Why do you think Hugh asked if we were married? He knows we're just friends.'

Toby shrugged. 'To embarrass us? Probably makes pretty gripping TV, making the contestants squirm.'

'You got your revenge with that *Cash in the Attic* crack though,' Joely said, smiling.

'Well. He gets my back up, that guy.'

'I hope we can find a good swap in Harrogate tomorrow. I've got six months to get a mortgage deposit together before I have to put the cottage on the market to pay off that equity company Dad took a loan from. I can't bear to think of strangers living there.'

'Joely...'

'Hmm?'

Toby took her elbow to stop her walking on.

'Look, I know buying back Bluebird Cottage has been top of your priorities since Ned died. But did you ever think that maybe selling the place was for the best?'

Joely frowned. 'What?'

'Well, there are so many memories for you there.'

'That's exactly why I can't lose it. The cottage is all that's left of... of my mum and dad.'

'I get that,' Toby said soothingly. 'But sometimes clinging to old memories stops us from moving on and making new ones. Don't you think so?'

'What, so I ought to forget them?'

'I'm not saying that. I just worry this obsession with buying back the cottage is stopping you from finding your own happiness.' He met her gaze. 'Perhaps from seeing what's right in front of you.'

'How do you mean?'

'Oh... never mind,' he said, breaking eye contact. 'Look, Jo, if this is what you want then you know I've got your back.'

'I know.' She patted his arm. 'You're a good friend, Tobes.'

A brightly coloured circus truck rolled past them towards the park. Gobbo's – a traditional circus with a huge Big Top – had pitched up there a few days ago. They watched as it disappeared down the road.

'What do you say we stop in at The Packhorse for a drink after our ordeal?' Toby said, summoning a smile. 'I'm buying.'

'Not now.' Joely patted the storybook under her arm. 'Better get this safely home. And my new clock too.'

'Odd little thing. Does it work?'

'I guess I'll find out.'

Chapter Three

Bluebird Cottage wasn't as idyllic as the fanciful name suggested – just a soot-blackened Victorian mill-worker's house, like so many others in the town – but it was home. The forget-me-not-blue door seemed to glow like a beacon whenever Joely returned.

She put her key in the lock, her gaze fixing on the wooden plaque with its carved bluebird. Dad had made that. He'd always been good with his hands, beaming with boyish delight whenever he stumbled over some prime piece of whittling wood.

So many memories. Joely remembered the door at Christmastime, merrily festooned with a fragrant wreath of pine, orange slices and cinnamon sticks. She remembered, too, the day her father had flung open the door, bursting with pride, one arm wrapped tightly around her mum's waist. The pink, wriggling bundle in her mother's arms had been introduced to Joely as her new baby sister.

She almost thought she'd stepped back in time when she entered the house to see another such pink, wriggling bundle snuggled into a Moses basket by the fireplace. Then Callie's head popped up from their mum's knitting corner.

'Hiya, Jo,' her sister said. 'Hope you don't mind us letting ourselves in. I needed some of Mum's yarn.'

'Of course not.' Joely gave her sister a hug, then bent to kiss Ivy, her baby niece.

Ivy greeted her aunty with a wet raspberry, making Joely laugh.

'Well, are you staying for a cuppa?' she asked Callie.

'Yes, please.' Callie nodded to the parcel she was carrying. 'Is that your starter item from Miss Moonshine?'

'No, this is.' Joely handed her the book.

Callie examined *100 Bedtime Tales*. 'This is what you're going on TV with? It doesn't look very valuable.'

'I know. It's been written in as well.'

Joely left the room to put the kettle on. When she came back in, Callie had the book open.

'"To my dear Stephen",' she read. '"I hope these stories give you hours of happiness. I'll miss you every single day. Lots of love, Grandma xxx"'

'What do you think?'

'Far be it from me to question Miss Moonshine's motives in giving people graffitied books. Still, I'm struggling to see why anyone would want to trade for this.'

'She seemed certain it was what we needed.' Joely unwrapped the clock. 'Look at this. She gave it to me.'

'Wow,' Callie said, blinking.

'It has to be this place, doesn't it? It's too similar to be just coincidence.' Joely looked from the clock to her sister. 'You don't think…'

'Dad made it?' Callie trailed her fingertip thoughtfully over the little blue door. 'It does look like his style.'

Joely turned a little knob to set the time. As soon as the hands reached the hour, 'Oranges and Lemons' chimed out. Two doors either side of the main one popped open and out came a pair of figures, a man and a woman. They bowed to each other and retreated back inside their house.

Callie laughed. 'Jo, look. It's Mum and Dad.'

Joely laughed too, turning the hands again so she could

watch the figures repeat their dance. 'Dad's in a bit of a state. He's lost all his hair.'

'I think he must have had a hat, once,' Callie said. 'I'll make tea.'

She disappeared into the kitchen while Joely glanced around the room, wondering where to hang the clock.

There was a mirror over the mantelpiece that she'd come to resent recently. Every time she caught a glimpse of her reflection, it reminded her how thin her face was now; how she had more grey than any woman her age ought to have, and crinkles at the corners of her eyes. She took the mirror down and put the clock in its place.

'That's better, isn't it, Ivy?' she said to the dozing baby, who responded by breaking wind noisily.

'She doesn't get her terrible manners from me,' Callie said, as she came back in with two steaming mugs. She nodded to the displaced mirror. 'Where will you put that?'

'In the loft. Then I don't need to see my haggard old face in it.'

'Don't talk daft.'

Joely sat down and hugged her tea. 'It's not daft. I'm looking seriously old before my time, Cal. I feel old.'

'Give over, you're only thirty-seven. Young enough to meet someone still.'

'What's the point? The people you love only go and die on you.' Joely lowered her eyes as she blew on her tea. 'Break your heart.'

Callie rested a hand on her shoulder. 'That's grief talking.'

'Doesn't make it less true.'

'Pain and loss are part of living, just like joy and happiness. If we hid from those things, maybe we'd never feel grief, but we'd never have love or companionship either. That's a hollow sort of life.'

'I know.' Joely closed her eyes. 'But it hurts so much to lose someone.'

Callie gave her a hug. 'I miss Dad too,' she whispered. 'But you've still got your life to live, Jo. Wouldn't you like to meet someone?'

'No, I've left it too late to go hunting for romance. Any allure I might've had once is long gone.'

'You look tired, that's all, which is hardly surprising. Half an hour with me, a bottle of hair dye and a bit of make-up and you'll be getting ID-ed at the off-licence.'

Joely gave a shaky laugh. 'It's so long since I went on a date, I'm not sure I'd know what to do with a man even if I did find one who fancied me.'

'Oh, it'll soon come back to you.' Callie swallowed down her tea. 'I'd better get home to Rich. He's cooking for our anniversary.'

'All right.'

Callie stood up. 'Why don't you redecorate if you're determined to stay? Get rid of this old wallpaper, put your own stamp on the place?'

'I couldn't do that. Dad picked that wallpaper.'

'Dad's gone, Jo.'

Joely blinked at her, and Callie sighed. 'I'm sorry, that came out wrong. All I mean is, it's a house, not a shrine. Dad wouldn't mind.'

'I can't,' Joely said quietly. 'It's different for you, Cal. You lived away for a long time.'

'But I moved back to Haven Bridge as soon as Dad got ill. I never expected you to do everything on your own.'

'Sorry, that wasn't a dig. I just mean, I've lived in Bluebird Cottage all my life. I can't imagine living anywhere else.' Joely pointed to their mum's old armchair, which even now, fifteen years after they'd lost her, still smelt faintly of her perfume.

'See, I look there and I can see Mum with old Mittens on her lap, knitting.' She swallowed hard. 'And this is where we had the Christmas tree – you remember? You used to put all your presents to one side and I'd put mine at the other, and we'd see whose pile was higher.'

'Yes, and here's the sofa we were sitting on when Dad told us about his diagnosis, and the bedroom upstairs where he died,' Callie said quietly. 'Bluebird Cottage doesn't just hold happy memories.'

'No. But those are the ones I see in it.'

'I know you do. And you're right, Jo, every memory of Mum and Dad is precious. But they're not here any more.'

'You sound like Toby. He thinks I ought to sell the place.'

'And you told him no chance, right?'

'Course I did. This is our home.'

'Not mine.' Callie lifted Ivy into her arms and rocked her gently. 'I've made a home of my own – one I hope this little monster will remember being just as happy and filled with love as ours always was. You ought to do the same.'

'I couldn't. It'd be like… like forgetting Mum and Dad.'

'No it wouldn't. Mum and Dad aren't in the house, Jo – they're in us. You should listen to Toby.'

'No.' Joely turned away as she felt the sting of fresh tears. 'I won't lose Bluebird Cottage.'

'All right.' Callie took her hand and gave it a squeeze. 'It was only a suggestion. Can you bring Ivy's basket out?'

Joely nodded, not trusting her speech while a lump still bobbed in her throat. She followed Callie outside with the Moses basket and put it in the boot while her sister strapped Ivy into her booster seat.

'I hope you haven't been snapping at poor Toby,' Callie said.

'I didn't snap.'

'He's a good friend, isn't he?'

'The best.'

Callie finished strapping Ivy in and turned to her. 'You ever think he might like to be more?'

'What, Toby?' Joely laughed as she pictured her friend, with his smiling, boyish face and messy brown hair. 'Don't be silly.'

'Why not?'

'Because he could do a lot better than me, for a start.'

'He doesn't think so.'

'How do you know?'

Callie shrugged. 'Little sister's intuition. He likes you, Jo.'

'I've known Tobes for seven years. If he wanted to ask me out, he'd have done it a long time ago.'

'I doubt he was allowed while he was Dad's nurse. I bet he wanted to, though.'

Joely thought back to earlier, and Toby's offer to buy her a drink. He couldn't have meant a date, could he? When Dad was here they'd naturally spent time together, and they'd grown close – very close, as friends – but there'd never been any hint of romance.

Well, why would there be? Toby was good-looking, funny, warm, kind – loads of women must fancy him. Callie was letting her imagination run away with her.

'We're just friends,' Joely said firmly. 'And please don't mention anything like that to Toby. He went bright red today when Hugh Waverly suggested we were a couple.'

Callie shrugged. 'OK. I'm right though.'

'You're not, but I know there's no point arguing with you,' Joely said, smiling as she gave her sister a hug. 'Bye, Cal. Tell Rich I wished you a happy anniversary.'

After her sister had gone, Joely went to her mum's knitting corner and carefully put the ball of yarn Callie had cut a length from back in the basket. When everything was as it had been, Joely examined her clock.

There was a key on the back to wind the thing and she soon had it ticking. A button on the side, Joely discovered, would pop out the two little figures.

She pushed it, and watched as the man and woman emerged to bow to one another.

'Poor little man,' she said to the male figure, whose bald head looked like the top of a dolly peg. 'I'm sure we can do something for you. Hang on a tick.'

Joely soon located a small, bare wooden bobbin, then a piece of cardboard, scissors, glue, and her dad's old paintbox. She cut a circle from the cardboard and glued it to the bobbin, then painted the whole thing black and left it to dry. And just like that, the man who lived in the clock had a stylish top hat.

She glued it on and, for good measure, gave his jacket a fresh coat of red paint. When he was dry, Joely pressed the button to watch him do his dance. The little man almost seemed to grin as, in his new finery, he bowed to his partner.

Chapter Four

Joely was jerked awake by the chimes of 'Oranges and Lemons'.

Ugh. She'd fallen asleep on the sofa. She had to stop doing that.

She'd expected her clock to wind down in the night, but it was still ticking away. Joely blinked groggily at the hands.

Eight o'clock! Good thing it had woken her. Toby would be here in an hour to drive them into Harrogate for the next round of *The Great British Antique Swap*.

Eight bongs followed the tune and the little couple glided along the garden path to bow to one another.

Joely frowned as she watched them. Maybe she was imagining it, but it felt like there was something… not quite right. The woman was still in her bonnet and navy dress with the white smudge on the front; the man in his red coat and new top hat. But the coat – she didn't remember it being that length when she'd painted it. It extended to his knees now in two tails. And… was that a cane he was holding? She didn't remember a cane.

But he must have had it, of course. Joely had been half in a daze yesterday. She couldn't have been paying proper attention.

What did he remind her of? A circus ringmaster, that was it. There was an air of the showman about him that she hadn't noticed at all yesterday afternoon.

Joely started as the landline rang.

'Hello?'

'It's Hugh,' came the host's polished tones. 'Change of plan. We need you and Toby to meet us at the shop.'

'Miss Moonshine's? Why?'

'Technical malfunction. None of the footage we shot yesterday recorded: we've got nothing but white noise. That miserable old hag probably put a hex on us. Anyway, we'll have to do a retake.'

*

When Joely arrived at Miss Moonshine's, Toby and *The Great British Antique Swap* team were outside.

'Morning,' Toby said. 'Get my message?'

'What message?'

He shook his head. 'You really ought to check your phone once in a while, Jo.'

Joely took out her mobile and discovered a video waiting to be viewed. She hit play and laughed at the sight of her friend doing some serious dad-dancing while he sang along to 'Ruby' by the Kaiser Chiefs.

'It's my lucky dance,' he said, smiling. 'With moves like that, we're bound to win.'

'You daft sod.' She kissed his cheek. 'I love it.'

Hugh was ranting at one of the crew, his voice getting steadily louder.

'For God's sake, Andy, just do it! Am I the only damn professional on this show?'

'What's up with him?' Joely asked Kevin.

'It's that music box he bought,' the cameraman told them in an undertone. 'Hugh was sure it was by some famous nineteenth-century manufacturer but turns out it's a copy, worth £50 at most. He's been stomping about all morning.'

'Ha!' Toby said. 'Serves him right for trying to swindle the old girl.'

'Right,' Hugh snapped when he reached them. 'Let's get on with it. Half an hour in here then we'll move on to the antiques fair in Harrogate.'

'Are you sure it's open?' Joely said. 'It's all dark.'

'It'd better open. That woman's lucky I haven't got my lawyer onto her, offloading her cheap, nasty stock on me.'

Joely smothered a smile. 'Well, she did warn you.'

Hugh ignored that and went to bang on the door.

'Come on, Moonshine, open up!'

But the shop remained as dark and silent as before.

'What's that bit of paper?' Toby asked.

Hugh pulled off the note pinned to the door. '"Gone fishing". What's that supposed to mean?'

'I think it's Miss Moonshine's way of saying she's not opening today,' Joely said.

'The hell she isn't! She owes me £85 and half an hour of footage.'

'What's written at the bottom?'

Hugh squinted at it. '"PS: no refunds. The house always wins."' He spluttered. 'I'll sue! I'll sue the pants off her.'

'On what grounds? She told you what it was worth when you bought it.'

'She tricked me. She deliberately conned me into thinking that was an original Nicole Frères.'

'Well, boss, now what?' Kevin asked, wisely changing the subject. 'Head to Harrogate and refilm the interviews there?'

Hugh was silent, glaring resentfully at the note. But Joely's gaze had been drawn to something in the distance – the red and white stripes of Gobbo's Big Top in the park. The little man and his ringmaster outfit were still fresh in her mind.

'What about filming over there?' she said, pointing it out. 'That'd make a good background for our interviews, wouldn't it? I'm sure the people who run it won't object to the publicity.'

Hugh shuddered. 'A circus?'

'Hugh's scared of clowns,' Kevin whispered to Toby.

Toby snorted. 'Is he? Why?'

'I reckon the white facepaint upsets him. He's essentially just a host organism for that tan.'

Hugh scowled at them. 'What are you two tittering about?'

'Nothing at all, boss,' Kevin said. Toby thrust his hands into his pockets and whistled innocently.

'Well, Hugh, wouldn't a circus backdrop work?' Joely persisted. 'It'll add colour, or whatever you telly people say.'

'Hmm. I suppose,' Hugh admitted grudgingly. 'All right, let's go.'

*

The circus was busy, although it was only breakfast time. A group of kids were being taught to spin plates as part of a Circus Skills workshop, while a hubbub of performers bustled about the Big Top preparing for their first show. Hugh shivered as a couple of clowns honked past him in their giant shoes.

A ringmaster with a huge curled moustache was overseeing things. He looked just like the figure in Joely's clock: top hat, red tailcoat, silver-topped cane and all.

'That looks like the man in charge,' Hugh said. 'I'll go chat him up. You lot get ready.'

'What's up?' Toby asked Joely, noticing her gaze fixed on the ringmaster.

'Tobes, do you believe in signs from the universe?'

'Like, horoscopes?'

'No. More like… I don't know. I've got the strangest feeling.'

'What sort of feeling?'

She hesitated, wondering whether to tell him about the clock. He'd only tell her she was imagining things. Maybe she was. Still, Joely was sure the little man had been different yesterday. Callie had said that if the house was Bluebird Cottage, then the figures must be…

'I just feel like this is where my mum and dad want me to go,' she whispered. 'Does that sound mad?'

'Well, yeah.' Toby gave her hand a squeeze. 'Then again, we do need a miracle.'

Hugh was deep in conversation with the ringmaster. After a while he came back, looking pleased with himself.

'Sorted,' he said. 'We'll film the interviews here, then get some footage of you two taking in the sights before we meet up with the blue team in Harrogate.'

Joely felt a little guilty. The other team were a married couple, trying to win enough for a second honeymoon to celebrate their Silver Anniversary. But if it was between them and Bluebird Cottage, well, all was fair in love and daytime TV.

When they'd finished refilming their interviews, Hugh instructed them to wander about while Kevin followed with the camera. They headed into the Big Top to watch the acrobats rehearsing.

'Oof.' Joely flinched as a trapeze artist leapt from his swing to catch his partner's hands. 'How can they do that?'

The ringmaster was nearby, observing the routine.

'That was me, once upon a time,' he said, smiling. 'It's not as easy as it looks.'

'You think that looks easy?' Joely turned to him. 'Weren't you scared to death?'

'Not really. I was born to it. My mum and grandma were both flyers.' He turned to look at them. 'So, what have you got to swap?'

'Here.' Toby handed him the storybook. 'God knows who's going to want this old thing, but we live in hope.'

The ringmaster frowned. '*100 Bedtime Tales*… hey, I used to have this book.'

'Really?'

The man stared at the cover, as if the pictures of dragons and wizards brought the memories flooding back. He laughed softly, running his fingertip over an illustration of a Big Top.

'My grandmother gave it to me when she retired from the circus,' he told them. 'Whenever I missed her, I used to read one of the stories and feel close to her again. She's passed away now. I often wish I had that book still, but we moved around so much, it got left behind somewhere.'

'Grandma…'Joely exchanged looks with Toby. 'Um, I don't suppose…'

'Stephen?' Toby asked.

The ringmaster frowned. 'How did you know my name?'

Toby reached over to open the book at the title page.

'Oh, my goodness,' Stephen whispered. 'This is… mine. My grandma wrote this.' After a moment's silence, he looked up at them. 'Is it for sale? I'll pay any price.'

'Well, we kind of have to swap it,' Toby said. 'That's the name of the game.'

'But what can I give you that could possibly…' He paused before unhooking the gold fob watch arranged across his chest. 'Here. Have this.'

Joely took the watch from him. 'Are you sure? This looks valuable. The book's worthless.'

'To anyone else, perhaps. To me, it's priceless.'

'If you're positive, then… well, thank you.'

'No, thank you.' He wrung their hands, then gazed at the book again. 'Thank you both, from the bottom of my heart.'

Chapter Five

When Joely went downstairs the next morning, she discovered her clock had wound down, halting when the figures had emerged to mark the hour. They stood frozen, staring into each other's eyes.

Joely had given herself a stern talking-to in the mirror before bed last night. 'Joely Fox, you need to get a hold of yourself. Magic clocks; fate; signs from the universe. Superstitious nonsense. You were lucky yesterday, with the watch, but if you want to win this thing then you need to get back to Planet Earth.'

'What about the watch though?' a little voice had murmured. 'Pretty big coincidence, right? That the book should find its way to the one person it was precious to?'

Perhaps. But coincidences happened every day, didn't they?

Anyway, the clock had stopped, and that proved there was nothing magical about it. Miss Moonshine's eerie shop had got under Joely's skin, that was all, and sent her still grief-afflicted imagination into overdrive.

Joely took the clock down to wind it.

The figures looked exactly the same as on the morning before. Of course she'd been imagining any changes. The circus truck that had driven by while she was walking home with Toby had lodged in her subconscious, combining with the top hat to produce visions of ringmasters.

Although she'd been mistaken about the white smudge on

the woman's navy-blue dress. Now she looked closely, it didn't resemble a blemish so much as an apron: faded with time, but with a distinct aprony shape. That made sense – a white apron to match the woman's white mobcap. Joely made a mental note to give it a fresh coat of paint when she got back from filming.

Their destination today was a vintage market near Skipton. Hugh had seemed peeved yesterday that they'd made their swap before arriving at the antiques fair they'd been destined for, but had grudgingly admitted there was nothing in the rules to say they couldn't swap with whoever they wanted – as long as they did it on camera. He'd instructed Kevin to shadow them whenever they left the house from now on, just in case they started swapping things when he wasn't looking.

Toby and Kevin picked Joely up at eleven.

'Hugh's hanging out with the blue team this morning, doing a *Through the Keyhole* job on their house,' Kevin told them as he drove.

'They're not going to do that to us, are they?' Joely's eyes widened as she imagined the TV crew traipsing around Bluebird Cottage, getting footage of her knickers drying.

'I don't think so. Hugh seems to have written the pair of you off as a dead loss – no offence.'

'None taken.' Toby's stomach rumbled. 'Man, I'm starving. Have we got time to stop for a bite, Kevin?'

'Well, Hugh goes ape if anyone's late.' He smiled. 'Let's do it.'

'I know a place near here,' Joely said. 'There's a café my mum used to take us to, if it hasn't closed down. Next left.'

Kevin followed her directions, and they were soon pulling up outside a traditional stone tearoom called Anne's Pantry.

'Hang on, just let me get my camera,' he said as they piled out.

Toby laughed. 'Who do you think we're going to swap with in here? It looks like we're the only customers.'

Kevin shrugged. 'I might as well get a bit of background footage though.'

They went inside and claimed a table. A friendly looking older lady in a navy-blue uniform approached them.

'Now then, my loves, what can I get you?'

Kevin, who was fiddling with his handheld camera, looked up. 'Ham sandwich and a coffee for me please.'

'Same, but make mine ham and cheese,' Toby said. 'How about you, Jo?'

Joely was staring at the waitress. The woman flashed her a bewildered smile.

'Joely?' Toby nudged her. 'Come on, we can't stay long.'

'That hat…' Joely's gaze was fixed on the woman's white mobcap.

The waitress laughed. 'I know, it's daft, isn't it? But if you own a place called Anne's Pantry, people expect a bit of olde-worlde.'

'You own this place?' Kevin asked.

'For my sins. I'm the Anne in Anne's Pantry.'

Joely was still staring. The navy-blue dress, the white apron, the mobcap… All just like the woman in her clock. Toby nudged her again, and she pulled herself together.

'Um, I'll have the same as him,' she said to Anne. 'Thank you.'

Anne disappeared behind the counter.

'I'd better check she's OK with me filming,' Kevin said. 'Back in a sec.'

'All right, what's up with you?' Toby asked Joely when they were alone.

'I just… That uniform. It… reminded me of something.'

'What?'

Joely grimaced. 'I can't tell you.'

'Why not? You tell me everything else. Even when I'm in the foetal position sobbing "TMI! TMI!".'

Joely took out the watch and laid it on the table. She ran a fingertip over the pattern on the gold case.

'Promise you won't laugh?'

Toby crossed himself solemnly. 'Cub's honour.'

'Well, you know that clock? I think… I think it's sending me messages.'

He snorted. 'You what?'

'You promised you wouldn't laugh!'

'Yeah, but I didn't think I'd have magic clocks to contend with. You're kidding, right?'

Joely let out a hollow laugh. 'No. I might be cracking up, but I'm not kidding. When the figures popped out yesterday, I was sure the little man had changed to look like a ringmaster. Then we met Stephen and he gave us the watch. This morning, the woman looked like she was wearing a maid's uniform with an apron and mobcap. Then we came here and…' She gestured helplessly to Anne, chatting with Kevin as she made their sandwiches.

Toby massaged her shoulder. 'Jo, have you been sleeping OK?'

'Not really. But that isn't it.' She held up a hand as he opened his mouth to speak. 'I know what you're going to say. Grief, right? Affects the brain. That's what I told myself too. But then…' She glanced at Anne again. 'Well, here we are.'

'Yes, but… coincidences happen all the time, Jo. Magic clocks… well, they don't happen all the time. In fact, I think I can safely say they never happen.' Toby lowered his voice as Anne approached with their lunch, Kevin following with the now rolling camera. 'Look, we'll talk about it later.'

Anne set her tray down.

'There we go,' she said. 'I'll just fetch the coffee pot and…'

Anne trailed off as her gaze fell on the watch. Joely watched her keenly.

'What is it?' she asked.

'That watch,' Anne said in a low voice.

Joely raised an eyebrow at Toby. 'Yes, it's the item we have to swap today.'

'It looks so much like…' Half unconsciously, Anne picked it up and ran the chain through her fingers. 'When I was a girl, my father had one like this. He used to sit me on his knee and teach me how to tell the time with it.'

Toby shook his head. 'You're kidding.'

'I'd swear it was this exact one.' Anne turned it over. 'In fact, I'm certain it is. There's a scratch that… This is my dad's watch.'

'How did he lose it?' Joely asked.

Anne lowered her eyes. 'He… pawned it. When his business went under. My family lost a lot of things.'

'You must want it back.'

'Yes,' she whispered, regarding it with a longing look. 'There are a lot of happy memories in this little watch.'

Toby met Joely's eye, shaking his head.

'Joely, don't,' he whispered. Joely ignored him.

'You could offer us a swap,' she said to Anne.

'But I've got nothing to swap. Nothing of value.' Anne was silent a moment, thoughtfully examining a charm bracelet on her wrist. 'This is the most expensive piece of jewellery I own.'

'What's it worth?' Toby asked.

'Not much, I'm afraid. I bought it at a jumble sale for £20.'

Joely opened her mouth to accept, but Toby cut her off.

'Would you mind if I discussed it with my partner here?' he asked Anne.

'Of course. I wish I had something else to offer, but business is… Well, you can see for yourselves.' Anne gave the watch a look of yearning before reluctantly putting it back on the table.

'Joely, what do you think you're doing?' Toby murmured

when they were alone – alone apart from Kevin, getting it all on film.

'You can see how much it means to her. We have to swap, Tobes.'

'For a £20 bracelet? The watch must be worth five times that. We're meant to trade up, not down.'

'Yes, but…'Joely rested a finger on the watch. 'I know it's the right thing to do. Trust me.'

'Am I trusting you, or am I trusting a –' Toby glanced at Kevin and lowered his voice – 'a supposedly magic clock?'

'Well, it was right, wasn't it? It sent us here, and we found the one person the watch is worth something to. Just like with the book.'

'OK, two issues. One, the clock did not send us here. My empty belly sent us here. Two, Anne is not the one person the watch is worth something to. It's worth at least a hundred quid to quite a lot of people.'

'Yes, but Anne's the one it means something to.'

'We have to take our best chance of winning, Jo. For Bluebird Cottage.'

'Tobes, I know I'm right.' She reached for his hand. 'Just trust me, OK?'

Toby sighed. 'I'm going to regret this.' He turned and beckoned to Anne. 'All right. Let's swap.'

*

The days leading up to the auction were like a dream. Every morning Joely noticed something different in the clock figures – not a big difference, but some subtle shift that seemed to guide her and Toby to where they needed to go. As item after item found the person it needed to be with, even Toby's diehard scepticism began to melt.

The day after swapping Stephen's watch for Anne's bracelet,

Joely noticed the cardboard of the clock man's hat had bent to leave just a front brim, giving him the appearance of a toy soldier. Later, when she and Toby stopped at The Nutcracker toyshop to buy a present for Ivy, a woman shopping with her grandchildren had cried out in delight at being reunited with the bracelet her late husband had given her on their wedding day. The same thing happened the day after, and the day after that. It was at a church hall jumble sale where they traded for the last item they had to swap – a delicate cloverleaf-patterned teacup and saucer.

'Are you sure this is where the clock wants us to go?' Toby asked on their final swap day as, with Kevin in tow, they once again crossed Miss Moonshine's threshold.

'Pretty sure.'

'How did it tell you?' Kevin asked. After days filming their swaps, the cameraman was now a fully converted follower of the clock.

Joely tried to remember what she'd seen that morning. The figures hadn't looked different really – well, they never did. Not so you'd swear they hadn't always been that way; tiny things that might have been there the whole time without you noticing. But this morning it had been more a feeling than anything specific. Something had told her they needed to go back to where it had all begun.

'It just did,' she said.

The old lady was nowhere to be seen. However, Napoleon jumped up to greet them, and a familiar voice sailed down from upstairs.

'It's on the counter, dear,' Miss Moonshine called. 'All wrapped up for you. Sorry, I've rather got my hands full.'

Joely shot Toby a puzzled frown.

'Um, what is?' she called back.

'Your last item. Leave whatever you have to swap and help yourself.'

'But you don't even know what we're swapping,' Toby called.

'Oh, that hardly matters. Just remember, no returns.'

Feeling dazed, Joely picked up the brown paper parcel on the counter and put the china teacup in its place.

'It feels heavy,' she whispered to Toby. 'That's a good sign.'

'Shall we open it?'

'Not here.' She cast a glance around the shop, which felt creepier when its proprietor wasn't present. 'Let's get it home.'

'But what if it's no good?'

'Trust the clock, Tobes.'

Toby and Kevin accompanied her to Bluebird Cottage and they unwrapped their final item. It was a brass kaleidoscope, patterned with winding vines.

'Well, it's nice,' Joely said after a minute. 'Good quality. I don't think it's genuine vintage though.'

Toby was already on his phone, googling. 'You're right, it's not. There's dozens like it on eBay.'

'How much are they going for?'

'Not loads. Seventy or eighty quid.'

Joely held the kaleidoscope to her eye, watching the colourful patterns form as she turned it. 'There must be something special about our one. Someone in the auction room will have a sentimental attachment to it, I guess.'

'I hope you're right. The teacup and saucer were worth a lot more than this.'

'The clock's guided you right so far,' Kevin said from behind his camera.

'I guess.' Toby gave the clock a wary look. 'You're absolutely sure it's magic, Jo?'

Joely smiled. 'After everything we've seen this week, you're still asking?'

'Well. I can't shake a lifetime of scepticism just like that.' He patted her knee. 'Come on, let me take you for that drink now.

Otherwise you'll just be fretting about the auction.'

'You and Kevin go. I've got my sister coming over.' She pecked his cheek. 'See you tomorrow. Cross everything, eh?'

Chapter Six

Joely squeezed Toby's elbow when she met him at the auction house next day.

'How are you feeling?' she whispered.

'Nervous.' He nodded to where the lots were laid out. 'The blues have done really well, Jo. They've got these antique silver binoculars.'

'Don't worry. We're going to win, the universe told me.'

'You genuinely believe that, don't you?'

She nudged him. 'Come on. You're still not a believer?'

'Well, yes, I am, but… just don't get your hopes up, OK? If we lose, we lose.'

'We won't,' she said firmly. 'There's a message behind the items we swapped. None of them worth wads of cash, but beyond precious to the people we reunited them with. It's a sign, you see? They mean just what Bluebird Cottage means to me.'

Toby didn't answer, but he did turn to look at her.

'You look nice,' he said.

'Oh.' She flushed. 'Thanks.'

Callie had come over the night before and the sisters had spent a fun girly evening messing around with make-up and hair dye. Joely had woken that morning to discover a fresh, rosy face looking back at her from the mirror, her grey all gone. When the figures popped out to chime the hour, they looked exactly as they had the day before. This time, it was Joely who was different.

'It's been fun, hasn't it?' Toby said.

'It has. It was incredible seeing people reunited with things that had so many memories for them.'

'I think my favourite part was spending time with you.' He smiled at her. 'So, how about that drink afterwards? You can't keep turning me down forever.'

The smile was the same as ever, boyish and open, but there was something in his eyes…

'Tobes,' she said slowly. 'When you say a drink… I mean, are you asking me –'

They were interrupted by Hugh Waverly.

'Come on, chop chop,' he said, clapping his hands. 'I need you and the blues together for a chat about how you're feeling. Play up the nerves, OK? It's a dead cert you're going to lose, but we want to keep a bit of suspense.'

The blue team's item was auctioned first, provoking a bit of a bidding war. In the end, the silver binoculars went for an impressive £350.

'Well, I think that's the biggest profit we've had in six years of *The Great British Antique Swap*,' Hugh purred to the camera. 'But it's not over yet. Let's see if our red team can pull off a miracle with their brass kaleidoscope.'

'Here we go,' Toby whispered to Joely. 'We'll be lucky to top their profit.'

'Don't worry. I told you, we can't lose.' Still, Joely grasped Toby's hand as the auctioneer opened the bidding.

'Ten pounds? Do I hear ten pounds for this fine item?' the man gabbled. He paused, but no hands went up. 'Five then. Come on, ladies and gents, a steal at five pounds.'

A hand was lazily raised, and Joely let out a sigh of relief. But a handful of half-hearted bids weren't enough to get them anywhere near the blue team's score. The kaleidoscope sold for a mere £45 – less than their original investment.

'Oh well, never mind,' Hugh said, as he patted Joely on the back. 'It was a worthy effort. And, ha ha, we won't even make you pay back the fiver.' He shot a sparkling grin to camera.

'Well, that's all, folks. Big thanks to both our teams for playing and we'll see you next time for another *Great British Antique Swap*!' He motioned to Kevin to cut. 'Weirdest episode we've ever shot. It's going to be a hell of an edit.'

Joely was still staring at the auctioneer. 'But… I don't understand. That wasn't… wasn't supposed…'

'Let's get out of here,' Toby murmured.

Feeling like her brain had floated out of her body, Joely let Toby guide her outside.

'What happened?' she whispered.

'We lost, Jo.'

'But… the cottage…'

'I know. I'm so sorry, love.'

'No.' Joely's brow knit into a determined frown as the reality of what had happened sank in. 'This isn't finished.'

'But what can you do? This was your one hope.'

'There are other gameshows, other ways to make money…'

'Joely, don't you get it?' Toby took her by both shoulders. 'Sweetheart, it's over. If this was a sign from the universe, then… well, perhaps the message was that it's time to let go.'

'No! I can't lose Bluebird Cottage.'

'Please, Joely. Just please, listen to me.' Toby's eyes had filled with earnest pleading. 'I hate having to say this, but Bluebird Cottage isn't healthy for you. You'll just be shut in that place like a ghost, running home videos in your head of happy times past instead of getting out and living your life. What sort of existence is that?'

Joely felt the sting of tears. 'Why do you keep saying these things?'

'Because someone has to.' He took her hands. 'Do you ever think about why you had such an amazing childhood in the cottage?'

'Well, because of my mum and dad.'

'Exactly. Because they loved you, and they filled your home with warmth. But you…' He dropped her hands to push his fingers impatiently into his hair. 'You know, Joely, you drive me insane. You could have that kind of happiness too, if you just opened yourself up to it.'

'Bluebird Cottage makes me happy.'

'So you're just going to live alone there for the rest of your days, numb to any feeling?' He sighed. 'I know it's hard. Grief is the worst – I see it at work every day. But I see love, too. Yes, people die but I've never met anyone who wished their loved one had never been born, just to spare them the pain of losing them.'

'Where are you going with this, Toby?'

'Jo, ask me what I was going to do with my half of the prize money.'

'You said you didn't know.'

'I did though. I was going to give it to you. For the deposit, so you'd have the full amount.'

She frowned. 'But… why? You told me I ought to sell the place.'

'Because even though I think staying in Bluebird Cottage is bad for you, I knew you wanted it more than anything. Because I want you to be happy.' He closed his eyes. 'Because I bloody love you, don't I?'

Joely took a step back. 'What?'

'Have done for years. I hoped you might notice, in the end.' He bowed his head. 'I'm sorry, Joely. I didn't mean to snap at you. Just forget I told you, OK?'

'But… you can't…'

'I'd better go. Bye, Jo. I hope you get your miracle. And I hope that whatever happens, you'll be happy.'

'Toby, wait!'

But he was already walking away.

*

Joely wasn't sure how she got home. She had a vague memory of passing Miss Moonshine's shop, seeing it as if in a dream, before the door of Bluebird Cottage loomed before her. She stumbled inside, staring numbly at the clock over the fireplace.

How could they have lost? She'd been so sure that someone, somewhere, had a plan for her. All the pieces seemed to fit together. The clock that looked like her house. The figures that she'd come to associate with her mum and dad, subtly guiding her. The memories that made each item special to the person it was reunited with. Everything had seemed to point to Bluebird Cottage, hers again, as it ought to be.

And Toby… she was still reeling from her friend's announcement. He loved her! Toby – caring, funny, warm-hearted Toby – loved her.

How did she feel about that? She'd never thought about it before, but the days she saw Toby were just *better* than other days. Along with Callie and Ivy, it was Toby who brought the sunshine into her life. And like a coward she'd let him walk away, so afraid of getting hurt that she'd rather live a half-life inside her memories than a full one in the real world. Her parents would never have wanted that for her.

There was a knock at the door. Joely wiped her eyes and went to answer it.

'Toby,' she whispered when she found him on the doorstep.

'Can I come in?'

'Of course.' She stood aside.

'I came to apologise,' he said, looking shamefaced. 'I had no right to go off on one like that when you were upset. And I guess I probably freaked you out when I said… what I said. I meant it – every word – but that wasn't the best way to tell you. I'm sorry.'

'I thought you were walking away from me for good,' she said with a watery smile. 'Tobes…'

'Let me get this out.' He took a deep breath. 'I've been thinking about what you said – the message behind those things we swapped – and I think you got it wrong, Jo. The message is that it's people who matter, not things. It wasn't the items that were precious: it was the memories of lost loved ones they brought back.'

'Right. Like Bluebird Cottage.'

'No. The memories don't belong to the cottage, Joely, they belong to you. Your parents filled this house with love, and they filled you with love. And their deaths made you afraid to give that love to anyone else. But I know you can, if you just understand that pain and joy together are what make us human – what make us alive. If you embrace that, life can be so, so sweet.' He took her hand and pressed it to his lips. 'We could make it sweet. Me and you.'

The clock chimed to mark the hour, and Joely watched the little figures emerge. It was funny, but they seemed back to normal now. Once again they reminded her of her mum and dad as they slid along the garden path.

They usually stopped a little distance apart, bowed and retreated. But today they kept going until they collided, their faces pressing together in a kiss. Then they drew apart, bowed civilly and went back into the house.

'That's weird,' she murmured.

'What?'

'The clock…' She turned back to Toby. 'I think it's trying to tell me something.'

He frowned. 'Still?'

'Yes. It's trying to tell me… I'm an idiot.' She laughed. 'I'm a massive, massive idiot, Tobes. That's my big, important message from the universe.'

She got it now. Toby was right, about the message behind the swaps. Joely's mum and dad weren't in the cottage: they were in her. In the life they'd given her to live, and the love they'd shown her how to share. A house was just a house, but people – they were what mattered.

Toby shook his head. 'She's a strange girl, but I love her.'

Joely smiled. 'Say that again.'

'I said, I love you. It's taken me years to get up the nerve to tell you that and now I can't stop.' He drew her gently into his arms. 'Well? Me and you, Jo, what do you think?'

Joely looked around the room. She thought about her parents and her sister. The laughter that had filled this house – and the tears. Pain, and joy, mingling together to make life as full and sweet as it deserved to be. Then she turned to Toby and answered his question by planting a soft kiss on his lips.

'I think it's high time I let you buy me that drink,' she whispered.

Mary Jayne Baker is a novelist from Bingley, West Yorkshire. Since her debut in 2016 she has published eight romantic comedies, including *A Question of Us*, **which was the winner of the Romantic Novelists' Association's Romantic Comedy of the Year Award 2020. Mary Jayne also writes humorous, emotional women's fiction under the name Lisa Swift, and World War Two sagas as Gracie Taylor.**

maryjaynebaker.co.uk

lisaswiftauthor.co.uk

Ginny's Ghost

By Helen Pollard

'It's driving me mad!' Ginny told Sandra over a dry cider outside The Packhorse Inn. 'I've been living in Haven Bridge Mill for six months, no trouble at all, and now I'm hearing all these weird noises.'

'What sort of noises?'

'Odd bangs, like doors or windows blowing shut – not ideal when your cakes are rising or you need a steady hand to pipe an intricate detail. I even made the building company come back to check if my central heating was faulty. Sometimes it's faint scraping noises. Sometimes voices, barely there.'

'Neighbours,' Sandra suggested.

'The noises aren't coming from their direction. And the flats above and to one side haven't sold yet.' Ginny sipped her cider. 'It's been going on for about three weeks now. If I didn't know better, I'd think there was a poltergeist loose!'

Sandra gaped. 'You think your flat's *haunted*?'

'No, of course not. I don't believe in that rubbish. Besides, there's barely a peep in the middle of the night, and that's when ghosts would be out and about.'

Sandra winced. 'Sounds like you need another cider.'

'Yes, please. No harm in enjoying the sunshine a bit longer. But only the one. Can't risk a hangover – I have a wedding cake to start on tomorrow.'

'I don't know how you have the patience.'

'It's my livelihood now.' Ginny smiled. 'And I love every minute of it.'

*

Ginny thrust the *Haven Bridge Gazette* at Sandra a few days later. 'Why is our private conversation plastered all over the local paper?'

Sandra swallowed. 'I… Er… Ah. Well, I was out with Barry a couple of nights ago, and he was complaining it was a really slow news week, so I joked around saying it was a shame he couldn't fill it with a haunted house story, and he asked why not, and I said because Ginny wouldn't like it, and he asked what a haunted house had to do with you, so I told him. Just for a laugh, of course.' Her panicked babbling tailed off. 'To be fair, I'd had three red wines.'

Ginny fixed Sandra with her steady gaze. 'Did you know Barry was going to print this?'

'Absolutely not. It was only meant to be a passing conversation,' Sandra protested. 'Look, the story's mainly about the history of the textile mill and existing ghost rumours, and Barry was already interested in that stuff. Your experience just put a new slant on it and gave it substance. At least he hasn't printed your name.'

'No, but he might as well have. He says I run a bespoke cake business, and since I'm the only resident in the mill conversion who does…' Ginny sighed. 'You *know* I value my privacy.'

'Look on the bright side. If people are intrigued, you might get more orders.'

'Firstly, it's wedding season, so I can't handle any more orders. Secondly, I'm not sure it'll do my reputation much good. Who wants to trust the centrepiece of their big day, costing hundreds of pounds, to a woman who's mad enough to think she has a haunted kitchen?'

'Ah. Hadn't thought of that.' Sandra bit her lip.

'Any chance you could get that lummox of a boyfriend of yours to print a retraction?'

Sandra thought about it. 'There's nothing to retract, though, is there? The history of the mill is what it is. The rumours have always been there. You hear noises and you don't know what causes them.'

Ginny sighed. 'I suppose I'll just have to put up with odd looks for a while and hope everyone forgets about it. Maybe Barry could make that happen sooner by finding some *other* titbit of idiotic gossip.'

'I'll use my feminine wiles to see what I can do,' Sandra promised. 'Sorry, Ginny. I didn't think it would lead to this.'

'I know.' Ginny gave her an exasperated look. *Sandra never thinks after three glasses of red wine. She should be banned from the stuff!*

Ginny's morning did not improve. As she'd predicted, even though the article didn't mention her by name, locals knew who Barry had meant. She got curious looks from shop owners. An old schoolfriend stopped her in the street to jokingly ask if middle age was robbing her of her marbles. And when she finally got back to her flat, relieved to be safe in her own domain, a client who had put two and two together – not difficult, since she generally met prospective customers in her home so they could see her pristine kitchen for themselves – phoned to anxiously wonder whether her cake would be affected by malevolent spirits and bring bad luck to her wedding.

Crossly bolting down a sandwich, Ginny distracted herself the only way she knew how – by working.

The knock at the door mid-afternoon came at a most inconvenient time. Ginny's stockist had sent her yellow sugar roses at the last minute instead of her bride's very specific shade of pale mint green. To make up for it, they had also sent her a small bottle of edible dye free of charge. *How helpful.* Painting the tiny roses was painstaking work and time that she couldn't charge her bride for.

When she opened the door to find Barry standing there, her mood took another dive. 'Go away.'

She made to shut the door, but he jammed his foot in it.

'Ow!' he yelped.

'Serves you right.'

'I suppose it does. Sandra said you're upset. I came to apologise. Can I come in?'

'No.'

'Why?' He looked offended. That little-boy-lost look was how he twisted Sandra around his little finger.

'Partly because I'm working on something delicate and don't need you crashing around the place. But mainly because you took a private conversation and printed it in your blasted paper without asking permission.'

Barry looked sheepish. 'I had an empty page to fill in a hurry, and the story fell into my lap. Sandra *hinted* you wouldn't want anything to do with it, but I figured most of it was old news anyway, and your experiences *are* in the public interest.'

'It's in the public interest to know that one flat in the whole of Haven Bridge Mill has trouble with the occasional banging noise? Really?'

'How do you know it's just one flat? Have you asked the neighbours? I could do that for you.'

'What do you take me for? Yes, I've asked the neighbours and no, I don't want *you* annoying them. Look, if this is your roundabout way of getting an interview, forget it. Go and crawl back under your rock, Barry, or so help me… I have some very sharp implements in my kitchen, you know.'

'OK, I'll go. But I *am* sorry. It seemed pretty harmless to me.'

'Not to me,' Ginny snapped. 'Neither the disturbances nor having my private life splashed across that sorry excuse of a paper of yours.' She sighed. 'But apology accepted. I don't want to fall out with you. For Sandra's sake.'

Barry nodded and left, but five minutes later, there was another knock.

'Oh, for goodness' sake.' Ginny steamed to the door and yanked it open. 'I told you to go *away*!'

The two bewildered faces on her doorstep stared.

'Ah. Sorry. Thought you were someone else.'

'Ms Roberts?' The man with grey hair and glasses, maybe in his late forties, spoke. His companion, a much younger woman with a blonde ponytail and wide blue eyes, remained silent.

'Yes. Can I help?'

'I hope so. Or perhaps we can help you.' His voice was calm and pleasing. 'I'm Graham Crowe. This is Megan Jackson.'

He held out his hand and Ginny shook it, although she had no idea who they were or why she should.

'I'm sorry, but I'm in the middle of something.' Ginny indicated her apron. 'I don't buy anything on the doorstep.'

Graham Crowe smiled. It was a very nice smile. 'We're not selling, and this *is* important. If we could come in, we'd be happy to wait while you finish what you're doing. It'll be to your advantage, I hope.'

'Well, I…' Ginny wasn't in the habit of allowing strangers into her home, but she needed to get back to the flowers, and the two of them were standing there as though their feet were cemented to the hallway, showing no sign of budging. Besides, they didn't *look* like axe murderers. 'Fine.' She waved them into the open-plan flat and pointed to the sofa. 'Take a pew. And please, no talking till I'm done.'

Her visitors sat, neither moving nor speaking, for the twenty minutes it took her to finish. Ginny was impressed. They must really want whatever it was they wanted.

'OK. Done. Thanks for not interrupting.' She almost offered them tea, then distractedly remembered she had no idea why they were here.

Graham Crowe took her words as an invitation to come over and see what she was up to. 'That's intricate work.'

'Yeah. My suppliers let me down at the last minute. The bride wants mint green. They only had yellow.' She rubbed her tired eyes. *Rats. I need a cuppa myself, anyway*. 'Tea?'

'Thank you.'

With the tray in front of them in the lounge area, Ginny said impatiently, 'I appreciate I asked you not to talk, but now I need to know why you're here. If it's double-glazing, you can go and take a running…'

Graham Crowe chuckled. 'Not at all. I doubt you need it in a brand-new conversion like this. We're paranormal investigators, for want of a better title. Megan is, anyway. She's doing a PhD on the topic. I'm a historical researcher and writer…'

But Ginny had stopped listening at '*paranormal investigator*'. 'Then I'm sorry, but you've had a wasted journey, a wasted twenty minutes' wait, and you won't have time to drink your tea, because I'd like you to leave.' She felt duped, and she felt like an idiot for letting them in at all. Just because the man had forest-green eyes behind those cute glasses and a smile that made you trust him didn't mean she should have let down her guard. Still, who expected paranormal investigators to turn up on the doorstep? She stood to emphasise that she meant what she said. 'Did Barry send you?'

'Who? No.' Graham Crowe looked disappointed at the turn of events but not surprised. Presumably he got this reaction quite often. 'We saw a story in the *Haven Bridge Gazette* online and happened to be in Halifax working on something. We decided to come and see if you'd talk to us or if we could help.'

Ginny gaped at him. 'If you could *help*? You're going to perform an exorcism on a ghost that doesn't exist?' *I'll throttle Barry when I next see him.*

'We don't perform exorcisms.' His lips pursed at the idea.

'Look, I think we've got off on the wrong foot. The article –'

'– was unwarranted and nothing to do with me,' Ginny interrupted. 'I told a friend in the pub about odd noises, she told Barry Blabbermouth, and the next thing I know, it's plastered all over the local rag.' Her eyes narrowed. 'How did you know it was me?'

'It mentioned a cake business. You advertise on the internet. It wasn't hard.'

Which is exactly what I told Sandra.

Graham Crowe shrugged. 'Well, if you really want us to go…'

He and his assistant both stood – and then Megan opened her mouth for the first time.

'Have the noises stopped, Ms Roberts?'

'No, but –'

'So, you're still being troubled by them? Wondering what they are, where they come from? It must be unnerving. And expensive, being made to jump at the wrong icing moment or having cakes fall flat.'

'That actually only happened a couple of times. The paper exaggerated.'

'You've investigated the noises?'

'Of course I have! I only have neighbours on one side and below. It's not them. The flat on the other side and the one above aren't sold yet. The construction company checked and they can't find anything wrong. Besides, I get different types of bangs. Some sudden and loud. Some quieter. Occasional whisperings.'

The young woman's eyes grew wide. 'The article didn't mention *whisperings*.'

'Thank goodness for small mercies,' Ginny retorted. 'Well, if you wouldn't mind…'

Graham Crowe looked wistfully at his undrunk tea,

hesitated, then picked up his mug and gulped at it with an apologetic shrug. 'Not had a cuppa since this morning. Sorry.'

He looked so woebegone, Ginny relented. 'Three minutes to drink it, then you can take your weird professions and wild theories away with you.'

'I don't think you really understand what we do, Ms Roberts,' he said gently. 'Or may I call you Ginny?'

'No need, since we won't be getting acquainted.' *When I've finished throttling Barry, I may move onto Sandra.*

'We could solve *one* problem for you,' Megan piped up. 'You say there's no ghost, and I'm sure you're right.' She put on an innocent expression that Ginny didn't trust. 'But in our experience, local interest only escalates after an article like that. Right, Graham?'

'Hmm? Oh, er, yes. True,' he agreed, as though Megan had kicked him in the shins to elicit the correct response.

'If you want to nip it in the bud,' Megan went on, 'the best way might be to pursue the idea.'

'*Pursue* it?' Ginny looked askance at her.

'Allow Graham and me to do our thing for a day or so. When we confirm what your intuition and common sense has already told you – that there's nothing here – you can go back to your newspaper friend –'

'He's no friend of mine.'

'Acquaintance, then, and tell him just that. We'd be happy to confirm it in an interview for you. How does that sound?'

Ginny had to admit Megan had a point. It might stop those curious looks. The ridiculous phone calls from clients.

'OK. Have a seat and tell me what you do. *Briefly.*'

'I did a module at university on parapsychology,' Megan told her. 'Now I'm doing a PhD looking into pseudo–' She stopped. 'Basically, I'm looking into phenomena that might seem psychic or paranormal but aren't.'

'Like mine.'

'Depends. A lot of phenomena do turn out to be paranormal, or at least unexplained. I have equipment that can amplify sound, find cold spots, measure electromagnetic fluctuations, there's thermal imaging…'

Ginny suppressed a cynical sigh and turned to Graham Crowe. 'And you?'

'I'm just along for the ride. Megan digs up a lot of interesting stories. Some of them have a basis, some don't. I research the background of a place, the people who lived and died there, then try to piece it together with her findings. Sometimes I find a likely story behind the phenomena. Sometimes it just turns out to be an interesting human story. I write articles and books about local superstitions, legends, history. Sometimes I guest lecture.'

'What would your "help" entail?' Ginny asked.

'We'd have to spend time here, obviously. Megan needs to bring her equipment in and take readings. I can research from anywhere, but I prefer to do it *in situ*.'

'Spirits are often more accessible at night,' Megan chipped in. 'We'd need to stay over.'

'*What?*' Ginny squeaked. 'I'm not happy about having you here in the daytime – I work from home, after all – but having two strangers stay at night? I only have one small guest bedroom.'

'That's fine,' Graham rushed to reassure her. 'Megan stays up half the night anyway, monitoring her readings, so she'd be in here. I could crash in the spare room. We're not together, you know.'

Megan blushed and stared at her feet.

Hmmm, no, but I have a feeling she'd like you to be?

'I honestly don't think this flat is haunted,' Ginny insisted. 'Your being here would be too inconvenient. I'm sorry.'

'I understand. Look, here's my number.' He handed her a business card. 'We'll be in Halifax for a couple more days. If you change your mind, let us know.'

'I will. But I won't. If you know what I mean.'

She saw them out, watching as they headed down the corridor.

Shame. Graham Crowe has looks and *charm. I almost wish the flat* was *haunted!*

*

The following morning, Miss Moonshine greeted Ginny with a warm smile. 'Hello, dear. How are you today?'

'Fine, thanks, Miss Moonshine. I delivered another wedding cake this morning.'

'That would scare me to death, trying to get it there without any disasters.' Miss Moonshine walked over to the window, her biker boots stomping under a floral 1940s-style summer dress. 'It's a fine day for it, at least. A June wedding doesn't always guarantee sunshine in good old Yorkshire.'

'Indeed.' Ginny chuckled as Napoleon, Miss Moonshine's ever-present chihuahua, looked up from his basket to yap his agreement. 'Has anything exciting come in lately?'

Ginny was in the habit of popping into Miss Moonshine's Emporium every so often. The shop's shelves and tables and alcoves were heaped with all sorts of interesting things, and a strip of vintage ribbon or silk flowers from an old dress could add an unusual and unique touch to one of Ginny's cakes – steam-cleaned first, of course.

'Not much, I'm afraid. Spring-cleaning season's over now. I did put these on one side for you, though.' Miss Moonshine rummaged in a drawer, then placed two porcelain lovebirds on the old, scarred wooden counter. 'The glaze is cracked, but I think that adds to their charm.'

'Oh, yes.' Ginny lifted the birds and examined them. 'They're beautiful. I'm dealing with a couple who hate traditional toppers and think flowers are boring. These might be perfect.'

'Good. And are these any use?' Miss Moonshine pulled out a long double string of artificial pearls.

Ginny gasped. 'How *do* you do it? Are you magic or something? I have a pearl wedding anniversary cake booked for September. These are perfect. And they look so real.' She fingered the pearls. 'If I colour the fondant icing a delicate shade of ivory pink, these will pop out against it. How much?'

Miss Moonshine told her, and Ginny happily paid the small amount she was asked for. How the woman made any money was beyond her.

'I see you were in the news,' the old lady said as she wrapped the items in tissue paper.

Ginny made a face. 'Not my doing, I assure you. An innocent chat in the pub, and the next thing I know...' She shook her head. 'Would you believe, I had two paranormal investigators on my doorstep yesterday?'

'That *does* sound interesting,' Miss Moonshine said.

She filled the kettle and made tea so Ginny would tell her all about it. Ginny was happy to perch on a stool by the counter and do just that. Miss Moonshine inspired confidences, somehow.

When she'd finished her tale, the old shopkeeper asked, 'You don't believe your flat's haunted?'

'Of course not.' Ginny frowned. 'Sorry. Do *you* believe in ghosts?'

Miss Moonshine cocked her head to one side like a bird, the white hair piled on top of it bobbing. 'Let's say I like to keep an open mind. There's so much in this world we don't understand; so much that can't be seen by others.' She stroked Napoleon, lost in thought for a moment. 'You won't ask them to come back? The writer and his companion?'

'Why would I?'

'She had a point about putting a halt to the rumours. If there's nothing to it, and they tell Barry that, and he prints it – which he owes you – then that would be an end to it. No more funny looks in the street. No more gossip.'

'You may be right, but… Two strangers in my home 24/7, with equipment everywhere, while I try to work and eat and sleep? No thanks.'

Miss Moonshine nodded, then startled Ginny by saying, 'Wait there.' She dashed upstairs, her flimsy dress flapping around her thin legs.

'I *thought* I had this in the second-hand books section,' she said as she came back down, brandishing a book. 'The name rang a bell – Graham Crowe. He writes about different environments and why they might be haunted. I have one of his on Lancashire and this on Yorkshire.' Miss Moonshine turned to the contents page. 'There's a chapter on mills and factories. You might find it interesting.' She jabbed at the author photo on the back. 'I recognise him now. He pops in here sometimes when he passes through Haven Bridge. Rather good-looking, if I were several decades younger.' Her hazel eyes twinkled. 'Why don't you borrow it?'

'Oh no, I…' But Ginny knew it was easier not to argue. 'That's very kind. Thanks for the tea. And for these.' She lifted her packages. 'See you soon.'

Ginny walked home with a light step, enjoying the warm summer breeze. She was happy with the wedding cake that had elicited such delight upon delivery, happy with her small purchases, happy she'd had a chat with Miss Moonshine – and happy with her decision to ignore Graham Crowe and his sidekick.

But her resolve was eroded all the way home. First, there was the overly sympathetic look in the minimarket from an acquaintance in the queue. That same woman nudged her companion, whispering loudly. Then she got, 'Well, if it isn't Haven Bridge's haunted homeowner. Bet you wish you'd bought a plain old terraced house now, don't you?' and a wink from the greengrocer.

As she crossed the bridge over the river on the way back to her once-prized home, admiring the huge stone edifice of the textile mill and its giant chimneys, Ginny thought things couldn't get any worse… until her mobile phone rang as she reached the communal door.

'Ginny? It's Gabby.'

Ginny racked her brain. *Gabby. Brunette. August wedding. Nature theme. Chocolate leaves and red berries and gold-sprayed twigs.*

'Hi, Gabby. What can I do for you?' *Please tell me you haven't changed your mind about which layers you want. Again.* 'I definitely think you should stick with fruitcake for the bottom layer to keep, the chocolate truffle sponge for the middle layer and red velvet for the top layer.'

'It's not that,' Gabby said. But Ginny's relief was short-lived. 'Jez's mother's worrying about your kitchen.'

'Gabby, you visited my home. My kitchen's state-of-the-art, I'm all registered, and it complies with regulations. I have certificates to prove it.'

'That's not the problem,' Gabby said. 'She read the article in the local paper.'

Uh-oh.

'And she was chatting with someone she knows who feels uneasy about it too.'

That would be the call I took yesterday.

'Gabby, that article had nothing to do with me. My home is not haunted. Even if it were, I don't see how it would affect your wedding cake.' Ginny struggled to keep exasperation out of her voice. 'There's been the odd banging door, that's all. So, are we good?'

'I'll speak to Jez's mother again.'

'You do that. Bye.' Ginny clicked off before she could blow a gasket.

Inside her flat, she needed a strong drink, never mind a cuppa. Allowing herself a shot of whiskey...*At three o'clock in the afternoon, Ginny? Seriously?*...she sank onto her sofa. Stupid bloomin' people. Stupid bloomin' Barry. She'd have no business left at this rate.

She jumped out of her skin as a loud bang shook through her ceiling.

OK, OK, I give in! She plucked the card from the coffee table, picked up her phone and dialled. 'Graham Crowe? Ginny Roberts here.'

*

Ginny looked around her once-peaceful home in dismay. Graham and Megan hadn't wasted any time. Two hours after she'd called, they'd turned up at her door, Graham claiming they'd more or less finished in Halifax anyway and that he was pleased she'd had a change of heart. And now her lounge area was cluttered with electronic equipment, boxes, files and laptops, and the sofa was piled with a sleeping bag and pillows belonging to Megan. Her small guest room had the same for Graham, who was insistent he wouldn't use her bedding and thereby cause her extra laundry.

'We do this all the time,' he told her. 'We travel prepared. Can't catch a ghost by staying in a nearby hotel, can we?'

He winked at Megan, who blushed.

Oh no. She really does have a crush on him. And he doesn't seem to have a clue.

When Ginny asked what they would like to eat, Graham was adamant. 'Takeaway is on us. Any suggestions?'

'The Mediterranean restaurant does takeaway, and the food's really nice.'

'Mediterranean it is, then.'

Opening a bottle of wine was a necessity – now the flurry of their arrival and setting up was over, the atmosphere had become stilted and awkward.

'What's all this for, then?' Ginny asked valiantly, wishing she hadn't as Megan spent the next twenty minutes enthusiastically explaining equipment that might catch otherworldly noise or movement or ectoplasmic something-or-other, until Ginny's head spun.

Graham gave her a sympathetic look. 'Don't worry. It's a bit beyond me, too.' When Ginny looked surprised, he said, 'I understand the principles, but it's not really my area.'

The arrival of the food was a relief, and they tucked in happily… until a loud bang made them all jump.

Megan's eyes were sharp. 'Is that the sort of thing?'

'Yes.' Ginny shrugged. 'Probably just a door.'

'But it came from overhead, and you said that flat's empty. Could someone be viewing the flat?'

'Bit late for that,' Ginny pointed out. "It's eight-thirty. I can't imagine the agents would work so late.'

Megan turned to Graham. 'We should ask the estate agent if we can take a look around up there.'

Ginny panicked. 'I'd rather you didn't. I don't want people knowing you're staying here or why.'

Graham nodded. 'There are ways around that.'

Two more bangs completed the evening's entertainment, but Ginny put paid to their interest in the final one.

'That's only my bathroom door banging closed. It does that if I leave the window open and a breeze blows up.'

Graham looked as disappointed as Megan, and Ginny wanted to put her head in her hands.

What have I done? All this so that wretched Barry will print something to stop people giving me funny looks?

'Well, if you don't mind, I need my bed,' she murmured. 'Goodnight.'

Megan waved a distracted hand, but Graham followed her into the hall.

'Is everything OK?'

'Fine. I just need an early night.'

He gave her a look that told her he knew she was escaping. 'I don't want you to feel uncomfortable in your own home, Ginny.'

His eyes were calm. Genuine. She felt she could be honest with him – so she was.

'Well, I do feel uncomfortable, but there's nothing you can do about it.' She sighed. 'Look, if you find a logical solution to this, I'll be happy – and not remotely surprised. If you find a supernatural solution, I'll eat my hat. And if you don't find anything at all, then I win anyway, because Barry's follow-up will have to say so, and my clients might stop phoning me about demonic energies wheedling their way into their wedding cakes.'

Graham's eyes widened. 'That's actually happened?'

'Two so far. Unbelievable – and the only reason you're here.'

He smiled in sympathy. 'Hopefully we can fix it for you.'

'Knock yourself out.'

Settled in bed, Ginny worried she'd come across as rude, or at least less than welcoming, so she reached for something to take her mind off it. Several books teetered next to the lamp, the top one being that day's acquisition – Graham Crowe's volume of Yorkshire phenomena, hauntings and the like.

'Seems I can't escape him,' she muttered. 'Even when he's at the other end of the flat.'

And he'll be sleeping on the other side of that wall tonight.

Ginny was surprised at how unsettled that made her feel.

Hmmph. Just my luck that the first bloke to stay in this flat since I moved in is someone like Graham Crowe, with his strange line of work and his besotted PhD companion in tow.

*

Ginny woke to a loud morning clatter from her resident whatever-it-was, with Graham Crowe's book on the duvet beside her. Had she really fallen asleep reading that thing?

Yes, she had. And it hadn't been the nonsense she'd expected. Graham Crowe, it turned out, was a serious writer who must do vast swathes of historical research. He would set out on a particular path due to a rumour he'd heard or one of Megan's investigations or a legend that took his eye, but once he was on that path, he made a thorough job of exploring it, and he made the journey very compelling for the reader.

Ginny had read his chapter on Yorkshire mills and was left with the feeling that if she did believe in ghosts – which of course she didn't – it wouldn't surprise her that old buildings like hers, whether still in ruins or renovated into smart homes, were the perfect place for an otherworldly being to reside. Poor working conditions and pay, callous owners and managers, casual cruelty, terrible accidents… A disgruntled ghost or angry poltergeist unable to 'cross over' might well choose to make a nuisance of itself there.

Bleary-eyed and in need of coffee, she staggered into the main room, remembering too late about Megan and Graham.

Megan wasn't around, but Graham was.

Great. My hair's a mess and I'm wearing the unicorn pyjamas that were too big for my teenage niece and somehow got donated to me.

'Cute,' Graham observed, nodding at her attire before handing her a mug of coffee. 'I hope you don't mind us helping ourselves?'

'Not at all. Thanks.' She sipped. *He makes good coffee. I like him more and more.*

'What's on your schedule today?' he asked.

'A retro seventies Black Forest gâteau for someone's sixtieth tomorrow night,' she told him, gulping down more coffee. 'Sponges today. Decorating tomorrow.'

'Sounds good.'

'Hope so. But the sponges need to be light, so I don't want either you or Megan blundering around while I'm baking.'

'No worries. I'll be out, researching. Besides, it's your ghost you need to worry about, isn't it?'

He said it so light-heartedly, she gave him a surprised look. 'If I didn't know better, I'd say you were a ghosthunter who doesn't believe in ghosts.'

Graham shrugged. 'I keep an open mind. I do believe in phenomena. And I do believe in other people's belief in ghosts.'

'Hmmm. Interesting.'

'That's me. An enigma waiting to be unwrapped.'

He winked, and Ginny dove into her coffee, not trusting herself to look him in the eye.

'Yes, well. Shower. Dressed. Cake,' she mumbled, turning.

'I think Megan's in the shower.'

'Wonderful.'

*

Ginny's day passed without incident. Her sponges turned out perfectly. Graham was out all day, researching in the Haven Bridge library. Megan spent her time fiddling with machinery, making notes and flicking through specialist magazines with bewildering subject matter. She looked fed up – hardly surprising, since nothing in the way of a ghostly manifestation had taken place all day.

Taking pity on Megan for her boredom and Graham for

the way he removed his glasses and pinched the bridge of his nose when he returned, Ginny brought them homemade white chocolate and raspberry muffins with a tray of afternoon tea.

'You're a baking angel,' Graham said as he bit into one. 'This is glorious.'

Megan gave Ginny a scowl before saying, 'We've heard nothing since first thing this morning. This is a wash-out, Graham. We should go back to Halifax and finish off there.'

'Not yet,' he said calmly, catching crumbs on his plate.

'How did you get on with your research today?' Ginny asked him.

'Oh, same old story. Textile mills had long hours and poor conditions. There were industrial accidents. One just a girl of twelve. The poor girl's hair came loose from its fastenings and got caught in the…'

Ginny held up her hands. 'Please, I don't want to know.'

'Understandable. Sorry.'

'I read some of your Yorkshire book last night,' Ginny admitted, to make up for her squeamish response. When he raised an eyebrow, she added hastily, 'It was foisted on me.'

He smiled. 'Of course. And?'

'It was fascinating,' she said grudgingly.

'High praise, indeed. Thank you. I went to the estate agent today.'

'You didn't tell them you were investigating ghosts?'

'No. I pretended to be a prospective buyer and spoke to the young man – Sam – who's dealing with those two flats. When I asked if he'd had many viewings recently, he said not, so that can't be what's causing your problem. He seemed a bit distracted when I asked for a viewing myself. Said he was too busy tomorrow morning, but he finally agreed to show me both tomorrow afternoon.'

'We can't go waltzing in there with our equipment if the

agent's with us,' Megan grumbled. 'Not if Ginny won't let us *say* anything.'

'No, but we can get a feel for the spaces.'

'I can't just sit around waiting for random noises, Graham,' she went on. 'I have my own work to do. I need to justify my trips, my time. *You* get something out of your research on this, no matter what – an interesting chapter for a book, maybe. I get nothing unless I prove something to marry up with my research.'

Graham looked suitably chastised. 'Sorry, Meg. Another twenty-four hours?'

Megan nodded grudgingly and turned to Ginny. 'Nothing happened during the day today. Is that usual?'

'The noises are mainly in the early mornings and the evenings. That's why I thought it was the neighbours at first – people coming and going to work, opening and closing doors, water pipes being used, the heating coming on and off. But if that was the case, I would have heard them long before now. And the noise doesn't come from their direction.'

'Noise carries,' Megan said as though to a child. 'You haven't kept a record?'

Tired of her attitude, Ginny said, 'It never occurred to me. I didn't know I'd have *experts* interrogating me about it.' She gesticulated at the mess in the living room.

Graham shot Megan a cautioning look.

'Sorry,' Megan said. 'I have a headache.'

Ginny berated herself for how ungrateful she must have sounded. Ever since their arrival, she'd taken the attitude that they were imposing their presence on her against her will. But it occurred to her now that she was getting their time and efforts for free.

'I'm sorry, too,' she said. 'I suppose some people charge for this sort of thing?'

'Yes, if that's how they earn their living,' Graham answered. 'In our case, even if we believe there's something here, we're ill-equipped to solve it. In that sense, we're not much use to you.' He grinned. 'We're happy to take advantage of you for our own research purposes, though.'

Well, he's nothing if not honest.

'Then thank you for what you're doing.' Ginny frowned. 'And I'm sorry if you feel you're wasting your time. To be honest, the noises have been less frequent since you arrived.'

'Or since the article in the paper?' Graham mused.

'Ha! You're not suggesting the ghost reads the *Haven Bridge Gazette*, surely?'

*

Unable to countenance another takeaway, Ginny cooked a salmon pasta dish, but halfway through, Megan pushed her plate away.

'I'm sorry. I can't eat this. I don't feel well.'

'Migraine?' Graham asked her, concerned.

'Yeah.'

She did look awful, Ginny thought – pale, her face pinched. A little green around the gills.

'Do you need to lie down?' Graham asked. 'Take my room. I'll stay on the sofa tonight.'

'What about the equipment?'

'I'll keep an eye on it.'

Too ill to argue, Megan nodded miserably and stood.

Graham picked up her holdall. 'I'll bring this through and get my stuff.'

Five minutes later, he was back.

'Does she get them often?' Ginny asked.

'Often enough. She won't be out here again tonight.' He gave her an apologetic look. 'And she may be sick, I'm afraid.'

'Can't be helped. Poor thing.' Ginny hadn't particularly taken to Megan, but she wouldn't wish regular migraines on anyone.

Graham cleared the plates and loaded the dishwasher. When they had mugs of tea in front of them in the lounge, he asked, 'How long have you lived here?'

'Six months. I moved here after my divorce. The kids are grown up – one in London, the other in Edinburgh. And before you start feeling sorry for me, so far I've had no trace of empty nest syndrome whatsoever. I love speaking with my kids and I see them as much as possible, but this is *my* time. Hence the new flat. The new business.'

'Have you always lived in Haven Bridge?'

'No. I was brought up here and had a hankering to come back. I saw this flat and decided it would be perfect.'

Graham gazed around the open-plan room. 'It is gorgeous. Spacious, with the high ceilings, but not cavernous. And that exposed stone wall over there gives a sense of the history of the building.' He walked over to the window to look out over the river. 'The view's terrific.'

'Yeah. I fell in love with it the minute I walked in. And because it was newly converted, I got to pick my own fixtures and fittings. Everything's to my specifications – a catering kitchen that conforms to standards.'

'Did you have a cake business when you were married?'

Ginny laughed. 'Not at all! I was a graphic designer. But my husband was away for work a lot – one of the reasons we grew apart, I suppose – and I took up baking and cake-decorating as a hobby. Friends and neighbours started to ask me to make their occasion cakes. When I was thinking about what to do after the divorce, I decided I wanted a completely new start – new place, new job.' She bit her lip, realising she was talking about herself too much. 'How about you?'

'I'm divorced, too. I'm afraid I'm probably the equivalent

of your ex-husband – my wife complained that I was away for work too often. Even when I wasn't, I'd get caught up in my research, my projects, to the exclusion of all else sometimes. At least, that's what Harriet told me when she booted me out. And she got fed up with my weird ideas. When we first got married, I was a straightforward history buff, but as you've gathered, my interests have expanded over the years. She didn't take to my "eccentricities", as she put it on her more polite days.' He shrugged. 'My kids always thought my work was cool, though. Still do.'

'That's…'

Ginny stopped as Graham put a finger to his lips. He crept from the sofa to Megan's equipment, staring at the screens intently. Then Ginny heard what he'd heard – a voice, so faint she could barely tell.

Crikey, he's got good hearing.

'It'll be someone out in the corridor, I bet,' Ginny decided. A wailing sound made her jump. 'But that's a new one.' Her eyes darted to the machinery.

'It is, but it's not your wandering spirit. It's Megan in the bathroom. Sounds like she's at the throwing up stage.'

'Poor Megan. I should go and see to her.'

'No. Let me.'

When he returned, he told her, 'She's settled back in bed with a cold flannel. I took her the bucket from the bathroom cupboard. I hope that's OK.'

'Of course.' *Does he often tend to Megan like this? It's rather familiar, isn't it?* 'How long have you two worked together?'

'Nearly a year. She propositioned me, so to speak, after she'd started her PhD – she said she admired my work, and she figured we'd complement each other with our different skills.'

'You spend a lot of time together?'

'Yes, we do.' He frowned as he read her expression. 'But there's nothing going on between us.'

Emboldened by the wine they'd had with dinner, Ginny said softly, 'You know she'd like there to be, right?'

'What?' Graham looked genuinely taken aback. 'No, it's nothing like that.'

'I'm not trying to stir up trouble, Graham. Honest. But I've seen the way she looks at you. She's hoping you'll make a move. I've also seen the way she looks at me. She's worried you fancy me, even though you don't.'

A loaded silence hung between them, until he said, 'Who says I don't?'

Does he? Ginny's heart thudded against her ribcage. 'What about Megan?'

'I'm twenty-five years older than her.' Graham's bewildered expression was endearing. 'I have grey hair, for crying out loud!'

Ginny gave him a pitying smile. 'Have you never heard the expression "silver fox"?'

'What?'

'Oh dear. You really have spent too much time in the library with your nose in old documents, haven't you? For your information, many women – younger women included – find grey hair and a slightly weathered face quite a turn-on.'

'Really?' He grinned. 'There's hope for me yet, then?'

'Indeed.'

'How about you?'

'Oh, I doubt it.' Ginny fingered the silvering strands near her ears, knowing the semi-permanent dye she favoured was no longer adequate and well aware that some of her assets were beginning to head south. And then there were the care lines at her eyes and mouth, courtesy of twenty-odd years of bringing up kids. 'I'm afraid "silver vixen" doesn't seem to apply the same way to women, more's the pity.'

'I wouldn't say that. But what I meant was, do you find that kind of man attractive?' Graham asked. 'A silver fox?'

'Oh! Well, I haven't much choice at my age, have I?' Ginny hesitated. 'Are you asking if I find *you* attractive?'

'I suppose so.' He moved closer.

Oh dear. This wasn't the plan at all.

Graham's lips lightly brushed hers… but then Megan's difficulties came back into earshot.

He disappeared again, and by the time he returned, Ginny assumed their tiny moment of madness was over.

But Graham had other ideas. 'You didn't answer my question.'

'Graham, we just almost kissed. I'm not in the habit of kissing men I don't find attractive.' She rolled her eyes. 'Not that I've had much practice in recent years, other than my husband. I'll discount his overzealous boss at a Christmas party once. Ugh.'

'Same.'

'You kissed your wife's boss at a Christmas party?'

'Very funny.'

This time when he kissed her, they were mercifully uninterrupted by retching noises.

When they broke it off, he touched the blue-green stone at her throat. 'This is pretty. What is it?'

'Amazonite. I bought it when I first moved here. Miss Moonshine said it would be perfect for a fresh start.'

'The emporium? I've been in there a few times. In fact, I was there this afternoon. It's amazing, isn't it? I love the building – the old stone is so handsome, and the roses climbing over the archway lead you through, drawing you in like magic. And once you're inside? I've never seen so much of… well, of everything. I could spend all day in there.'

So, we do have something in common after all.

Ginny smiled and kissed him again.

*

Miss Moonshine looked up as Ginny entered the emporium. 'I'm glad you popped in, dear. I have something for you.'

Miss Moonshine had gone for a totally different look today and wore a pretty vintage lace blouse over jeans.

Anticipating something unusual for one of her cake creations, Ginny was nonplussed when Miss Moonshine handed her a bunch of something dried and gnarled, bound with thin twine.

'What is it?'

'It's sage for smudging. You light the end until it smokes, then you waft it around every corner of your flat. It dispels negative energies. Might be helpful after your guests have gone, especially if you haven't enjoyed having them there.'

Startled, Ginny wondered how Miss Moonshine knew that Graham and Megan were now staying with her. She hadn't told a soul – not even Sandra, lest Barry should broadcast the information via his paper. And she trusted Graham not to have said anything on his visit to the emporium the previous day.

She stared at the sage. Although she was unnerved by Megan and her equipment, Ginny wouldn't say that Graham's presence brought negative energy. Quite the opposite, in fact. There had certainly been no negative energy during their kisses last night!

'I got it from a shamanic practitioner here in town,' Miss Moonshine added, as though that explained things.

'Uh-huh.' Ginny gave Napoleon a look as if to say, *'You know your owner's batty, right?'*

Miss Moonshine shot her a knowing smile. 'How's the research going? Any joy?'

'Oh, the usual – textile mills weren't the nicest places, so Graham reckons there could be any number of reasons for a manifestation. I don't believe that sort of guff, of course. But there were a few nasty accidents over the years, apparently.'

'Yes. I had friends who worked there,' Miss Moonshine murmured.

Ginny frowned. 'But that place hasn't operated as a mill for decades.'

'I'm very old, Ginny.' Miss Moonshine's eyes went distant. 'So many memories over so many years.'

Perhaps the old dear ought to take a leaf out of Napoleon's book and have a nap, bless her. I'd better leave her to it. 'How much for the sage?'

'No charge, unless you feel it does something for your flat.'

'Oh. Well. Thank you.'

Miss Moonshine came out of her reverie. 'Graham Crowe was upstairs in my second-hand book section yesterday, looking for something useful to help you out. It's good of him, isn't it?'

'I suppose so.'

'Handsome, too, with those gorgeous green eyes. About your age, I reckon.'

Ginny couldn't help but smile. 'You're not matchmaking, are you, Miss Moonshine? I haven't been rid of my last bloke for long. I'm not looking for another yet.'

Miss Moonshine stroked Napoleon absentmindedly. 'We don't always get to choose when people turn up in our lives.'

'It's his *reason* for turning up that bothers me,' Ginny said. 'I don't believe in half of what he writes about.'

'I've seen a lot over the years, dear – enough to know that opposites attract. Not just in looks and interests, but in beliefs as well.' The old lady cocked her head to one side. 'I see you still wear your amazonite. The one you bought for your new beginning here in Haven Bridge.'

'Yes. I've been here six months now, though.'

'It doesn't only have to be for a new place. It can be for other new beginnings.' Miss Moonshine made no effort to hide her heavy-handed hinting. 'And it can give you faith in the choices you make. Remember that.'

Ginny sighed with relief when another customer entered the shop. *Off the hook.* 'Well, goodbye. Thanks for the sage.' *I think.*

*

Megan remained in bed all morning and into the afternoon. With Graham at his laptop, quiet as a mouse, Ginny spent the afternoon putting together the Black Forest gâteau.

'All done.'

Graham came over to admire the three-layered concoction topped with cherries and piped cream. 'Wow! You'll slap my hand away if I try to dip a finger in the cream, right?'

Ginny laughed. 'Yes, but don't worry, I made you a little one of your own. And one for Megan, of course,' she added hastily, reaching under the counter to lift up two mini versions.

'You are my idea of the perfect companion,' Graham said without thinking, making them both shuffle with embarrassment. 'I'll save it till I come back from viewing the flats.'

'And I need to get this to my client. Reconvene for a cuppa after?'

*

Later, drinking tea, Ginny asked Graham, 'So? How were the viewings?'

Megan had forced herself out of bed and was attempting peppermint tea, looking wan. Her gâteau was understandably rejected.

Graham, however, tucked into his with gusto. 'This is out of this world.'

Megan glared in Ginny's direction.

'Interesting,' Graham told them, oblivious to the atmosphere.

'The flat to the side' – he waved vaguely at the wall – 'was as I'd expected. Bare. Not fully fitted out yet. Cheerless, until it finds its owner. The one upstairs, though?' He paused as he bit into his cake and savoured it. 'It had a different feel, somehow.'

Megan perked up. 'What kind of feel? I wish we could take our equipment up there.' She shot another glare in Ginny's direction, this time presumably less about Ginny taking up Graham's attention and more about her insistence that nobody should know she had paranormal experts on the case.

'Not that kind of feel,' Graham said, making Megan's face fall. He turned to Ginny to explain. 'I don't always subscribe to the things we investigate, but I do sometimes feel there's something "off" about a place. Something otherworldly. This wasn't like that, though.'

'In what way?'

'The windows were wide open. When I asked the estate agent why, he said he was taking the opportunity to air it out. But he hadn't done the same with the flat on this floor.'

Megan curled her lip. 'That's it? Open windows?'

Graham shrugged. 'I can't explain it. Only that one flat felt different to the other.'

'We're wasting our time,' Megan grumbled.

'Very probably. But we'll stay a couple more nights, I think.'

'*What?*' Megan looked seriously unimpressed at that idea.

Ginny gave him a sharp look, too. Why was he bothered about staying so much longer than planned?

Or did her gut know the answer to that already?

*

The following morning, Sandra was on the phone before Ginny had the chance to get to her first and vent her spleen.

'I know, I know. I'm sorry, Ginny. Nothing to do with me, I promise.'

Ginny closed her eyes in despair – and to avoid looking at the new article in the paper, in which Barry told the citizenry of Haven Bridge that she now had ghosthunters staying in her flat.

'I've a good mind to take this paper and shove it –'

'I told him you wouldn't like it,' Sandra said defensively.

'That's an understatement. Apparently, I'm being *menaced* by my ghost. Apparently, I'm *terrified*.' Ginny blew out a breath. 'How did Barry know they're here?'

'He spotted Mr Crowe going into the library and recognised him from the cover of a book he'd borrowed from Miss Moonshine a while ago. Then he asked Mrs Dawlish the librarian, and she said Mr Crowe had been there for hours looking at the old mill archives, and Barry began to wonder. So, he staked out the entrance to your building and saw him coming and going.'

'He had no right, Sandra.'

'It's his job.'

'What about *my* job? I had two customers on the verge of cancelling after Barry's first article. What'll happen after this one?'

'Really?' Sandra sounded shocked and upset. 'I had no idea.'

'Yes, well, perhaps you could point it out to Barry. And tell him I expect a full backpedalling from him the minute my "ghosthunters" agree there's nothing here and leave – which will have to be sooner rather than later now.'

'I'll tell him. I'm really sorry, Ginny.'

'Yeah. Me too.'

And not only because of the damned article. Now I have to tell Graham I want him out as soon as possible. And it turns out I kind of liked having him around.

*

Ginny tried to hide her sadness later that day as she said, 'Graham, you have to leave.'

He skim-read the article. 'I thought the idea was for us to disprove this?'

'We have, haven't we?' Megan said sulkily. 'Or we're getting nowhere, which amounts to the same thing.'

Graham looked torn.

'Megan's right,' Ginny said gently. 'All you've heard is a few household noises. You've no readings to speak of.'

'The least we can do is to see your favourite reporter tomorrow before we go,' Graham said. 'We'll tell him we found nothing and insist he prints that.'

'Hardly our job,' Megan complained.

'I'll cook,' Ginny offered, hoping that good food would improve the atmosphere.

She put together a lamb tagine and couscous, which Graham complimented several times.

Clearly the way to a man's heart is *through his stomach, after all.*

After dinner, Megan fiddled with her equipment. 'Nothing.'

Graham stared at her. 'You're right.'

'Of course I'm right.'

'No, I mean there's been nothing *at all* today. Not one single noise. I hadn't realised that until now. There's always been *something*.'

'Maybe the ghost read Barry's article and decided it'd better scarper, quaking in its boots at the thought you might bring in an exorcist,' Ginny quipped.

Megan narrowed her eyes at her, but Graham just laughed. 'Maybe.'

*

When he came back from their interview with Barry the next day, Graham greeted Ginny with, 'Do you want the good news or the bad news?'

'Where's Megan?' she asked.

'She fancied a wander around town. And she didn't want to hear the story all over again.'

Or she didn't want to be here as we said our goodbyes? 'Well, the good news first, obviously.'

'Barry's going to print a new article saying there are no ghosts in this building.'

'Great!' Relief flooded Ginny's system. She'd taken a second call from one of her nervous brides already. 'So, why is there any bad news?'

'We found out the source of the noises. Well, Barry did.'

'And that's not good?'

'Not if someone lost their job. Remember I told you that Sam, the young estate agent, had been odd about me viewing the flats?'

'Yes.'

'It turns out he's been squatting in the one above you for the past month.'

'*What?* But how on earth did he manage? Surely there's no electricity or water yet? How did he cook? What if he'd been seen?'

'If he was seen, he could say he was checking on the flat. There is electricity – they need lights for showing clients on a dull day – but he didn't dare use it in case it was spotted on the meter readings. It's midsummer, so he didn't need the lights, and he got his meals from takeaways, which is why the windows were wide open when I went, in case any smells lingered. And he didn't want anyone to view in the mornings because he needed time to move his stuff back into his car. You're right about no water, so he showered at the gym. The noises were mostly mornings and evenings because he was at work during the day. The reason for doors banging was because he had the windows open when he was there. The occasional voice or whispering? If he was on the phone. He didn't realise the noise would carry so much, but there are no carpets or rugs yet to dull the impact. When he saw the first article Barry wrote, he shrugged it off and tried harder to be quiet, hence fewer incidents once we arrived. But when he read the second article yesterday, he recognised the photo of me from my viewing and panicked. It was getting too risky, so he left – which is why we heard nothing after yesterday morning.'

'But his employer found out and fired him?'

'Yes. Barry was investigating, too, and he tried to view the flats, but Sam knew who he was and tried to put him off. Barry peered into his car outside, saw his stuff in the back – sleeping bag and whatnot – and went back in to ask him about it.'

'That Barry's like a bull in a china shop!'

'To be fair, he thought the lad was alone, but the boss was in the back office and overheard.'

'So Barry effectively got him fired?'

Graham shrugged. 'Sam wasn't just squatting, Ginny – although that's bad enough. He was deliberately discouraging viewings so he could stay longer.'

'But why did he need to camp out there, anyway?'

'His girlfriend lives in Skipton and he'd got a new job there, due to start next month. They've rented a flat together, but the lease doesn't start yet and his old lease here had run out. He had the bright idea of bridging the gap by using the flat above you without anyone knowing, to save money on temporary accommodation.'

'But where will he live now?' Ginny asked, dismayed.

'His girlfriend's parents have taken pity on him and agreed to put him up. They feel sorry for him – the reason he was so keen on saving money was because he wanted to buy an engagement ring.'

'Oh, the poor boy. What about his new job? Will getting fired affect that?'

'It *would* have done. His current employer had given him a reference, so according to Barry, they felt obliged to inform Sam's new employer in Skipton about all this.' Graham smiled. 'But a certain someone found out about it and stepped in on the young man's behalf – an old lady who says she's seen plenty of young people make unwise choices over the years and feels that everyone deserves a second chance.'

Ginny grinned. 'Miss Moonshine, by any chance?'

'You got it.'

'I don't know what Haven Bridge would do without that woman!' Ginny sighed. 'You know, I'm almost disappointed. I didn't believe in all that paranormal stuff, but with you here, I'd begun to think there might be something in it. Turns out there's no real story here, though, is there?'

Graham held her gaze, his own that cool green she liked so much. 'No, there's no story here.' He hesitated, then pointed between them. 'But there *is* a story here, isn't there? You and me? Or there could be, if we choose to write it?'

Ginny's pulse began a slow, strong thrum in her veins. 'You don't want to be tied down, Graham. You travel around.'

'I'd like to do a bit less of that. A bit more research and writing. Besides, you're enjoying your newfound freedom. We don't want to be under each other's feet. But we *could* see how it goes, couldn't we?'

'You need to let Megan down gently.'

'I will. Telling her I don't want to travel around so much is the perfect excuse. I honestly didn't realise how she felt, Ginny, or I would have done something about it sooner.' He lifted her chin. 'I'm more interested in how *you* feel.'

Ginny touched the amazonite at her throat. '*It can give you faith in the choices you make*,' Miss Moonshine had told her.

'I'm willing to give it a go, if you are,' she murmured.

His face lit up, and then his lips were on hers for a long kiss that held promise and possibilities.

'You don't care about my weird ideas and eccentricities?' he asked her.

'Opposites attract,' she echoed Miss Moonshine. 'You don't mind my line of work either?'

'Your line of work, I can happily live with.' Graham smiled. 'Do you have any cake to go with a cuppa? I'm starving!'

As a child, Helen Pollard had a vivid imagination fuelled by her love of reading (long past her bedtime!) so she started to create her own stories in a notebook. Now a best-selling author of contemporary romance, she believes that good characterisation is the key to a successful book and loves infusing her writing with humour and heart. Helen is a member of the Romantic Novelists' Association and the Society of Authors. You can find more about Helen's books on Amazon.

amazon.co.uk/Helen-Pollard/e/B00O2E0BRC

I Shall Wear Purple

By Melinda Hammond

Chapter One

Haven Bridge 1998

It was the Art Deco tea set that stopped him in his tracks. Clarice Cliff. He had first seen that geometric pattern on the table at Prospect View: cups, saucers, plates, all covered in the same bold orange and yellow shapes. Jeannie had registered his look of surprise and been defiant.

'It's not new, and maybe it is a bit garish for a funeral tea, but I like the colours. It's my own little rebellion against living here amongst these dark, satanic mills.'

Forty years on, most of the mills were gone, smoke in the valley was a thing of the past and many of the sandstone houses, having been cleaned of their sooty coating, glowed a warm honey-gold on summer days like this.

'I am so sorry if I kept you waiting.'

He jumped and turned to see a small lady at his side. He couldn't determine her age and, in his younger days, he would have called her a hippy, with her colourful, slightly exotic clothes. Her white-blonde hair was cut short, giving her dainty features an elfin look, enhanced by the bird-bright eyes that twinkled with merriment.

'I usually open up much earlier.' She gave him an engaging smile. 'But I'm here now, so won't you come inside?'

'Erm, yes, thank you.' He'd only been whiling away time, window shopping, but it seemed churlish to walk away now. He looked at the sign above the door. Miss Moonshine's Wonderful Emporium. He thought, but couldn't be sure, that the shop had been there when he was a boy.

'You were looking at the tea service,' she said, preceding him into the cool, shadowed interior. 'There wasn't room for all of it in the window, so the rest is displayed over there.'

She pointed to the small gate-leg table against the wall. It was covered with bright crockery, the vivid colours contrasting strongly with the polished mahogany. He went over and picked up one of the plates, turning it over in his hands. He could have sworn it was the very same set. The porcelain felt cool against his fingers. So fragile, delicate, and yet it must be strong as well as beautiful. Like Jeannie.

They had been childhood sweethearts, growing up on the hills above Haven Bridge. Jeannie's mother died when she was twelve and she hadn't flinched from looking after her father while keeping up with her schoolwork. She was the star pupil, passing her exams seemingly without effort, while Dan had always struggled to get the grades he needed. But where he had achieved his dream of becoming a vet, Jeannie's father had refused to let her go to university. Girls didn't need an education, he'd said. Girls needed only to know how to keep a nice house for their husband.

'You look familiar. Do you live in Haven Bridge?' The shopkeeper's soft voice dragged his attention back to the present.

'No, just passing through.' Her eyes were fixed on him and something in her kindly smile encouraged him to say more. 'I live in Bakewell now, but I grew up in Cragg Royd. Lived there until I went off to university.'

He felt a tiny glow of pride. Local boy made good. But there was a tinge of dissatisfaction, too, because by the time he went off to university Jeannie had been working for three years at Grassholme Mill. They'd talked of getting married, but they knew that was impossible until he was working, and Jeannie wouldn't let him give up his dream.

'You go off and become a vet, Dan, and when you've made your fortune you can come back and marry me!'

They had written, of course, but his life in Edinburgh was a world away from Haven Bridge. His visits home became more infrequent and the letters had dwindled away, the very last of them coming from Jeannie, telling him she was getting married. After that he spent the vacations with friends, returning home only for a few days at Christmas to see his family. By the time he'd finished his six years of study and had letters after his name, Jeannie had been married for three years and was expecting her second baby.

Dan carefully replaced the plate on the table. Time to go. He could do without these old memories. The shopkeeper caught his eye as he made for the door.

'Thank you, sir. Do call again.'

He nodded but he wouldn't be coming back.

*

On waking, Jeannie's first thought was 'I'm still at The Rowans.'

It was the same every morning. Her gaze moved down over the pale green walls to the boxy wardrobe and chest of drawers. Institution furniture.

She looked around her room, thinking it was very like Sam's first halls of residence. That had been a brand-new building, the rent far higher than a shared flat in one of the converted houses that littered the university town, but Bill hadn't minded paying the extra. Nothing was too good for his son, he said. Nor for Alison and Brenda. They hadn't gone to university, although Jeannie had encouraged them to think of it. Instead they had both married young, and the money Bill lavished on their weddings was equal to the cost of putting their brother through university.

Bill could deny them nothing. Jeannie had tried to remonstrate, but he had merely laughed at her.

'Why shouldn't I buy them nice things? I can afford it.' Then he uttered the clincher: 'Now then, Jeannie, I don't keep you short, so why do you want me to refuse our children? That doesn't seem right to me.'

It was true. He never questioned her spending, although he refused to leave Prospect Villa or to replace the Victorian furniture they'd bought when they were first married. Jeannie had bought herself the colourful tea service, knowing it would look well against the polished mahogany, but Bill had never liked that set. Garish, he'd called it, but Jeannie had loved the bold pattern and bright colours.

It was gone now, taken to the hospice charity shop, along with all the other much-loved china she had collected over the years. Jeannie sighed and threw back the covers. Ah, well. Time to move on.

She was washing her face at the sink in the corner when there was a knock on her door and a young girl looked in.

'Morning, Mrs Sowerby, you OK today or d'you need me to help you dress?'

'No, I'm fine, Gulnar, thank you.'

'Right then, we'll see you at breakfast.'

The door closed, she heard Gulnar's footsteps padding away to the next room, heard her cheerful voice raised in greeting. 'Good morning, Elsie. Time to get up…'

Jeannie gripped the edge of the sink and stared into the mirror. Was this it now for the rest of her life? Funny, at sixty-two she hadn't considered herself old, yet here she was, in The Rowans Residential Home.

It was all a blur, the fall, being taken into hospital. She had felt so tired and confused, she let the children deal with everything while she struggled to get well.

'You should sell Prospect Villa,' Alison, her eldest, had told her. 'We've been telling you since Dad died it's too big. You need something more manageable.'

'Yes, now is the time to sell,' agreed Brenda, who was receptionist for an estate agent in Leeds. 'The market's booming and we can get you a good price.'

Only it wasn't her house. When Bill died, he left her a lump sum – which was now paying for her stay at The Rowans – and instructions that she should have the use of the house as long as she required, but when it was sold, the money was to be split between the children.

'That won't be a problem, Mum,' Sam had assured her at the time. 'We'll see you right. We'll start looking for somewhere, just as soon as you're well enough.'

Well, six months on and she *was* well enough, she thought, walking over to the wardrobe. She had kept up the exercises the physio had recommended and she was as fit as ever. A sudden chill ran through her as she stared at the clothes hanging in the wardrobe. Shapeless dresses in pastel colours, clothes the children had chosen for her. Clothes suitable for an old lady living out the last of her days in a home.

Was it only a week since Sam had dropped the bombshell? He'd arrived promptly at two-thirty and Jeannie had accepted his dutiful peck on the cheek.

'Can't stay long, I'm afraid. Michelle's car has packed up and she's having a bikini wax, so I have to collect her at four. It's at least a forty-minute drive.'

'That's a new excuse.'

Sam had the goodness to flush, but he said irritably, 'Come

on, Mum, 'Chelle and I are very busy. It's all right for you, sitting here all day with nothing to do!'

And whose fault is it I don't have a proper home?

She let that go and said, 'The sun lounge is empty, let's sit in there.'

'Well, this is very pleasant,' he said chattily. 'I'd love a brew, wouldn't you?'

'No, I wouldn't actually.' For once she didn't feel like being hospitable. 'There's a machine for visitors, in the kitchen.'

It made her sad to see how shocked he looked at the thought of paying for his own drink, rather than charging it to her account here, but after a moment he laughed and settled back in his chair.

'Ah, well, I mustn't waste precious visiting time fetching tea. How are you?'

'Fit enough to leave here. Have you found me a house yet?'

'I'm afraid not,' he responded sadly. 'Brenda is keeping an eye on the new properties, but there's nothing suitable.'

'I see.'

'You're not unhappy here, are you, Mum?'

'It's not where I want to end my days. Doctor Ellis says I'm quite fit now.'

'Oh? I didn't know he was coming to see you.'

'He was here earlier to see Mrs Norris so I spoke to him then.' She sat forward in her chair. 'You promised me you would buy me a small place of my own, Sam, or I'd never have agreed to move out of Prospect Villa.' She picked up the newspaper she'd earlier left on the table. 'Look. I've marked three or four properties that would be suitable.'

He studied them in silence. 'They're all on the tops.'

'Is that a problem? I still have my driving licence.' She smiled. 'When I really am old and infirm then I shall have to resort to taxis. Or ask you to take me out. Now, how soon can we arrange to view them?'

Was it her imagination, or had his cheeks turned white?

'We should wait until you're stronger, Mother.'

Mother? She pursed her lips then replied with equal formality.

'I'm serious about this, Samuel. I've been here long enough.'

'Ah.' His eyes slid away from her. 'The thing is, we can't afford any of them.'

'But Prospect Villa fetched a very good price!'

'I know, but Brenda dipped into her share to pay off some debts, and Alison has moved house –'

Her brows snapped together. '*What?*'

'It was all a bit sudden. She had tickets for Eurovision in Birmingham this year and thought it would be easier to get there from Edgbaston.'

'*Edgbaston*! Houses there cost an arm and a leg. Good heavens, Sam, how much *can* you all afford then, to buy me a house?'

He was staring at her like a hunted animal. 'There was my golf club membership, and Michelle's new car…'

Now it was her turn to stare. Sam avoided her gaze and twisted his hands together nervously.

'You've spent it all. You thought I wouldn't be coming out of here again.' She pushed herself out of the chair. 'I think you'd better go now, before I say something I might regret.'

The alacrity with which he jumped up would have amused her, had she not been so angry.

'Yes, yes, I'll be off then. I'll come back next week and we'll have another talk about it.'

'Is there really any point?'

He gave a little laugh, as if he thought she was joking, and hurried away. Jeannie sat back down and dropped her head in her hands. She should never have agreed to them selling the house. She should have seen this coming. Looking back, she knew how utterly selfish the children had become. It was not entirely their fault, she should have stopped Bill from giving in to them so much, but it had been simpler to let it go.

*

Dan glanced at his watch. Was it only eleven o'clock? He had the whole day ahead of him. He walked along Market Street, but somehow the shop windows couldn't hold his attention now. He kept thinking about Jeannie and wondering what had happened to her.

Some said she had done all right for herself, marrying Bill Sowerby. He owned a large Victorian mansion that towered over the neighbouring terraced houses clinging to the steep hillside. Dan knew the house, of course. Everyone in Haven Bridge knew it because of its prominent position overlooking Market Street, but he'd only been inside once, when he returned to Haven Bridge for the funeral of Jeannie's father. Bill Sowerby had deemed his father-in-law's cottage in Cragg Royd too small for the funeral tea, so friends and family had been invited back to Prospect Villa.

That had been a dark October day, Dan recalled. The euphoria of England winning the World Cup had faded with the summer and a blanket of grey cloud rested on the hills above the valley, trapping Haven Bridge in a dreary half-light. Jeannie had looked tired and very pale, her green eyes dull and her curly dark hair scraped back under a small black hat. She was wearing a black coat, too, which didn't suit her. He remembered her wearing bright colours, even if it was only a shocking pink scarf or scarlet gloves purchased at a jumble sale. She'd said it made her stand out from the crowd. It was probably that splash of colour that had attracted Bill Sowerby's notice.

The funeral tea was spread over the table in the dining room, the usual sandwiches, sausage rolls and cold quiche. The church hall had loaned them extra crockery, thick off-white earthenware plates and teacups that contrasted starkly with the glorious colours of Jeannie's tea service.

That was when she'd made her comment about the Clarice Cliff being her small rebellion and her mother-in-law, coming in at that moment, added sharply, 'Aye, lass, and it's those same dark, satanic mills as paid for this do, and don't you forget it.'

Dan gave a grim, inward smile. Who could forget that funeral?

The funeral procession in particular had been designed to attract attention. People in the street had stopped and men had doffed their caps as the coffin went past in the hearse, a black Austin Princess which, as Bill Sowerby explained to anyone who would listen, was the same model that had carried Sir Winston Churchill through the streets of London the year before. The whole thing had been designed for show, to reflect Bill's status as part-owner of Grassholme Mill.

'It's not what Dad would have wanted,' Jeannie told Dan in a burst of confidence, when old Mrs Sowerby had moved off. 'He wasn't one for show, he'd have preferred a quiet service, just family and close friends.'

'I hope I would still have been welcome,' he replied, and she put her hand on his sleeve.

'You would always be welcome, Dan.'

His reaction to her touch shocked him, sending the blood pounding through his veins. He left soon after, knowing it was too dangerous to see Jeannie again.

Dan had reached a turning, the road leading up to Prospect Villa. He guessed Bill Sowerby had retired by now and surely they would have moved. He remembered Jeannie had disliked living in the valley. Nevertheless, he felt a strong curiosity to see the old place. The hill was steeper than he remembered. Last time he'd walked up here he'd been a young man of thirty and it had been a cold October day. Now he had the June sun beating down upon him. He stopped to take off his coat then carried on, puffing slightly. He was rewarded by finding that Prospect Villa still loomed over the valley, but it looked different. Less imposing. Brighter. He crossed the road and strolled past the house, noting that the windows had been replaced and the front door was painted scarlet. The roses had gone from the small walled area at the front and, tucked down behind the wall, was an estate agent's board, a 'Sold' banner proudly displayed across it.

She'd moved then. Dan felt a sudden and unexpected stab of disappointment. It shouldn't matter to him, but somehow it did.

*

It was such a lovely day that Jeannie found her cardigan quite sufficient for her usual morning circuit of the garden, and afterwards she ran upstairs to her room to fetch her book. It wasn't safe leaving anything outside her room; some of the residents here were a little confused, and often carried things off. One poor old dear had even tried to eat one of her paperbacks.

Most of the residents were watching daytime television in the lounge, staring at the moving images on the screen as Jeannie walked through to the sunroom, where she found old Mrs Norris asleep in her usual corner.

Jeannie sat down and opened her book, but somehow today she couldn't concentrate and she stared out at the view. It was pleasant enough, looking out over the garden, but the hills rose steeply beyond the wall and in the winter, they blotted out the sun. Jeannie wanted to be back at Cragg Royd, high above the valley, where you could hear the skylarks and see for miles across the hills. Even in winter you could watch the sun make its way across the sky all day until it went down in a blaze of fiery light. She sat back and closed her eyes. If only.

Jeannie refused to give up her dream and she hadn't been idle since Sam's disastrous revelation. She went to see the council and made an appointment with the bank's customer relations officer, a girl young enough to be her granddaughter, but it only confirmed what she feared. With just her widow's pension and her savings, she couldn't afford to buy a house.

'Lunchtime!' trilled a cheerful voice. 'Oh, did I wake you, Mrs Sowerby? I am sorry, but lunch is ready.'

'Yes, thank you. I will come,' said Jeannie, although her appetite had quite disappeared.

The assistant beamed at her and went to rouse Mrs Norris from her slumbers and help her to the dining room.

*

Dan made his way back down the hill. He had talked himself out of knocking on the door of Prospect Villa and asking about Jeannie. He hadn't seen or heard of her for thirty years. She might have moved away years ago. The sun disappeared behind the clouds just as he reached the valley bottom and he shrugged himself back into his jacket, feeling suddenly dispirited. He should never have come here. Never have scratched at the old wounds and opened them up again.

'Dan? Dan Hartley?' He looked up to see a man in tweed coat and moleskin trousers grinning at him. 'Eeeh, lad, I'd've known you anywhere!'

'Joe Crawshaw!' Dan stuck out his hand and it was taken in a strong, calloused grasp. 'How are you?'

They had been neighbours in Cragg Royd and even gone to the pub together when Dan had made his infrequent visits home from university.

'Oh, I aren't so bad, old lad. Just doing a bit of shopping. Well, well, long time no see!'

Dan glanced at his watch. 'I was going to grab a spot of

lunch at The Old Bull… are you rushing off or do you fancy coming with me? We could catch up on old times.'

A slow grin spread across Joe's features. 'The missus is visiting her mother so I've nothing to go home for yet. Come on, then, I'll buy the first pint.'

The Old Bull had changed a lot since Dan had last been in there. The interior had been gutted, the separate bars and snug giving way to a large airy space with plenty of tables and chairs and a large blackboard now displayed the pub food on offer. They found a spare table by the window and ordered their meals, Joe fetching over two pints of real ale to keep them going until the food arrived.

'Still got your veterinary practice in Derbyshire?' Joe asked him.

'No, I've retired now.' Dan lifted his glass and took a long draught. 'Sold the business, but I'm still living in Bakewell.'

'I wondered if you might be thinking of moving back, with all the work our kid's done on your parents' place this year.'

Dan grinned. 'Knew I shouldn't have used your brother!'

'Our Ken's the best builder in the area,' Joe retorted. 'You'd be a fool to use anyone else. It's a shame your mum and dad didn't get longer to enjoy it. Just three years, wasn't it, before that winter flu bug hit them both? Bad business.' He shook his head sadly. 'Those last tenants of yours fairly trashed the place, I hear.'

'That's why I'm putting Harebell Cottage on the market. I've had enough of renting it out.' He cocked an eyebrow at his old friend. 'Interested?'

'What, live up on the tops again? No, thank you. We've got a nice little place along the valley. No more worrying about the weather, wondering if the gritter's been up the hill and digging ourselves out when it snows.'

Dan nodded and sipped his beer. Personally, he wouldn't

want to live down here. It felt too closed in. On the hills there was room to breathe. A waitress came over with two plates of fish and chips and put them on the table.

'So,' said Joe, reaching for the salt. 'Have you been seeing the estate agent this morning?'

'Only dropping the keys in. I checked the property and went through everything with them yesterday, intending to drive home this morning, only my car wouldn't start. Managed to get Morton's to tow it to their garage but it needs some new part and won't be ready until tomorrow. Had to book another night at the B&B.'

The conversation petered out. Dan hadn't realised he was so hungry. He soon cleared his plate and sat back

'So, you retired now, Joe?

'Aye. Finished at the rope factory last September.'

'Oh? I thought you worked at Grassholme Mill.'

'Not for twenty year. I could see which way the wind was blowing.'

Suddenly Dan was interested. 'What happened to Grassholme?'

'Sowerby didn't keep up with the times.' Joe pushed his now-empty plate away. 'There was no investment in the mill for years.' He drained his glass. 'The saying is clogs to clogs in three generations, but the Sowerbys'll make it in one, I reckon. They're too good at spending.'

Intrigued, Dan rose and picked up the empty glasses. 'I'll get us a refill.'

'Just a half for me,' said Joe quickly. 'I'm driving.'

Five minutes later, they were nursing full glasses and Dan gave Joe a gentle nudge.

'Tell me what happened at Grassholme.'

'Bill Sowerby had a heart attack and died about ten years ago. The children weren't interested in the business and sold it to a company in Huddersfield. Kept going for another couple of years but finally had to shut the doors. Must be five years since. I suppose you don't hear anything now your mum and dad are gone.'

'What happened to Bill's widow?'

'Jeannie?' Joe sighed. 'Pity about her. Nice lass. She had a bit of a turn at Christmas and had to go into hospital. She never came home again. '

'She's dead?' A cold hand clutched at Dan's heart.

'Oh, no. She's at The Rowans now. The missus had it from a neighbour that it wasn't anything serious, but the kids persuaded her to sell the house.'

That explained the 'For Sale' sign, thought Dan.

Joe hesitated. 'I don't know if it's true, but…'

'Go on, man.'

'Well, it's probably just gossip, but the missus heard she doesn't really need to be there, but the three kids spent the money from the house so she can't go anywhere else now.'

'They wouldn't do that to their own mother!'

Joe shrugged. 'Like I said, probably just gossip.' He pushed his empty glass away. 'Thanks for that, mate. I suppose I'd best be going.'

They both rose and walked towards the door, Dan still thinking about Jeannie.

'She was never one for living in the valley,' he mused. 'I wonder how she's coping at The Rowans?'

'No reason why you couldn't go and see her,' said Joe, holding open the door for him. 'I expect she'd be glad of a visit. Her family don't call much, from what I hear.' He paused. 'I'll drop you off there on my way home, if you like?'

*

By the time Jeannie had finished her lunch, the latest edition of the local paper had been delivered and she carried a copy off to her room. She scanned the property pages, her heart sinking further as she took in the prices, and by the time she reached the final page, she was ready to cry with frustration.

'Mrs Sowerby?'

The door opened and Jeannie summoned up a smile. 'Yes, Gulnar?'

"There's a visitor for you.'

'For me?' Jeannie followed the girl down the stairs.

She could see someone was standing in the hall, but it couldn't be Sam: the staff knew him by now. She could only see his feet and legs. From the casual shoes and trousers, she guessed it wasn't someone from the council to tell her she did qualify for a council flat, after all. Although these days you couldn't be sure what an official would be wearing. She continued down the stairs, watching the rest of the figure appear from the knees up. Long legs. A tall man, she thought. Lean and upright. Broad shoulders, too. Finally, she saw he had thick silver hair, neatly brushed.

He had his back to her, reading the notices on the wall, but as she reached the bottom step, he turned towards her, his blue eyes crinkling as he smiled.

'Hello, Jeannie. I would have known you anywhere.'

Her hand tightened on the banister rail.

'Dan?' Her voice was a croak, then the delight of seeing him again flooded through her and she went forwards. 'Dan! After all these years, what a surprise!'

He took her hands and squeezed them, still smiling. 'I was having lunch with an old friend and he told me where you were. Joe Crawshaw, remember him?'

'Why, yes. His daughter was in the same class as Alison. How is he?'

'Very well. Retired now.'

Jeannie knew she must be grinning like an idiot. 'Have you time for a cup of tea?'

'I'd love one!'

She looked around and saw Gulnar hovering close by.

'Would you be a dear and bring us two teas, please? We'll be in the sunroom.'

She led the way through the lounge, trying not to shuffle as she walked. She didn't want Dan to think she was like the poor old dears who spent their days in front of the television. Once they were sitting down, Jeannie felt a sudden shyness and resorted to her mill-owner's wife manner. 'Well, this is a pleasant surprise, Dan. I haven't seen you for years.'

'Thirty-two years,' he said. 'It was your father's funeral.'

'Ah, yes.'

She was gratified he remembered so well. She'd been worn out that day, after six months of going up to the cottage to nurse her father, as well as looking after the large house, her husband and three young children. Bill had just taken out a loan for the mill and money was tight. He was working all hours, so she didn't think it was right to ask for paid help.

It was only after Bill died she learned that those late nights had not been spent at the factory, but in Dale Street with Dot Tingley, known locally as the merry widow. Jeannie gave herself a little mental shake.

'That was a long time ago,' she said briskly, and invited him to tell her all about himself. Over tea she learned he'd been a widower for thirty years, was retired now and had no children.

'And what of you?' He sat back, the teacup cradled between his long fingers. 'How have you been, Jeannie? How's the family?'

'Oh, everyone's very well,' she replied. 'I have two lovely grandchildren, who I don't see as often as I'd like, but they do ring me every week, which is good of them.'

She sipped her tea, knowing she would have to answer his unspoken question.

'I had a fall last Christmas,' she said at last. 'After I left hospital I needed to be looked after for a while so I booked myself in here and,' she summoned a bright smile, 'here I am still.'

'You sold the house.'

It was a statement, not at all judgemental.

'Yes. It was too large for one person. I believe a family have bought it now. I wish them well.'

'And how long are you staying at The Rowans?'

'I'm looking for something suitable.' Another bright smile. 'It's quite exciting. The children are helping me.'

That was a lie, but Jeannie didn't want to admit the truth to anyone. She quickly changed the subject and began talking about the past. The years slipped away and they chatted easily, like the old friends they were.

At last Dan looked at his watch.

'That can't be right. I've been here two hours!' He gave her the lopsided grin she remembered so well. 'Time flies when you're enjoying yourself. But I must go. Thanks for the tea, Jeannie. No, don't get up, I can see myself out.'

But she insisted on accompanying him to the door.

'Thank you so much for coming,' she said, when they were once more back in the hall.

'It was a pleasure,' he said. 'Truly.'

'Safe journey home.'

'Thanks. May I phone you?'

'If you'd like to.'

After a slightly awkward pause he nodded and went out. Jeannie watched him walk up the path. He waved as he shut the gate behind him and she raised her hand in response. Then she straightened her shoulders and went back to the sunroom to collect the cups. No point in leaving them for the girls when she was perfectly capable of carrying them to the kitchen.

Dan Hartley. Fancy him remembering her after all these years. His visit had cheered her up no end and there was a positive spring in her step as she walked back through the lounge.

*

Having started venturing out, Jeannie continued to walk regularly through Haven Bridge, doing a little shopping, checking with Swinburn's and looking in the newsagent's window for accommodation to rent. On her very first outing, she remembered Miss Moonshine's, a fascinating shop on Market Street that she had visited many times over the years. The sun glinted off something in the window and, since she was in no hurry, she decided to take a look. A chill ran down her spine as she stared at the display and the next minute she was pushing open the door.

Inside, the shop was cluttered with all sorts of furniture and bric-a-brac. Clocks ticked from every wall; Meissen figurines danced between grinning Toby jugs. The smell of beeswax took her straight back to the dining room at Prospect Villa. Miss Moonshine was sitting in a rocking chair in one corner and she didn't look a day older than the last time Jeannie had been in here, which must have been at least five years ago. She was feeding treats to a tiny dog on her lap, but when Jeannie came in, she put the dog down and came forward, saying with a smile that robbed her words of offence, 'You strode in here with a purpose, dear. How can I help you?'

Jeannie's mouth was dry and she had to run her tongue around her lips before she could speak.

'That tea service. The Clarice Cliff. May I look at it?'

'Why, certainly.'

'It's the teapot I particularly wish to see,' said Jeannie.

'Ah, of course.' Sharp, birdlike eyes regarded Jeannie with a twinkle before the lady went over to the window and carefully extracted the teapot.

'Here you are.'

Jeannie took a deep breath, steadying herself before she took the teapot in two hands. She gazed at it, taking in the geometric blocks of vivid colour. It couldn't be the same one. Carefully she removed the lid. There, just beneath the rim, were two little marks. It had happened on one of the rare occasions she had been ill and had asked the children to wash up. Alison had been angrily banging pots around in the sink and chipped the teapot lid. Jeannie had never forgotten it.

'How long have you had this set?' she asked.

'Two ladies brought it in last March. They looked very alike. Sisters, I should think. I remember because they brought a box full of ornaments as well. Clearing out for an elderly relative, they said.'

An elderly relative! Was that how her daughters thought of her?

Still struggling to recover her health, Jeannie had not felt up to making many decisions about the contents of Prospect Villa. There was very little she wanted to keep. The photographs, some books and jewellery. She'd told the children to take what they wanted and send the rest to the hospice shop.

Miss Moonshine said quietly, 'I think this set meant a great deal to someone.'

It did. The Clarice Cliff set had been an extravagance. Bill had never seen the point of it. He had objected, but for once Jeannie had been adamant. Anger welled up. The tea set had been her pride and joy. She could only bear to part with it knowing it would provide money for a cause she'd supported for years. Instead, Alison and Brenda had sold it and she was pretty sure they hadn't donated the proceeds to charity. She imagined having it out with them, seeing their sullen looks and hearing them say, 'Well, it's gone now. No point arguing over it, Mum. Let it go.'

But this time she wasn't going to 'let it go'. She reached for her purse.

'If I give you a deposit, can you put this aside for me? I have nowhere to store it at present, but I hope to have somewhere soon.'

Miss Moonshine smiled, took her money and wrote her out a receipt. 'I'll keep it safe for you,' she said.

Jeannie left the shop, anger still fizzing inside her, but soon it transformed into a newfound energy. She bought herself some new clothes, smart trousers, a jumper and two shirts in jewel-bright colours. She wasn't yet ready to be anyone's elderly relative.

Chapter Two

The storm hit Haven Bridge three weeks later. Gale-force winds and torrential rain lashed the valley, but it was even worse on the surrounding hills. The first Dan knew of it was a phone call from the estate agent. He listened as they described the damage to Harebell Cottage. Tiles dislodged, chimney-pot toppled and windows smashed by a falling tree.

'Rain damage inside, I'm afraid,' an apologetic voice crackled down the line. 'We'll get someone to shift the tree and secure the building, but it will need some remedial work and internal decoration before we can have any more viewings.'

'OK. I'll come up as soon as I can to take a look.'

Dan put down the phone. It seemed he would have to go back to Haven Bridge again after all.

And the strange thing was, this time he was looking forward to it.

*

A week later and Harebell Cottage was as good as new. Dan stood on the drive and surveyed the house. The only thing left to do was to paint the water-damaged lounge wall and he'd pop back to do that tomorrow. He took one final look before he drove off. He'd forgotten what a lovely house it was.

Dan glanced at his watch. It was only eleven o'clock. He wondered what to do for the rest of the day. Lunch first, he decided, but for once the idea of eating alone didn't appeal to him. He thought of Jeannie. They'd spoken on the phone several times since that first meeting and he felt no qualms about ringing her at such short notice.

Jeannie was waiting at the gate when he pulled up outside The Rowans. He jumped out and walked around to open the passenger door for her. There was something different about her today. She had more colour in her cheeks, and in her clothes. She looked younger and more… alive, somehow. But then, he had caught her rather unawares that first time.

'I saw you coming along the road,' she greeted him. 'How nice of you to invite me out to lunch.'

'Ulterior motive,' he said. 'I didn't want to eat alone.'

Half an hour later they were seated outside The Packhorse Inn, at one of the wooden benches between the pub and the river. Jeannie insisted on buying the drinks, a small glass of wine for her and a half of cider for Dan, and they sat in companionable silence while they waited for their meals.

'I didn't think you were coming back to Haven Bridge.'

'I hadn't intended to, but Harebell Cottage was damaged in the recent storms. I could have left it to the agents to sort it out but, well…' He shrugged. 'I wanted to see it was done right.'

'Of course.' She nodded. 'How long are you staying?'

'Only until tomorrow. I've got to do a bit more painting and then that's it.'

The food arrived, causing a welcome diversion, and the talk became more desultory until they'd both finished, then Jeannie sat back and gave a satisfied sigh.

'I really enjoyed that. Thank you.'

'Good.' He hesitated. 'I wondered if they would let you out.'

'Oh, yes. I'm allowed to come and go as I please.' His surprise must have shown because she laughed. 'It's not a prison!'

He grinned. 'Sorry. I know very little about these things. Mum and Dad both enjoyed very good health, until the end. They never needed to go into a home. But, have you not found anywhere else to live yet?'

'Not yet. In fact –'

She stopped as the waitress came at that moment to take away their empty plates, and afterwards asked him about his life in Derbyshire. He found himself telling her about his veterinary practice, recalling any number of anecdotes to amuse her. It was very comfortable, sitting there beside the river, the sun shining down on them, and Jeannie was very easy to talk to. They were able to discuss anything; everything. Even his marriage, short-lived because Mary died of cancer.

'She was a lovely woman,' he said, a little wistfully. 'You would have liked her. She would have made a wonderful mother, but sadly we couldn't have children.'

'I am sorry. Although children aren't always the comfort one hopes they would be.'

She responded to his startled look with a shake of her head and began to talk of something else. He followed her lead, until the tables around them began to empty and she glanced at her watch.

'No need to worry on my account,' he told her. 'I'm in no hurry to go. Funnily enough, I've enjoyed being back in my old haunts.'

'Well, if you aren't in a hurry….'

He caught her eye and laughed. 'I remember that look of old! What is it you want to ask me, Jeannie?'

She blushed a little, which made her look younger than ever. 'If you don't have to dash off, I wonder if I could ask a favour of you? Because you have a four-by-four.'

'A throwback from my veterinary days,' he said, grinning. 'It suits me, and there's plenty of life left in the old girl yet. Go on then, what is it you want?'

'I'm supposed to be going up the hill this afternoon, to look at a house to rent. It's a little off the road and the local taxis don't like going along there…'

'You'd like a lift? No problem. What time's your appointment?'

'The agent said I can collect the keys and go at any time, as long as I drop them back before five-thirty.'

'And it's three now. Shall we go?'

She stood up, her green eyes twinkling. 'All right, but I insist you let me pay for the lunch as a thank you.'

Half an hour later they had reached Cragg Royd, which comprised little more than two lines of terraced houses.

'They look very different to when we lived there,' Jeannie observed, looking at the hanging baskets and brightly painted doors. 'I expect they're very sought-after now.' She glanced at the directions in her hand and sat forward. 'Take the next turning right.'

A stony track led to an even smaller hamlet which had obviously not yet been discovered by the young families and business professionals. As the track curved away towards a cluster of substantial farm buildings, there was a terrace of four tired-looking houses, one of which had a 'To Let' board nailed to the front.

Dan frowned and glanced uncertainly at Jeannie. 'Do you still want to look inside?'

'Of course! It would be a shame not to, after coming all this way.'

They both climbed out of the car and stood looking at the

houses. The end house was boarded up but the next was clearly occupied, with bright curtains at the windows and a child's pushchair outside the door. The other end terrace was also occupied, for Dan had seen the curtains twitch as they drew up.

Jeannie pulled the keys from her pocket. 'Would you rather wait in the car?'

'And let you go in there alone? No way!'

He said nothing as they walked around, but it didn't take a genius to know the house wouldn't do. It smelled of damp, the electrics needed replacing and there was no central heating, only open fireplaces in the downstairs rooms. The only thing in its favour were the views over the surrounding fields and, from an upstairs room, one could see the distant moors.

Neither of them spoke as they went back to the car but once they were inside, Dan couldn't keep quiet any longer.

'You can't live there, Jeannie.'

'No.' She sighed. 'It's a shame, because the rent is dirt cheap.'

'And now you know the reason.'

'Yes. I like my home comforts these days and it would take far more than I can afford to make it liveable. Ah, well. Back to the drawing board.'

She smiled bravely and Dan's heart ached for her. He was tempted to drive to Harebell Cottage, it wasn't far out of their way, but that would be cruel. She obviously couldn't afford to rent anything much. It would be like showing her the prize she hadn't won.

Back at The Rowans, he accepted her offer of a cup of tea. Nothing was said about the rental house but he could see Jeannie was disappointed, even though she tried to hide it.

'Thank you for coming, Dan,' she said, going with him to the door. 'I do appreciate your help today.'

'It was a pleasure. What will you do now?'

'Keep looking. Something will turn up.'

'Surely the children will help you find something.' He thought a shadow flickered across her face, but it was gone in an instant and she smiled.

'Yes, of course they will. Safe journey home, Dan.'

He hesitated then kissed her cheek. He didn't want to go. He wanted to say – He didn't know *what* he wanted to say. At that moment an assistant came bustling down the corridor, so he muttered a quick 'Goodbye' and left.

*

Jeannie went slowly up to her room. She and Dan had always been best friends as children, and even at their respective grammar schools the buildings were next door to one another, so she and Dan walked home together most days. At least they did until Dad put his foot down. She remembered his words as if it were yesterday.

'You're fifteen, our Jeannie, and there's a place at t'mill waitin' for you. Learning's all very well but it won't put bread on the table!'

There had been rows and tears. Her teachers had tried to talk Dad round, telling him she could get a place at university. Even Dan had tried, until Dad had shouted at him not to get involved in what didn't concern him. In the end Jeannie had given in. What else could she do?

It wasn't as if Dan had abandoned her after that, but she'd soon known there was no future for them, and once he went off to university their worlds became very different. To her eighteen-year-old self, stuck in Haven Bridge, six years waiting for him to become a vet was a lifetime. She was lonely, too, since all her friends had boyfriends. Then Bill had asked her out and she was flattered enough to go…

It hadn't been a bad marriage, even though she'd realised too late that Bill was not the love of her life. Jeannie put a hand up to her cheek, where Dan had kissed her. She'd had her chance with Dan Hartley forty years ago and she had thrown it away. Best to forget him now and get on with her life.

*

'Are you sure you have no new rental properties this week?' Jeannie saw the receptionist hesitate and guessed the reply. She'd looked in vain at the private ads in the paper and the newsagent's window.

'I'm sorry, Mrs Sowerby, there's nothing.' Nicola gave her a sympathetic smile. 'I'll go and see Mr Swinburn, ask if there's anything we haven't put on the system yet.'

She disappeared into the back office and Jeannie sat down on a chair to wait. She kept her eyes turned resolutely away from the revolving boards with their enticing pictures. Places that were completely out of her reach. In fact, it looked as if everything was out of her reach, unless she was prepared to live in a poky little bedsit, so she might as well stay at The Rowans until her money ran out, then the council would have to rehome her. She couldn't ask the children to help. Her little outburst over the tea service had shaken them, and every time she saw them now they made it clear they had no money to spare. She pressed her lips together. If they were struggling to make ends meet after sharing out the cash from Prospect Villa, then she had no idea how anyone else managed!

The doorbell tinkled and a rainbow floated in. It took Jeannie a moment to realise it was Miss Moonshine, wearing a very floaty summer dress made of some brightly coloured material, a matching turban perched on her white hair. Jeannie nodded towards the empty desk.

'I'm afraid Nicola has gone off to find some information for me.'

'I can wait. I'm just dropping off a brooch she bought from me.'

As she placed a small box on the desk, Jeannie said impulsively, 'I do love your outfit.'

'Thank you.' Miss Moonshine gave her a twinkly smile and Jeannie continued, 'I read a poem once. Something about when I am old, I shall wear purple.' She flushed. 'I wanted to do that. I thought I would wear bright colours and do all the rebellious things that I didn't do when I was younger. Silly, isn't it?'

'No. Not silly at all. And that lovely green jacket you're wearing is an excellent start. But you're nowhere near old yet.' Miss Moonshine tilted her head to one side. 'It's Mrs Sowerby, isn't it? I have the Clarice Cliff tea set put aside for you.'

'That's right.'

Conversation flagged. Miss Moonshine walked over to look at the houses for sale.

'There are some lovely places here, aren't there? Here's one that I particularly like.'

It was only polite to get up and look. Miss Moonshine was pointing one dainty finger at a very pretty little house of local stone, glowing golden in the sunlight. The garden was all lawn and shrubs, and Jeannie began to imagine flowerbeds under the two front windows and a vegetable patch at one side. Then she stopped herself, turning away with a sigh.

'Is it not for you?' asked Miss Moonshine. 'Some people wouldn't dream of living up on the hills.'

'I dream of nothing else. But it's not to be.'

'I am so sorry, Mrs Sowerby,' Nicole came hurrying back to her desk. 'Mr Swinburn says if you leave your details, he'll let you know as soon as something comes in.'

Jeannie wrote her name and telephone number on a notepad, then she and Miss Moonshine left the shop together. As they stepped out into the sunshine Jeannie came to a decision, and she turned to her companion.

'I think it only fair to tell you that I can't take the Clarice Cliff after all.' There was something constricting her throat and she swallowed to clear it. 'At least not for a very long time. I think you should put it back on sale.'

'Oh, there isn't any need for that just yet.'

'But there is!' cried Jeannie. 'I have nowhere to store it and… no use for it. I know I'll lose the deposit, but –'

A gentle touch on her arm stopped her. 'It's perfectly safe with me for a little longer, my dear.'

'I don't think you quite understand!' But looking into Miss Moonshine's bright eyes, Jeannie had the strangest feeling that the old lady *did* understand. She said slowly, 'Well, if you are sure?'

Again, that twinkling smile appeared. 'Oh, I am very sure. Now, I hear that Wendy's Wardrobe has a rather good selection of new clothes just in. I suggest you go and treat yourself to something nice and stop worrying.'

Chapter Three

Dan was worried. August was coming to an end; Harebell Cottage had been back on the market for a month and there was no interest in the house at all.

'Sometimes it just happens like that,' said Jack Swinburn, when Dan phoned him to find out what was going on. 'Of course, empty houses never sell quite as well as furnished ones. People find it more difficult to imagine what it would be like to live in it. Something obviously doesn't appeal to prospective buyers, but it's nothing that we can pinpoint.'

Frustrated, Dan decided he needed to go and check the house out for himself. He thought about ringing Jeannie, but in the end decided against it. Since that last trip to Haven Bridge, she had become rather elusive. Whenever he phoned she was either not available or had some excuse to keep the call short. Dan was disappointed. They'd slipped back into their old easy friendship so quickly that he missed chatting with her. Very much.

'You're an old fool, Dan Hartley,' he muttered. 'She's got her own life now, and her children to look after her. She doesn't need you.'

He reached Harebell Cottage by ten o'clock in the morning and tried to look at it impartially. Everything looked fine to him, but he'd designed the house, so maybe he just couldn't see its faults. He needed a second opinion and after an inward struggle, he reached for his phone.

'Jeannie? Really sorry to bother you.' It had taken some time for the girl who answered the phone to fetch her and she sounded a little strained. 'Is everything all right?'

'What? Oh. Yes. The children were here, but they've all left now. How are you?'

'I'm well, thanks. Erm, Jeannie, I was wondering if you would do me a great favour…' Dan explained quickly. 'What do you think?'

There was a long pause, then, 'Of course I'll come, Dan.'

He gave a relieved sigh. 'Excellent. We can have lunch first –'

'No.' She interrupted him. 'I have a few things to do. It would be best if you picked me up around two, if that's OK with you?'

Everything agreed, Dan said goodbye and put his phone away. Jeannie had sounded a little distracted and he hoped she was OK. He didn't like to ask over the phone, but it would be easier to talk face to face.

He decided to grab a sandwich from the café in Market Street and as he walked back to his car, he passed Miss Moonshine's and glanced at the window. The colourful china wasn't there. Without thinking, he went in.

Miss Moonshine emerged from the back, carrying her little dog under her arm, and her face lit up with gratifying recognition.

'Oh, look, Napoleon. It's the gentleman from Bakewell. Welcome back.'

'The Clarice Cliff tea set,' he said. 'The one that was in the window…'

'Oh, that's put aside for someone,' replied Miss Moonshine. 'Were you interested?'

'I don't want to buy it,' he said hastily.

'Because I think it might be available again very soon.' She continued as if he hadn't spoken. 'The lady has been looking for a place of her own, but I'm afraid she isn't having much luck. And that's a pity,' she continued, fixing him with her strangely compelling gaze. 'She is such a lovely lady; it will be very sad if she has to give up on her dreams.'

Dan murmured a few words and retreated, feeling vaguely uneasy. It seemed such an odd thing to say. Also, he couldn't shake off the suspicion that Miss Moonshine had been talking about Jeannie.

*

When he reached The Rowans, Jeannie stepped out before he'd even reached the door. He gave her a cheery wave and, taking in her neat ankle boots, slim black jeans and purple jacket, said teasingly, 'You look very smart. Going somewhere nice?'

Her smile was perfunctory. 'I bought these clothes a few weeks ago and this is my first chance to wear them. To be honest, I've been wondering if they're too young for me. The children think I'm mutton trying to dress as lamb.'

'Not a bit of it,' he said bracingly. 'Come on. Your chariot awaits, ma'am.'

'It's very good of you to do this for me,' he said, as he set off. 'You sounded a little hesitant when I phoned. I wondered if you thought I was being a bit cheeky.'

She disclaimed quickly but didn't elaborate. Something was bothering her and he really wished she'd tell him what. But it wasn't his business. He had no right to ask, so he kept quiet.

*

'I shouldn't have come,' thought Jeannie, staring out of the window at the familiar landscape, wind-blown hills and small fields edged with ragged drystone walls. All her dreams of living up here were at an end and she really should have made some excuse not to come, but the thought of seeing Dan again had been too strong to resist. As they drove through the pretty hilltop village of Ryeden Dan slowed and, as he turned onto a gravelled drive, Jeannie's heart sank. It was the house of her dreams. The one Miss Moonshine had pointed out to her in Swinburn's.

'What's the matter? Don't you like it?' There was concern in Dan's voice.

'Oh no!' she said. 'I mean, I do like it. It's beautiful.'

He looked relieved. 'Good. Let's go inside. I'm afraid it's just empty rooms. I wanted to get rid of every trace of the tenants so I threw out all the furniture and had the house completely renovated, a blank canvas so the new owners can put their own stamp on the place.'

*

The house was built on a slight elevation and almost every room looked out across the fields or the moors. They were the sort of views Jeannie had dreamed of for so many years. She followed him around, mentally filling the rooms with colour, adding warm carpets to the bedrooms, stocking the bathrooms with thick, fluffy towels and imagining a dog lying on a bright rug in front of the wood-burner in the lounge.

When they'd seen everything, she shook her head. 'I honestly can't understand why no one has snapped this place up, Dan.'

'Could it be the kitchen, do you think?'

'No. It's beautifully done and the views from there across the valley are just stunning.' Jeannie had a sudden image of sitting at the breakfast bar, drinking her tea from a Clarice Cliff teacup with the morning sun streaming in. She swallowed a sigh. 'I couldn't imagine anyone wanting anything better. I suppose the right person hasn't come along yet.'

'The right person,' he repeated, slowly.

He was frowning at her and Jeannie realised she was being no help at all. She shouldn't have come.

'I don't suppose –' He stopped and shuffled awkwardly. 'I don't suppose *you'd* like to live here?'

For a moment she felt quite dizzy at the thought. Then common sense asserted itself. She couldn't afford to buy it. Or even to rent such a place. She wanted to weep with frustration, but pride came to her rescue.

'Oh goodness me, what a thought!' She managed a very creditable laugh. 'I know, I did say I wanted to live somewhere like this, but one has to be practical, in the end. And I have other plans now,' she continued, feigning cheerfulness. 'I told you I saw the family this morning, didn't I? Well, you'll never believe it, but they've come up with the very thing for me. I'm going to live with Alison at her new house. Won't that be wonderful?'

'Really?' His brow cleared. 'Well, that's good news.'

'Yes.'

Jeannie kept her smile in place. She'd never tell anyone Alison was only taking her because she needed a lodger to help pay her mortgage. When questioned whether the new house had taken all her share of the money from Prospect Villa,

Alison's perfectly shaped brows had shot up. 'Edgbaston's not cheap, you know.'

Dan was looking delighted. 'That will be the very thing for you. I'm glad your family has stepped up at last.'

'Yes.' She kept smiling but inside she was crying at the thought of it. 'Now, I really must get back. There's a lot to sort out before Alison returns to fetch me at the weekend.'

'You're going so soon?'

'No point in paying for The Rowans when there are two perfectly good rooms I can have in Edgbaston, is there?' she said brightly, echoing Alison's words.

They went out to the car, where Dan opened the door for her, and she thought once again what a kind, courteous man he was.

When they reached The Rowans, she climbed out quickly, saying, 'No, please don't get out. You'll be wanting to get back home.'

'Thank you for coming with me, Jeannie.'

'I'm really sorry I couldn't be more help.' She gave him her bright smile. 'We probably won't be seeing one another again, but it was nice to catch up with you, Dan.'

She shut the door and stepped back for him to drive away. When he glanced in the rearview mirror she was still standing there, her purple jacket making a brave statement.

Brave! That's the word that had been eluding him. Jeannie was being brave. She didn't want to live in a granny flat in Edgbaston. She wanted a house on the hills. Good God, they were the same age and he certainly wasn't ready to give up on life yet, or to let go of his dreams.

He slammed on the brakes.

Epilogue

It was the last week of September: a cool blustery day of showers and fitful sunshine that made shoppers in Haven Bridge scurry about their business. One couple hurried along Market Street hand in hand and almost ran into Miss Moonshine's Emporium, laughing as they struggled to close the door against an exceptionally strong gust of wind.

'What a day!' exclaimed the woman, laughing and throwing back the hood of her bright yellow raincoat to disclose dark curls lightly peppered with grey.

Miss Moonshine put Napoleon down in his little basket and went forward to meet them.

'You're back!'

'We are indeed.' As the woman removed her gloves, a sudden burst of sunlight glinted from the gold band on her wedding finger. 'Dan's house in Bakewell is on the market and we're on our way to Harebell Cottage.'

'The house of our dreams,' said the man happily, putting his arm around his wife. 'We just stopped off to collect the tea set, if you still have it?'

'I parcelled it up last night for you, Mr and Mrs Hartley.' Miss Moonshine gave the happy couple a beaming smile. 'Welcome home.'

Melinda Hammond is a West Country girl who spent thirty happy years in the Yorkshire Pennines walking the moors and thinking up her stories. In 2018 she decided to realise a lifelong ambition to live by the sea and now writes her award-winning romantic historical adventures from her new home in the Scottish Highlands. Melinda also writes as Sarah Mallory for Harlequin Mills & Boon and has published more than fifty novels.

melinda-hammond.co.uk

Music, Love and Other Languages

By Helena Fairfax

Chapter One

There was the noise of a whistle blowing and doors slamming. Someone entered the carriage, pushing past Edith and knocking her shoulder. She opened her eyes with a start and glanced round, blinking. She must have nodded off. She hoped she hadn't been drooling. Or even worse, snoring. Thank goodness the seats across from her were empty.

Edith sat up quickly. There'd been a woman and her little boy opposite, chatting about getting off the train at Halifax. She turned to the window. Had she missed her stop? The train was picking up speed and, with a sinking heart, she watched the sign for Halifax flash past.

Overhead, the tannoy whirred. The conductor, in a broad Yorkshire accent, announced their next station stop would be Haven Bridge. Edith thought this over for a minute or two. *Haven Bridge.* She sank back in her seat again. Actually, the name had a nice sound to it. And after all, it didn't really matter where she got out. In fact, the more she thought about it, the more Haven Bridge sounded just right. A *haven* was what she was looking for.

The train clattered over the rails, leaving the stone houses of Halifax behind, and soon they were entering a wonderful landscape of high, rolling hills and green moorland. There was a wild energy in the view, a feeling of space, and for the first time in a long while, Edith's spirits began to lift.

Before long, they started to slow for the next station. Edith slipped her feet back into her trainers, pulled her hair into its ponytail and stood to retrieve her things. For a second, her heart stood still. Her rucksack was there on the rack – but there was no sign of her violin! And then she remembered. Of course. Her violin was safe where she'd left it, still in its case, in the house she shared in London with three other students. She'd deliberately placed it in her wardrobe, out of sight, before she left.

She swung her rucksack down from the rack, feeling strangely bereft. This was the first day she'd been without her instrument in… how long? Her mum had bought her a tiny violin before she even went to school. That must make it at least fifteen years. Too long to think about.

The carriage door swished open. A young man about Edith's age was sitting on an enormous suitcase, waiting to get off. He was tapping his knee with long slender fingers, his eyes closed. Edith couldn't hear the music from his tiny earbuds, but it only took her a bar or two to work out the beat. His fingers were tapping in seven/four time.

Then she rolled her eyes at herself. Here was a perfectly nice-looking boy, and all she could think about was music. And on closer inspection, he was a *lot* more than just nice-looking. Dark hair that curled a little; cute stubble; fine cheek bones; eyes of an unusual hue. Were they dark grey? Grey flecked with blue?

Oops. Eyes that were now *open.* Open and looking right back at Edith, and brimming with lively amusement. A dimple appeared under his cheekbone.

Flustered, Edith turned quickly and pretended to search her pockets for her ticket.

The train came to a halt with a rattling *hiss*. When the door clanked open, the boy stood and gestured politely for Edith to go first. As she passed him, she caught a delicious smell, like wood and oranges. She nodded her thanks, but Music Boy, as she'd silently called him, was bending to wrestle with his case.

Edith stepped out into blue skies and a glorious sun. Haven Bridge was a small station, with an exit leading onto a cobbled square. She looked around curiously. The green hills ranged all around the town, with rows of quaint stone terraces rising up. Which way to go? Everywhere looked enticing. There was a map on a display board next to a bus stop. She was just about to make her way to it, when she came to a halt.

In one of the drop-off car-parking bays was the most amazing vintage car, its top turned down to reveal tan leather seats. But it wasn't the vehicle that caught Edith's eye – in London she was used to odd sights – it was the woman standing next to it. She was dressed in a long purple jacket, with a jaunty peaked cap perched on top of her white hair. In her hand, which was gloved in black lace, she held the lead of a tiny chihuahua, who sat at her feet, looking about him with a faintly bored air.

The woman fixed her clear hazel eyes on Edith. 'Oh, you've come today,' she said. She beamed. 'I was hoping you would.'

Edith looked behind her. The woman couldn't be talking to her – could she? Edith hadn't known she was coming herself until she missed her stop.

She was saved answering, because at that moment Music Boy appeared through the station arch, pulling his suitcase behind him. He caught sight of the elderly lady, and an attractive smile spread across his face.

'Miss Moonshine,' he said.

Edith couldn't place his accent. Was it Yorkshire? But she didn't have time to wonder, because Miss Moonshine – for that seemed to be her name – was looking from one to the other of them. She clapped her gloved hands together in a way that tugged the chihuahua to attention.

'Two of you,' she cried. 'Isn't this perfect?' She turned to the boy. 'I haven't driven the Osbornes' car in, oh, I don't know how many years. And I do enjoy a trip out, especially on such a glorious day.' She glanced down at the dog. 'And so does Napoleon.'

Napoleon – who appeared to be the chihuahua – didn't seem as enthusiastic as his owner made out. Edith could swear he rolled his eyes. She realised she was staring again and quickly gave herself a shake. She hitched her rucksack more firmly and was about to walk on, when Miss Moonshine called out, 'Can we give you a lift, dear? There's plenty of room.'

Edith turned her head. What sort of place was this, where strangers offered you a lift? In London it would be unheard of.

'Oh, thank you,' she said politely. 'But I don't know where I'm going yet. I'm looking for a B&B.'

Miss Moonshine bent to pick up the chihuahua, with a surprisingly sprightly movement for someone her age. 'We pass one on our way,' she said brightly. 'And your rucksack looks heavy. You sit in front with Napoleon –' she held the tiny dog out, leaving Edith no choice but to take him – 'and we'll drop you off. They're sure to have room at The Old Smithy.'

Edith clutched the dog to her, wondering what to do. But Miss Moonshine was already bustling round to the driver's seat, with a quick, brisk step. And Music Boy was holding the passenger door for her. His eyes were dancing again, in such a merry way she found herself smiling back, despite herself.

'Are you sure this is OK?' she asked, climbing inside. Music Boy heaved his case onto the back seat and clambered in to sit on top of it. 'I mean –'

Miss Moonshine was already reversing, with a jolt of gears that caused Edith to clutch the dog tightly. The engine stuttered and then they were juddering over the cobbled stones of the car park, and over a little bridge, beneath which was a canal, with lots of brightly coloured narrowboats.

'Hold on to your hats,' Miss Moonshine cried cheerfully. As far as Edith could tell, there was no real need to hold on to anything, as the car didn't appear capable of more than ten miles an hour, but it was very pleasant to see all the little shops and cafés of Haven Bridge go by. Miss Moonshine was clearly well known, as many of the shoppers on the pavements waved and smiled as they passed.

The chihuahua looked at Edith as though to say, 'See what I have to put up with?' Then he turned himself round a couple of times and settled on her knee. Edith turned her head to look at the boy in the back. He was sitting perched high on his case, gazing around with lively curiosity. His bright eyes met hers, his dimple reappearing.

'Hello,' Edith said, just as though they were meeting at a student social, and not jolting along in a vintage car being driven by a crazy woman. 'My name's Edith O'Brien. What's yours?'

The boy leaned forward, as though he hadn't quite caught what she'd said. But whatever answer he was about to give was lost in an ear-splitting *ho-o-o-nk* as Miss Moonshine pressed the horn. And then another *h-o-o-onk* as she drew up beside the pavement.

'Edith O'Brien,' the old lady said. 'What a lovely name. Here's The Old Smithy.'

There was a flight of stone steps leading up to the B&B. A red-haired woman in a blue-striped apron flung the door wide at the sound of the horn.

'Hello, Miss Moonshine.' The woman took in Edith and the boy in the back seat, her expression inquisitive. 'You've got a carful.'

Miss Moonshine took the chihuahua from Edith's knee. 'This is Edith O'Brien,' she explained. 'She's looking for a room.' She patted Edith's hand. 'This is where I'll leave you, dear. Christine will look after you.'

Edith was relieved to see Christine seemed quite down-to-earth, in her pinny and slippers. But the real clincher was the delicious smell of baking scones wafting out of the door. She remembered she hadn't eaten anything since a hurried croissant that morning in King's Cross station. She opened the car door and stepped out onto the pavement. She was just turning to say thank you, when Miss Moonshine said, 'Oh, just a minute.' She reached to rummage around the glove compartment for a while, before drawing out a business card. She passed it to Edith. 'Come and see me later,' she said. 'I have something you might like.'

Edith looked down at the card. *Miss Moonshine's Wonderful Emporium* was printed in swirling type, against a drawing of an old building, its lights glowing invitingly. She opened her mouth to ask what Miss Moonshine meant, but the old lady parped the horn again and began to drive off. The boy in the back called something to Edith as he passed, but she couldn't make out a word above the stuttering engine. She gave him a wave, and he gave up the attempt at speech, spreading his hands wide with a hopeless grin. The car rounded a corner and they began to climb the steep hill out of the town.

Chapter Two

An hour, two scones and several cups of tea later, Edith was sitting by the window in a tiny but cosy room at the top of The Old Smithy guesthouse. Christine had plied her until she couldn't eat any more, chatting pleasantly about the glorious summer they were having, and not seeming to mind when Edith only nodded and drank her tea. The guesthouse owner seemed to sense that she preferred not to talk, and, apart from asking her where she'd travelled from, she merely said, after the final crumbs of scone had disappeared, that she expected Edith could do with freshening up, and showed her to her room.

There were lots of shoppers bustling about on the street below. It had seemed like a long day, but it was still only mid-afternoon. The reality of running away began to hit. It was all very well leaving everything behind, but what was she going to do now? Edith took a deep breath. Her conscience was already pricking her, even though she'd been gone less than a day. One of the first things she needed to do was switch on her phone.

She fished her mobile out of her bag and reluctantly pressed the button. Even the glow of the logo made her heart beat faster with anxiety. She closed her eyes, breathed deeply again, and opened her messages. There were several from her student flatmates.

'*Hey, Edith, whatever you need to do. We're here for you, OK?*' followed by lots of hearts.

'*Edith, you're doing the right thing. This can't go on xxxxx*' followed by a caring emoji.

'*The orchestra's not the same without you, hun :(*'

Edith's eyes started to swim. Then she swiped up her phone log, and her heart began its erratic beat again. Several missed calls from her mother, and three voicemails.

Her palms were sweating. Time to face the music. The irony wasn't lost on her as she pressed her mum's number; it was music she was running away from.

Her mum picked up on the very first ring. 'Edith. At last! Why aren't you answering my calls? I've had David on from the college with some crazy tale about you walking out. And in the middle of an important rehearsal! What on earth is going on?'

Edith closed her eyes as, without pause, her mother continued her barrage of exasperated questions. She felt again that terrible churning sensation of dread, as though her mouth were literally taped shut. It was the same sickening emotion she felt day after day in the rehearsal room. David Costa, her college tutor and the orchestra's conductor, was one of her mother's closest friends in the music community. How to explain to her mum that she felt constantly intimidated by him, worthless – *fearful*, even.

Things had come to a head during the previous day's rehearsal. She'd tried her best to play the Bartók the way David wanted, but each time she started, the music spilled out of her in a particular way. In an exuberant way. In a way that made her heart lift and the notes swell with feeling – until David's baton had slammed down on the stand.

'No, no, *no*, Edith!' he'd shouted, making her leap, and her bow scrape violently across the strings, and the rest of the orchestra come to a shocked hush.

And now here was her mother, echoing the anger in David Costa's voice. 'What do you mean by this nonsense, Edith? All that practice I've put in with you! Years and years of it, and you get this great opportunity, and throw it all away.'

'I was playing the Bartók the way I felt it –' Edith began.

'The way *you* felt it?' Her mother's voice rose. 'David Costa has *decades* of experience and you're a student. Do you seriously think you know better than he does? You need to stop being silly and get back into the rehearsal room and learn from him. And that means playing the way he tells you.'

Edith's hand on the phone was shaking. She opened her mouth, but found herself unable to say a single word. She wanted to tell her mother that she just couldn't. She simply could not play the notes of the score the way the conductor told her, because she felt the music in her very being. Everything was connected: her emotions, the minims and quavers leaping off the page, her hands, the bow, the violin itself. She couldn't stop the way the music flooded out of her. It was like trying to dam a waterfall.

Edith wanted to say all this, but instead said nothing. Just as David Costa had stopped her playing, her mother seemed to have stopped her ability to voice her feelings.

The silence continued for a beat or two more. Then, as though perhaps realising she may have gone too far, her mother spoke more gently.

'Well, there's no real harm done. Perhaps some time away might do you good. You've been working hard, I do know that. And David told me he thinks you have an exceptional talent. You just need to harness it.'

Harness. The very word made Edith think of a wild horse being tamed and forced where it didn't want to go. She swallowed.

'Where are you, anyway?' her mum asked finally.

Edith registered how this question came right at the end, as though Edith's whereabouts weren't particularly important; as long as she went back to fulfil her mother's ambition to have a concert violinist for a daughter, it didn't matter where in the world she was at this moment.

She looked out at the hills and the sun dropping down onto the cheerful little town of Haven Bridge. 'I'm somewhere I can have a rest, Mum,' she said. 'I'll call you when I've decided what I'm going to do next.'

She cut the call and exhaled: a long, deep breath. Had she really just told her mother the next decision would be hers? Not David Costa's? Not anyone else's?

For the first time in her life, Edith was going to do things the way she wanted.

Then her throat tightened. But what would that be? If she couldn't play the violin – and despite what he'd said to her mum, David Costa had made it quite clear she couldn't – then what else did she have? The violin was all she knew.

She switched off her phone and was placing her mobile back in her bag when she noticed the little card she'd dropped inside. She drew it out.

Miss Moonshine's Wonderful Emporium

The old lady had told her she had something for her. Edith couldn't imagine what that might be. Miss Moonshine was clearly a little bit batty. But running away was proving more difficult than she'd anticipated. She'd thought a rest from music might do her good, and hadn't imagined being away from her violin would mean brooding and getting anxious. Miss Moonshine had seemed a kindly soul. Besides, Edith might get to find out more about Music Boy.

She put the card back in her pocket and made her way down the three flights of stairs to the dining room.

Christine wasn't there, but sitting at one of the tables was a stout-looking woman, around the same age. There was a laptop in front of her and a look of concentration on her face. She glanced up as Edith peeped round the door.

'Hello, love, you must be our new guest. Edith, isn't it? My name's Gloria. I'm Christine's wife. I hear she's been plying you with her scones. If you stay here much longer, you'll be as round as I am.' She laughed, and her ample bosom wobbled.

Edith couldn't help smiling back. 'The scones were delicious. I haven't eaten anything as good in ages.'

Gloria looked at her over her glasses. 'Well, you've come to the right place. You'll find plenty of good food in the cafés in the town.'

'Actually, I was wondering if you could help.' Edith neared the table and handed Gloria the card. 'I met this lady as I was coming out of the station.'

Gloria chuckled. 'Christine told me Miss Moonshine bowled up outside, peeping her horn. I hear she offered to pick up the Osbornes' cousin, and she was driving their car. She loves a vintage car, does our Miss M, and any excuse to drive one. Though between you and me, the town doesn't love her driving.'

Gloria proved as chatty as Christine. And who were the Osbornes? Edith's mind wandered back to the cheerful grey-eyed boy. Was he the cousin? She indicated the card. 'So does Miss Moonshine own a shop near here?'

Gloria gave a half-snort, half-giggle. 'Well, I suppose you could call it a shop. Sometimes it's open, and sometimes it isn't.' She handed the card back. 'But if Miss Moonshine's invited you specially, I expect you'll find her shop open. Just turn right out of here and keep going. After a while you'll come to a building with an archway in front of it, covered in flowers. That's Miss Moonshine's Wonderful Emporium.'

Edith pushed the card into the pocket of her denim skirt. It all seemed very strange. But she couldn't face the thought of sitting alone in her room worrying. She had to admit she was intrigued to know more about Miss Moonshine's Emporium. And OK, maybe she wanted to know more about the Osbornes' cousin, too, if that's who Music Boy was…

Gloria gave her a friendly goodbye, and Edith made her way out of the B&B, following the directions she'd been given. The town was still busy, but despite what Gloria had said, she began to wonder if the emporium really would be open. If Miss Moonshine had had to drop the Osbornes' cousin off, would she be back by now?

It wasn't long before a glorious arch of flowers came into view. This must be the place. Edith stood outside the little yard in front of the shop. It didn't really look like any shop she'd seen before. The windows were set quite high up, and there were one or two dusty items on display. A large drum, like a soldier boy in Wellington's army might have carried, and an old rocking horse. The year 1777 was inscribed in gold over the door. What an odd place. But there was a beautiful rowan tree curving its graceful branches to one side of the building. Edith was particularly fond of rowan trees – she'd always heard they brought good luck – and so she stepped right up to the heavy door and pushed it open.

Chapter Three

After the bright summer afternoon, the interior of the shop seemed rather dark and dismal. Edith didn't know what she'd been expecting but felt a bit disappointed as she took in the piles of scented soap, the tallow candles and the rack of postcards. It seemed just like any other shop in a tourist town, only a bit dingier.

Miss Moonshine herself, though, was anything but dingy. She'd taken off her purple jacket and peaked cap, and was standing behind the counter wearing a glittery silver dress, like something from a 1920s' movie. She was deep in conversation with a young couple. There were several other people in the shop, too, browsing the shelves of knick-knacks and ornaments. Edith took another look around. What brought so many to this unremarkable place? Even Napoleon the chihuahua, who was lying in a basket to one side of the counter, opened one eye at Edith with a sort of 'I wouldn't bother' expression, before closing it again.

Oh dear, Edith thought. There was bound to be a pub somewhere in Haven Bridge. A couple of hours in a sunny beer garden suddenly seemed a much better idea than getting to know Miss Moonshine's shop. She was about to make a hurried turn, hoping to leave unnoticed, when the old lady's sharp gaze landed on her.

'Oh, you've come.' She sounded flustered. 'I'm a little busy. But take a look around, dear.' She waved a hand towards an opening. 'There's plenty more upstairs.'

Edith felt trapped. Too polite to say she was sure there was nothing at all in the shop she could ever possibly need, she made her way, despite herself, past Napoleon the chihuahua and up a flight of stone stairs.

The first floor seemed even dingier than downstairs, if anything. The sun filtered through the branches of the rowan tree outside, lighting up shelves of old medical books, a mechanical monkey riding a bicycle, a porcelain doll lying next to a bugle, and all sorts of other random… *tat*, was the only word Edith could think of to describe it.

She wandered past the bric-a-brac, aimlessly passing a feather fan, a set of opera glasses and a big mug shaped like an ice-cream cone, with 'A present from Scarborough' painted in pink letters round the rim. When she picked it up, it played 'I Do Like to Be Beside the Seaside'. Edith chuckled. Her flatmates would love it. She put the mug down and was still smiling when she rounded a corner… and came to an instant halt. She blinked twice. There, hanging on the wall at the back of the room, was a violin.

The branches of the rowan tree stirred in the breeze, and a ray of sunlight touched the instrument, giving it a warm, amber glow. Edith had made up her mind she would never play the violin again, but something impelled her forwards, and despite everything, she found herself moving across the stone-flagged floor to where the violin was hanging. She reached a hand up to touch it. Although the shop was dusty, the wood beneath her touch was polished and gleaming. She tucked a nail under one of the strings and plucked it gently. The sound rang, clear and sweet, and she gasped. The instrument was in perfect tune.

'Beautiful, isn't it?'

The voice behind her made her jump. She turned to find Miss Moonshine, head tilted to one side, looking at her for all the world like a curious bird.

'Do you know, I rather thought it might be you it found,' she said thoughtfully.

'Found me?' Edith's eyes widened. What a strange thing to say. It was Edith who'd found the violin, surely, and not the other way round?

But Miss Moonshine carried on, as though she hadn't spoken. 'This violin was left here – oh, when would it be now?' She moved past Edith to lift it down from its hook. 'A long time ago. The years become so complicated. It was Gyuri who brought me it. Such a charming young man. Of course I never sold it. I told him I'd keep it for him.' She glanced down at the instrument in her hands. 'But he never came back.'

'I'm sorry,' Edith said. But perhaps she'd imagined the fleeting sadness on the old lady's face, because now Miss Moonshine was looking at Edith, bright and smiling, and then she said something extraordinary.

'This violin needs someone who knows how to play it. And since you're the one it found, something tells me that person is you.'

Edith gasped, but Miss Moonshine came nearer, and the next minute the violin was in her hands.

'No, you've got it all wrong,' Edith cried. 'I *can't* play. And a violin is exactly what I *don't* want.'

'Oh, my dear.' Miss Moonshine put her head on one side again. 'What we want and what we need are often very different things.'

Edith opened her mouth, but Miss Moonshine was ready.

'Even if you don't want the violin,' she said, 'the violin needs you. It hasn't been played in – oh, it must be more than eighty years.'

'Didn't you say a man called Gyuri gave it to you?' Edith asked. 'Didn't he play it?'

A dreamy look came over Miss Moonshine and she clasped

her hands together in front of her. 'Oh, he played this violin like an angel.'

Edith frowned. If the instrument hadn't been played in eighty years, how could Miss Moonshine have heard this Gyuri playing it? None of it made sense at all. She held the instrument out. 'I'm sorry,' she said. 'I can't possibly take it. Especially if it belongs to someone else.'

Miss Moonshine gave her a smile. 'Just think of it as a loan, dear, and look after it as long as you can. The right owner will find it, don't you worry. And if he doesn't, well,' she held her hands wide, her eyes all innocence, 'you can always bring it back.'

'But Miss Moonshine –'

But the old lady was moving off, with brisk strides. 'If you'll just follow me,' she said over her shoulder, 'I'll see if I can find the case for it.' She stopped, as though a thought had struck her. 'Why not play a few folk songs in the town? People love a bit of music, especially on such a lovely day as this.'

*

Twenty minutes later, Edith was standing at the end of an old stone bridge that spanned a narrow, cheerfully bubbling stream. The violin case lay in front of her, and she was turning the instrument over in her hands. Where the strings met the base there was a tailpiece intricately carved in the shape of a golden sunflower. She'd never seen anything like it before. It was the work of a master craftsman. If the truth be told, she hadn't needed much persuading by Miss Moonshine to borrow the instrument. She'd never held such a wonderful violin, and as soon as the shopkeeper had placed it in her hands, she'd felt the strangest connection. It was almost as though, after eighty years of silence, the violin was urging her to play it.

She plucked each string again, checking the tone, expecting

to have to tune them, but all four notes rang out in perfect pitch, their sound rich and full.

Edith took up the bow and placed the violin under her chin. She'd never learned any folk music – her teaching and practice had always been classical – but she knew many Schubert songs, and so she decided to play one of these.

She raised the violin and held the bow over the strings, ready to play the first note.

And then the most extraordinary thing happened. Instead of the Schubert, the bow moved of its own accord, taking her fingers with it, making her arm swoop into a tune she'd never heard before. And what music! It was literally as though she were possessed. An exuberant folk song burst forth from the strings, the notes darting and laughing and dancing, as though the violin itself had come to life, after many years abandoned, and was filled with joy. Edith could do nothing. She didn't even want to stop. She was caught up in the song, feeling such happiness rush through her, it was as though her feet had left the ground and she was flying.

The bow whirled its magic and when the song finally came to an end, it drew a long, last, trembling note that floated into the air. Edith dropped the bow to her side, breathless and elated. To her surprise, there was a round of applause from a handful of people leaning over the bridge.

'That was grand,' cried an old man. 'Can you play us some more?'

'Aye, give us another, love,' said a woman pushing a pushchair. 'My Emma loved that.'

The toddler in the pushchair gave a dribbly smile and clapped her hands, and the woman dropped a pound coin in the case, where, to Edith's astonishment, several coins were already lying. People were paying her to play! She'd been so swept away by the incredible music, she hadn't noticed.

She looked around at the waiting faces, her breath coming in gasps, enjoying the wonderful sensation of connection with her audience. How different this was from her soulless and stressful rehearsals with David Costa. To feel that people were enjoying her playing! She lifted the bow, took a deep breath, and again tried for the first notes of the Schubert. Again, the music rose of its own accord, and the bow played something else entirely. Another unfamiliar folk tune whirled merrily as the bow danced over the strings, and as Edith played, eyes closed, she had a vision of dancers in red woollen dresses, skirts flying, and boots stamping.

When the last notes died away, the onlookers burst into a round of applause and whistling. The toddler sitting in the pushchair jerked forward and cried 'More! More!', and there was a chorus of laughter.

Edith took in a breath. At college, lessons had always been about playing the music *correctly*, getting the notes *right*, but here she felt for the first time an amazing energy. Who cared if she played properly? The whole magical, impossible music was crazy, but the audience *loved* it.

She wished she could see the violin from the outside – see how the bow flew over the strings of its own accord – and then a thought struck her. She drew her phone out of her pocket and stepped up to the young mother, asking shyly, 'Please could you do me a favour? When I play the next tune, could you take a video?'

The woman nodded. 'Course, love. You've kept our Emma entertained. It's the least I can do.'

Edith stepped back to take up her position, violin tucked under her chin. When the woman signalled, she lifted the bow. The music spilled out a third time, more gently this time, as though the first rush of notes through a dam had ceased, and now the instrument was taking its time, enjoying every long, drawn-out sound from each string. The notes rose in a swell of music and Edith closed her eyes to listen. When the last bar fell away, in a long, sweet note, she dropped the bow to her side and stood still. For a second or two, there was silence around her, and then the crowd – grown again – began to cheer.

The mother passed Edith her phone back with a smile. 'You should put that on YouTube, love,' she said. 'People would pay to see music like this. Thanks for cheering up my day.'

Edith blushed and tried to say it wasn't really her, it was the violin, but that would have sounded ridiculous, and in any case, the woman was already pushing the pushchair away, her toddler fast asleep.

At the crowd's urging, Edith played several more tunes, until she began to feel weary. As though sensing her tiredness, the bow stumbled once or twice with a soft rasp, and she decided it was time to put the instrument away.

She took a small, shy bow as the audience gave a final round of applause. The ancient case lying on the ground was now filled with coins, and even a few notes. The people watching began filtering away, and she tipped the money she'd made into her bag, tucked the violin back into the case and fastened its leather buckle.

As she stood, she thought of Miss Moonshine. Everything had begun with the strange old lady – the trip in the vintage car, the guesthouse, and then the emporium. Suddenly, she needed to know more about this Gyuri. She picked up the violin and made her way purposefully back over the little stone bridge, heading for the archway of flowers. She ducked through and strode up to the door, and this time, with no hesitation, made to push it open. But the door was locked. Edith knocked a couple of times, and called out 'Miss Moonshine!', but there was no response.

Chapter Four

Later that evening, Edith lay in her bed in the attic of the guesthouse, replaying the video the young mother had taken. After her vain attempt to see Miss Moonshine, she'd gone to a supermarket and bought herself something to eat and then taken a picnic to a park situated beside the canal. There she'd sat on a bench, taken her phone out of her pocket, and watched the video over and over again. No matter how many times she saw it, she couldn't work out where she, Edith, stopped, and the music took over. The Edith moving the bow was her, but the music – the incredible music – was all the violin's.

Finally, when she couldn't keep her eyes open any longer, Edith uploaded the video's opening bars to her TikTok account, with the caption: '*Anyone know this music?*' Then she switched off her phone, flicked off the bedside lamp and lay looking at the moonlight filtering through the window. Running away was proving exciting, but very tiring.

It was also proving a hungry business. Edith slept so deeply, when she woke the next morning the aroma of breakfast cooking was already filtering through the guesthouse. Remembering the delicious scones, she leapt out of bed, scrambled into a pair of cotton trousers and the daisy-print shirt she'd brought with her and clattered down the stairs.

The dining room was full, and Christine was busy, and so Edith applied herself for the next hour to doing justice to the glorious breakfast. After grapefruit and cereal followed by scrambled eggs, she was just wondering whether it would be too greedy to have a slice of toast and honey and another cup of tea, when she finally took stock, and realised several of the other guests were casting curious glances her way. She glanced down. Had she dripped orange juice on her shirt?

An elderly man stood and approached. 'Excuse me,' he said.

'Are you the girl who was playing the violin by the Packhorse Bridge yesterday?'

Edith nodded, feeling her cheeks go pink.

'I just wanted to tell you how much I enjoyed it.' He beamed at her.

'Oh, but it wasn't –' Edith began. But it was impossible to say it hadn't been her playing, but the violin, all by itself. Her cheeks turned pinker as the man waited. 'It wasn't something I learned at college,' she finished lamely.

There was a chorus of questions from the room. Where was Edith studying? Was she professional? When even Gloria came through from the kitchen to join in, Edith began to feel more and more uncomfortable. She needed to get straight back to Miss Moonshine's and return the violin as soon as she could. Everything was getting out of hand!

She rose to her feet and, after thanking Gloria for the delicious meal, hurried back to her room. If the emporium was shut, Edith decided, she would camp outside until the old lady reappeared.

This was her plan. That is, until she picked up her phone, which she'd left charging on the bedside table. To her surprise, her screen lit up immediately with dozens of messages.

'*Wow, brilliant, hun… I thought you'd left your violin behind?*'

'*Edith, this is **** awesome!*'

One of her flatmates had messaged: '*Hey. Wait till old Costa sees this. Good for you!!*'

Edith replied '*???*'

Her flatmate came straight back, '*Check out your TikTok!!!!!!!*'

Edith opened up the TikTok app. And almost dropped her phone. The video of her playing, which she'd captioned '*Anyone know this music?*', had been shared over and over and over again. Someone had created a duet with her on the cello, and their duet had been shared, and again until it was a whole string quartet. And then other musicians had taken the song in a completely different direction, with a folksy accordion, a drum, tambourines and a guitar. Edith scrolled through, her eyes wide with amazement, until her fingers stopped on the latest video. The one that was trending. The best video of all.

@Gyuri had posted a montage, with Edith's violin and the stone bridge in the foreground, then sampled it with all the other musicians, and added a video of women dancing. Women in red dresses, their skirts swirling, boots flying. The same dancers Edith had imagined when the bow had taken over as she played.

She sank down on her bed. Under her video two messages were blinking:

@Gyuri *I know this music*

@Gyuri *You are playing my violin*

*

A few minutes later, Edith was running down the street, violin case in hand, heading towards the arch of flowers outside Miss Moonshine's Emporium. Edith had excellent recall. She needed it in order to commit pages of musical score to memory. Everything the shopkeeper had said about the violin – which, to be honest, wasn't much – was clear in her mind.

'*It was Gyuri who sold it to me… It hasn't been played in – oh, it must be more than eighty years.*'

Eighty years ago? He'd just sent her a message on TikTok. It was impossible. Edith hurried underneath the blossoms and came to a panting halt at the door, to find it shut. *Again.*

'Miss Moonshine!' she called. She banged once or twice, but was met with silence. She went to the window and jumped up, trying to catch a glimpse of the interior, but the windows were too high to let her see much, apart from the soldier's drum, still there on display.

'Well then, I'll wait,' she said out loud. She sat down on the doorstep, placed the violin carefully beside her, and folded her arms. 'No matter how long it takes.'

Quarter of an hour passed. Several of the passers-by on the other side of the archway cast inquisitive glances in Edith's direction, but she continued to sit on the step, determined not to leave until Miss Moonshine either opened the door, or returned from wherever she'd gone. It was tempting to while away the time looking at her phone, but she felt overwhelmed by the stir her video had caused. Then it dawned on her that at this rate it wouldn't be long before her mother found out about it, and David Costa. She could imagine the uproar. Her hands became clammy, and she wiped them on her trousers. She was just wishing she'd had the forethought to bring a bottle of water to wet her dry throat, when a car pulled up at the kerb. The sun was now over the houses opposite. Edith shaded her eyes as the car drew off again, and a silhouette stepped through the archway.

She scrambled to her feet. The boy from the train. Music Boy. The Osbornes' cousin. He was looking at her, a curious expression on his face. In one hand he carried a violin case, in the other a mobile phone. His attention switched to the violin case Edith had placed beside the stone step.

'My name is Gyuri,' he said, in accented English. His clear grey eyes met hers. 'You are playing my violin.'

Edith's mouth fell open. 'You're Gyuri? But – But Miss Moonshine said you were old!'

He continued to regard her a moment or two, as though struggling with something. Then he put down his violin and flicked on his phone.

'Siri, *fordítás huszonhárom éves vagyok*.' He stepped forward to show Edith the screen, and at the same moment, Siri's chirpy electronic voice said, 'I am twenty-three.' The young man spoke into it again, and Siri translated, 'I am Hungarian.'

The boy called Gyuri smiled, his eyes brimming amusement at Edith's expression, as they had done when she first saw him on the train. It was such a cheerful, friendly look, Edith couldn't help smiling back, despite her astonishment. After a moment's hesitation, she came closer to speak into his phone.

'Siri, translate "I'm pleased to meet you. Would you like your violin back?"'

The electronic voice began to speak, but before it finished, there was a rattling of a key behind them, followed by the door opening, and there stood Miss Moonshine, smiling widely on the doorstep.

'So here you both are,' she said. 'I've been expecting you.'

Chapter Five

A short while later, Gyuri, Edith and Miss Moonshine were sitting at a little table behind the counter in the emporium. Miss Moonshine had ushered them inside, looking from one to the other of them, the smile never leaving her face.

'Well, don't we have a lot to talk about?' she'd said. 'What we need first is some tea and biscuits.'

And so there they were, a blue-and-gold teapot on the table in front of them, and a cup of tea each. Miss Moonshine laid an iPad beside the plate of biscuits. Gyuri said something in Hungarian as he placed his phone next to it.

'Chocolate digestives,' Siri translated helpfully, 'are my favourite English biscuit.'

'Help yourself,' Miss Moonshine said, her eyes twinkling as she pushed the plate towards him. 'And I'll tell Edith all about the violin.'

The old lady picked up the iPad and began to flick through the screens until she came to an old black-and-white photo. 'Ah, there we are.' She turned the tablet so that Edith could see.

Edith leaned forward. 'But this is the car you were driving

yesterday,' she said in surprise. 'Didn't you say it belonged to the Osbornes?'

'That's right.' Miss Moonshine looked at her, impressed. 'You have a very good memory.'

The photo showed the vintage car outside a building which, Edith was amazed to note as she peered closer, was Miss Moonshine's Emporium. It must be a very old photo. The rowan tree was still only small, but there was the same distinctive archway of flowers. In front of the car stood a woman in a calf-length print dress and a fetching hat. Beside her stood a young man in a stylish double-breasted suit and a trilby. He was holding a violin under his chin, with the bow poised over it, as though about to play. Edith recognised the distinctive sunflower tailpiece immediately. But it wasn't this that struck her. The man was gazing directly at the camera, a cheerful smile on his face.

Edith glanced from the photo to Gyuri, who was sitting beside her. He caught her eye and smiled, and she gasped.

'The man in the photo,' she said to Miss Moonshine. 'He looks just like Gyuri!'

'That's Gyuri's great-grandfather,' Miss Moonshine explained. 'Also called Gyuri. And this is his great-grandmother, Evie Osborne. The photo was taken shortly before they married.'

'But how –'

'Well, you see…' Miss Moonshine placed her cup back in its saucer. 'It's like this…'

Edith heard how some time in the 1930s Evie Osborne had fallen in love with a Hungarian musician.

'It was a whirlwind romance, my dear.' A shadow crossed Miss Moonshine's face. 'But then everyone started talking about another war, and Gyuri wanted to go back to his family in Hungary, and Evie – well, she insisted on going with him, and nothing her father could say could stop her. She loved

Gyuri, and that was that. Gyuri brought me the violin – to raise money for their passage home, he said, but really I think he wanted me to keep it safe. And so they both went to Hungary. When war broke out, they couldn't get back. And although they were both safe, of course after the war the Iron Curtain came down, and there was no chance of them ever returning. And so we never saw them again.'

Gyuri must have understood some of this, because his expression was solemn. But Miss Moonshine patted his hand, telling him, 'But after your great-grandmother Evie went to Hungary they had a baby, your grandfather. And then your father was born. And then you. And so if they'd never gone to Hungary, you wouldn't have been born at all.'

Again Gyuri seemed to understand, and he nodded. He turned to Edith and began to speak, in slow, careful Hungarian, while Siri translated.

'My grandfather, the son of Evie and Gyuri, died a few months ago.'

Edith murmured how sorry she was, and, in case he hadn't understood, she reached over to press the young man's hand. He returned her clasp briefly, a fleeting touch of his fingers on hers that left a lingering warmth.

Gyuri went on to explain how, while sorting out his grandfather's effects, he'd come across this same photo of his ancestor Gyuri, playing a violin. None of the rest of his family was musical. It was the first he'd heard that his great-grandfather played. The violin was a distinctive one, with its sunflower carving.

'It was strange,' Siri translated, 'but something drew me to this violin. I couldn't rest until I'd found it.'

Gyuri asked his parents where it now was, but too many years had passed, and neither of them knew anything. And then his mother said she thought she recognised the building in the photo, and the archway of flowers. In the 1990s, a few years after the Berlin Wall came down, she'd gone to England, curious to discover her ancestors. She'd been amazed to find there were still Osbornes, distant cousins and descendants of Evie's brother, living in the very same house Evie had grown up in, in Haven Bridge. And Gyuri's mother was sure this was the strange little emporium she'd visited in the town.

Edith turned her attention back to the photo. Everything was now falling into place for her, too. Sort of. But there was still the question of how Miss Moonshine could possibly have known Gyuri's great-grandfather, all those many years ago.

'But how?' she began.

But Miss Moonshine was already rising from her chair. 'So, that means young Gyuri has come for his family's violin at last. And something told me the violin would find you, too. Isn't it wonderful that it's brought us all together?'

'But that still doesn't explain –' Edith began.

'Now, I'm sure you two have a lot to talk about,' Miss Moonshine went on. 'And I really must open up the emporium. Perhaps you'd like to go upstairs and chat?' She glanced at Siri, and then at the pair of violins on the counter. 'Or else play some music?'

Gyuri evidently understood the last question. He rose eagerly to his feet, holding his hand out to Edith, his expressive eyes full of question. Edith took the proffered hand immediately. With the idea of playing the fabulous violin, all thoughts of Miss Moonshine's impossible history were forgotten.

And Edith and Gyuri may not speak the same language, but with their music, so much could be said.

*

Later, Edith would often think of the hours that followed, in the upstairs room of Miss Moonshine's Wonderful Emporium, as among the happiest of her life. The late-morning sun streamed through the window as she took out the violin that had belonged to Gyuri's ancestor and held it out for his great-grandson to see. Young Gyuri ran his slender fingers over the carved sunflower. He turned it in his hands, admiring the beautiful patina of the wood, just as Edith had done, before plucking each string gently in turn. As the notes rang out, Gyuri lifted his eyes to Edith's, and she could see exactly the same emotion in them as she'd felt herself.

Gyuri signalled for her to take the instrument back, and then took up his own violin. Edith picked up her bow. Their eyes met, and Gyuri nodded. He began the first bars of a folk song, and Edith followed. This time, the bow and the violin moved completely at her own will, as somehow she'd known they would. Whatever had possessed the instrument the previous day was gone, as though released. There was no moment when Edith didn't feel the music was all hers – or rather, that the music belonged to her and Gyuri together. Sometimes Gyuri led with a tune of his own, while Edith answered with the counter-tune, and sometimes Edith took the lead, the sweet notes of his ancestor's violin filling the room.

For hours they played, with no words between them, working out by instinct what the other was trying to convey in the music. For Edith, it was a liberation. There was no one to tell her she was doing everything wrong. Playing with Gyuri, the music rose from the violin in a way that felt completely right. Their notes followed one another in the final bars of a particularly intricate and tender song, and Edith felt so happy – so relieved to be able to play the way she wanted, with no questions, with someone who understood her every move – that as she dropped her bow to her side, a tear rolled down her cheek.

Immediately, Gyuri put down his instrument. '*Mi a baj, drágám*?' he asked, concerned.

'Nothing.' She gave a watery smile. 'There's nothing the matter at all. I'm just really happy.'

Gyuri reached out his hand to wipe the tear away. For a second or two, the slender fingers that had held his bow cupped her face. His expression was solemn, the grey of his eyes darkened to charcoal.

'You play like an angel,' he said, in English.

And then his dimple returned, and the old merry look. He turned to Siri and asked her to translate: 'You are tired. Would you like something to eat?'

Edith glanced at the time on her watch. 'Wow, I didn't realise it was so late. I'm starving. I've never been so hungry since coming to Haven Bridge.'

The machine translated, and Gyuri laughed. He answered in Hungarian, and Siri's chirpy voice translated, 'Your Shakespeare said music is the food of love. But your English fish and chips are also good.'

They made their way back down the stairs and found Miss Moonshine still sitting at the table behind the counter, a dreamy expression on her face. The emporium was empty, apart from Napoleon, who was lying in his basket, chin on his paws, looking… *blissful*, was the only word Edith could find to describe him.

'Thank you for playing for us,' Miss Moonshine said. 'It was absolutely wonderful. Your great-grandfather would be very, very happy.'

Chapter Six

Gyuri told Edith his English cousins had recommended a pub that served the best fish and chips, and so they made their way over the Packhorse Bridge towards it, carrying their violins. They found a table in the beer garden, where Edith left Gyuri to look after her instrument while she went to the bar to order.

She insisted on paying, telling Gyuri she still had lots of money from her busking, and it was the least she could do, considering she'd earned it playing his violin.

When she returned, carrying their drinks, Gyuri looked up from his phone and pushed it across the table towards her.

'Look, Edith,' he said in English.

Edith liked the way he pronounced her name: Édit. She took the phone from him with a smile. On the screen a video was set up to play. She pressed the arrow, and there was Gyuri, standing on a stage, violin in hand, striking the first note of a tune. He was joined quickly by a double bass, and then a percussionist with a small drum, and another girl behind him on the violin, and a boy on a guitar. The camera turned, moving away from the stage to a sunny park by a lake, filled with young people, whirling round and round in time to the music.

'You're in a band,' Edith cried. 'This is amazing!'

Gyuri watched, a shy smile on his face, as Edith immersed herself in his videos, asking him excited questions about the other musicians, where they played, how they knew each other, and soon they were chattering away, speaking so rapidly Siri often failed to keep up, and the electronic voice would ask them crossly to speak more slowly, which made them both laugh.

The afternoon was well advanced, and their fish and chips long finished, when Edith finally told Gyuri about how she'd run away. She kept her eyes fixed on the table as she told him how the conductor had shouted at her when she couldn't play the Bartók.

'I don't understand,' Gyuri said.

Edith began to repeat what she'd said, but Gyuri broke in, 'I understand the words. I don't understand *why*. You play like an angel.'

They were the same words he'd used before. Edith turned to look at him, and found the same solemn expression on his face. 'Come with me to Hungary,' he said in English.

Edith's heart jumped a beat. Something in her expression must have made him think she hadn't understood. He turned to his phone and spoke rapidly in Hungarian.

'Come with me to Hungary,' Siri repeated. 'Come and play with us. You will love it. They will love you.'

'This is crazy,' Edith said, but found she couldn't stop beaming. Her face felt like it would split in half with her smile. 'But I can't speak Hungarian.'

Gyuri wasn't smiling. His face was as serious as it had been before, when he'd reached out to touch her cheek, upstairs in Miss Moonshine's Emporium. 'Music is a language,' he said, through Siri. 'You speak it more fluently than anyone I know.'

His phone vibrated with a message, and he bent to pick it up before Edith could answer. Not that she could think what to reply. So much had happened in the past two days. She'd gone from believing she should never play the violin again, to finding a soulmate who spoke exactly the same musical language.

Gyuri rose to his feet, explaining that his cousins, the Osbornes, had planned to take him to Halifax that afternoon, to show him the old Piece Hall, and that he should go back.

Edith stood, too. Was it only yesterday she'd missed her stop? It seemed like a lifetime ago.

A thought struck Gyuri, and Siri translated, 'Would you like to come with us?'

Edith considered for a moment, then said, 'It would be lovely to meet them. But I'd like some time to think things over. And I really should make some phone calls. Let my mum and my tutor know what's going on.'

Gyuri nodded, then caught hold of both her hands in his. 'Remember what I asked you. Come and play with us in Hungary. Think about it.'

Even Siri sounded earnest as she translated Gyuri's words. Edith returned his warm clasp. 'I will,' she promised. Then she bent to pick up the old violin. 'Here,' she said. 'This is yours. You must take it.'

But Gyuri lifted up his hands. He smiled. 'You keep it for me,' Siri translated for him. 'Then I know one day you will bring it back. Whatever happens.'

*

The guesthouse was quiet when Edith returned. She made her way straight upstairs to her room, took a seat by the window and fished her phone out of her bag. Then she took a breath, readying herself to face the clamour of messages. Time to face the music yet again.

She pressed the button. Sure enough, the screen lit up. Edith went first to her TikTok app. Her mind was blown when she saw that Gyuri's video of her by the Packhorse Bridge, with the accompaniment of musicians and exuberant dancers, had now been shared hundreds of thousands of times. It was impossible to visualise such an extraordinary number.

Underneath the video was a message from Gyuri, sent just a few minutes before. '*I told you they would love you*!'

She smiled, but the smile faded when she flicked off the app. There were numerous voicemail messages from her mum, as well as from David Costa at the college. She pressed to listen. Better get it over with.

'Hello, Edith, I hope you're well,' came David's voicemail.

Edith almost dropped the phone. Was this definitely him? Asking after her health? She stared at the speaker. David's plummy voice continued, 'Could you give me a ring back when convenient? There's something I'd like to discuss. *Ciao*.'

When convenient? *Ciao*? For months David had put Edith down, making her feel stupid and talentless in rehearsals. She'd expected an angry message telling her how childish she was, and how she was wasting time on social media when she should be practising.

She was about to press replay on his astonishing voicemail, to check it really was him, and not one of her friends playing a joke, when at that very same moment the phone rang in her hands, making her almost jump out of her skin.

'Hello,' she said tentatively.

'Edith!' David boomed. 'I've been trying to get hold of you. Popular girl. Ha ha ha!'

Edith didn't know what to reply. She listened in silence as David told her he hoped she was enjoying her 'break'. And then he said jovially, 'I've seen your video –'

Edith stiffened.

'– and it's quite the little success! I've had enquiries about you. Not to put too fine a point on it, a gentleman from Sony has been in touch –'

She leapt to her feet. 'Sony Music?'

David gave a patronising chuckle. 'Now don't get your hopes up, but I may be able to get the orchestra a recording contract. You'll be first violin, of course. I thought I'd suggest the Bartók. You just need to work a little more on the expression –'

Edith drew in a breath. All was now clear. So *that* was what his sudden friendliness was all about. He wanted to cash in on her playing, and on Gyuri's viral video. If her mind wasn't already made up before, now it definitely was.

'I'm afraid I've already been offered a job,' she said coldly.

There was a silence at the other end of the line. 'I'm sorry,' he said, with a genial laugh. 'I didn't catch that.'

'I have a job,' she repeated. 'In Hungary. I'm coming back to London to see my mother and settle a few things, and then I'll be leaving.'

'Edith, you're making a very silly mistake –'

She pressed the button to end the call, feeling liberated. This felt like the best decision of her entire life.

The Final Chapter

The next morning, after a last hearty breakfast in the guesthouse, Edith said goodbye to Gloria and Christine, took up her rucksack and old Gyuri's violin, and made her way back to Miss Moonshine's Wonderful Emporium. Somehow she knew this time the shop would be open, and sure enough, the door swung wide when she turned the handle.

Miss Moonshine was standing by the window, arranging a feather boa on a mannequin. She turned as the door opened.

'I've come to say goodbye,' Edith said, smiling.

'I was hoping you would.' The shopkeeper left the mannequin and moved to the counter, where a photo in a silver frame was propped against the till. 'I have something for you.'

Inside the frame was the photo of Gyuri's great-grandfather, standing beside Evie. Miss Moonshine had had the image coloured, and now Evie's dress was a delicate rose-pink, patterned with cream flowers, and Gyuri's eyes twinkled the same grey as his great-grandson's. It was as though the photo had just been taken yesterday.

'Oh, this is lovely,' Edith breathed. 'Thank you! They look so young.'

Miss Moonshine's gaze softened. 'We were all young once, my dear.'

There was the parp of a horn outside, and Edith turned her head. 'Oh, that's my lift,' she said. 'Gyuri has come in the vintage car to take me to the station. I'm going to London to see my mum, and then I'm travelling with Gyuri to Hungary. To play wonderful music.'

Miss Moonshine pressed the frame into Edith's hands. 'Then this is for you both. With best wishes on your adventure.'

'Thank you,' Edith said. The horn parped again, and she made quickly for the door, turning as it swung open, letting in the sunshine. 'Thank you, Miss Moonshine. For everything!'

Helena Fairfax is a freelance editor and author of romantic fiction, as well as a non-fiction social history called *Struggle and Suffrage in Halifax: Women's Lives and the Fight for Equality*. **Readers can keep in touch on social media, where she's the only Helena Fairfax, or subscribe to her newsletter for book news, photos of her beloved Yorkshire moors, and the occasional free stuff.**

t.co/8WkjaK3b3B

*****

Thank you so much for reading *Midsummer Magic at Miss Moonshine's Emporium*. We hope you enjoyed our collection of stories. If you did, please consider telling your friends or posting a short review on Amazon or Goodreads. Word of mouth is an author's best friend, and much appreciated!

ABOUT THE AUTHORS

Midsummer Magic at Miss Moonshine's Emporium is an anthology put together by a group of romantic novelists and short story writers from Yorkshire and Lancashire in the north of England. The group meet regularly in the little town of Hebden Bridge, and this location, lying as it does on the moors near the border between the two counties, led to the group name Authors on the Edge, and to the inspiration behind this collection.

Much cake was consumed by these authors in the making of this anthology.

Top: Mary Jayne Baker, Sophie Claire, Jacqui Cooper
Middle: Helena Fairfax, Kate Field, Melinda Hammond
Bottom: Marie Laval, Helen Pollard, Angela Wren

More by the Authors on the Edge...

Miss Moonshine's Emporium of Happy Endings

Sometimes what you need is right there waiting for you...

Miss Moonshine's Wonderful Emporium has stood in the pretty Yorkshire town of Haven Bridge for as long as anyone can remember. With her ever-changing stock, Miss Moonshine has a rare gift for providing exactly what her customers need: a fire opal necklace that provides a glimpse of a different life; a novel whose phantom doodler casts a spell over the reader; a music box whose song links love affairs across the generations.

One thing is for certain: after visiting Miss Moonshine's quirky shop, life is never the same again...

Christmas at Miss Moonshine's Emporium

When the magic of Christmas is just what you're looking for... There's something magical about Miss Moonshine's Wonderful Emporium, and at Christmas she brings an added sparkle to the inhabitants of the pretty Yorkshire town of Haven Bridge. Customers who step over her threshold find an eccentric collection of gifts, but Miss Moonshine has a rare knack for providing exactly what they need: a strange Advent calendar whose doors give a glimpse of a happy ending; a vintage typewriter that types a ghostly message from Christmas past; a mirror in a silver case that reflects the person you'd like to be. Step inside Miss Moonshine's quirky shop, and the thing you need most for Christmas will be right there waiting for you...

Printed in Great Britain
by Amazon